After the Cold War

Library of International Relations: Volume 6

After the Cold War

Security and Democracy in Africa and Asia

Edited by

William Hale and Eberhard Kienle

Tauris Academic Studies
I.B. TAURIS LONDON • NEW YORK

Published in 1997 by
Tauris Academic Studies
An imprint of I.B. Tauris & Co. Ltd
Victoria House
Bloomsbury Square
London WC1 4DZ

175 Fifth Avenue
New York NY 10010

In the United States of America
and in Canada distributed by
St Martin's Press
175 Fifth Avenue
New York NY 10010

A full CIP record for this book is available from the British Library
A full CIP record for this book is available from the Library of Congress

ISBN 1 86064 136 9

Typeset in Adobe Caslon by Hepton Books, Oxford
Printed and bound in Great Britain by Bookcraft, Bath Ltd

Contents

Part II Democratisation and the Fate of Leftist Movements

Notes on the Contributors

Harihar Bhattacharyya is Senior Lecturer in Political Science at the University of Burdwan, West Bengal. He is the author of *Micro-Foundations of Bengal Communism* (Ajanta, Delhi, forthcoming) besides several papers on communism and nationalism in Tripura.

Michael Bratton is Professor of Political Science and African Studies at Michigan State University, He has written extensively on African politics and development, most recently with Nicolas van de Walle in a forthcoming book on *Democratic Experiments in Africa: Regime Transitions in Comparative Perspective.*

Christopher Clapham is Professor of Politics and International relations at the University of Lancaster. He is the author of *Third World Politics: An Introduction* (1985), *Transformation and Continuity in Revolutionary Ethiopia* (1988) and *Africa and the International System: the politics of state survival* (1996). He is currently preparing a book on guerrilla warfare in Africa.

Rosemary Foot is the John Swire Senior Research Fellow in the International Relations of East Asia at St Antony's College, Oxford, and the current director of the College's Asian Studies Centre. Her most recent book is *The Practice of Power: US Relations with China Since 1949* (Oxford: Oxford University Press, 1995).

Graham Fuller is Senior Political Scientist at the Rand Corporation in Washington DC and former Vice Chairman of the National Intelligence Council at the CIA for long range forecasting. He is author of several books on Iran, the geopolitics of Turkey, a book on Islam and the West, and numerous monographs for Rand on ethnicity,

Islamist movements, studies on Central Asia and the Caucasus, and on the new world order.

William Hale is Reader in Politics with reference to Turkey at the School of Oriental and African Studies, London. He is the author of *The Political and Economic Development of Modern Turkey* (1981) and *Turkish Politics and the Military* (1994) besides numerous papers on modern Turkish politics.

Fred Halliday is Professor of International Relations at the London School of Economics and Political Science. His publications include *The Making of the Second Cold War* (2nd edition, 1986); *Cold War, Third World* (1989); *Islam and the Myth of Confrontation* (1996).

Eberhard Kienle is Lecturer in the Politics of the Middle East at the School of Oriental and African Studies. He is the author *Ba'th versus Ba'th: The Conflict between Syria and Iraq* (1990) and editor and contributor to *Contemporary Syria Liberalization between Cold War and Cold Peace* (1994) besides numerous papers on political and economic liberalisation and international relations in the Middle East.

David Shambaugh is Director of the Cigur Centre for East Asian Studies at the George Washington University, Washington D.C. He was formerly Reader in Chinese Politics in the University of London and editor of the *China Quarterly.* He has published widely on Chinese domestic politics, foreign relations, military affairs, and the international politics of Asia. His is presently writing a book on *The Chinese Military in the 1990s.*

Charles Tripp is Senior Lecturer in Politics with reference to the Near and Middle East at the School of Oriental and African Studies. He is co-author, with Shahram Chubin, of *Iran and Iraq at War* (1988) and of *Iran–Saudi Arabia Relations and Regional Order* (1996).

Introduction

William Hale and Eberhard Kienle

Not surprisingly, the much celebrated end of the Cold War, its causes and consequences, rapidly emerged as a key topic of analysis during the early 1990s. This literature addressed many of the practical political, as well as the conceptual and theoretical aspects, of the so-called 'new world order'. However, its focus is very largely on global systemic change, or on what, in the days of the Cold War, was termed East–West relations. This book seeks to redress the balance by analysing the transformations now taking place in those parts of the world which – with some exceptions like Korea – did not normally occupy centre-stage in the global Cold War conflict. At the same time, the countries of Asia and Africa were certainly affected by the Cold War, and have been equally affected by its end. They include regions which are likely to attract increasing attention – either in a spirit of desperation (as in much of sub-Saharan Africa) or one of hope an promise, as in that of the Pacific rim.

The future of these parts of the world also poses a host of unanswered questions. Have the Asian and African states gained or lost international influence, with the end of Cold War rivalries? Have regional conflicts become easier to settle, or have new conflicts arisen to take their place? Alternatively, have some regional conflicts remained unaffected? How has the end of the superpower conflict changed the relative power of Asian and African states, within their own regions? How has it affected their internal political structures – in particular, has the victory of liberal democracy at the global level really enhanced its prospects outside Europe? How have communist and leftist movements in Asia and Africa adapted themselves to the transformed global environment? These are some of the questions which this book seeks to answer.

Like the political transformations which have affected the former

Soviet Union and Eastern Europe, as well as their relations with the Western powers, the simultaneous or subsequent changes in the domestic politics and international relations of Asia and Africa may not be final or definite. They may be the prelude to further change, or they may turn out to be reversible, and thus no more than an interlude before the outbreak of another Cold War, perhaps less ideologically determined than its predecessor. Even if it is only temporary, however, change has nonetheless occurred, and it needs to be evaluated and explained.

This book grew out of a conference held in October 1994 at the School of Oriental and African Studies of London University and the chapters have been updated since then. Reflecting the thematic subdivisions of the conference, Part One discusses the relevance of the end of the Cold War for the dynamics of regional conflicts and security. Part Two considers its effects on change commonly summed up as 'political liberalisation' or 'democratisation'. Issues discussed in this section include political participation, human rights, and the new constraints and opportunities for leftist movements. This thematic division may be criticised on the grounds that it reflects an out-dated distinction between international and domestic affairs. To make the whole manageable, it was nevertheless clear that dividing lines had to be drawn somewhere. The division, however, has not been rigidly applied. As an example, intra-state conflicts have been dealt with in the first section rather than the second. In effect, the distinction drawn is one between conflicts, on the one hand, and longer-run change and processes, on the other.

Global Peace and Regional Conflict

The end of global conflict between Moscow and Washington, first with the advent of Gorbachev, and then with the decline and ultimate demise of the Soviet state, did not have a uniform effect on conflict and cooperation elsewhere in the world. While some existing conflicts, such as that between Israel and most of the Arab states, came closer to a definite settlement, others, such as those in Kashmir or the Sudan, have remained immune to such influence. New conflicts, though arguably latent and hitherto suppressed, erupted or escalated only after the end of the Cold War, and mainly or partly because of it. As Graham Fuller observes, an essential distinction can be drawn between conflicts taking place outside the former communist bloc, and those within it.

In the first category, regional or intra-state conflicts were often long-standing and usually openly recognised. In the second category, however, their very existence was denied, as part of the old communist orthodoxy. The removal of Soviet power released new forces and contests which had not been predicted or expected – as in the cases of the former Yugoslavia, Transcaucasia, and Central Asia.

Against this background the first section first seeks to explore why conflicts in Asia and Africa have been differentially affected by global change. As some writers suggest, the definition of conflict cannot be reduced to openly violent behaviour. The analysis thus has to extend not only to cases marked by visible hostility, but also to others marked by increasing political tension, tending, possibly, towards violence. All the conflicts considered are regional conflicts in the sense that the major or direct participants operate in geographical proximity, and that the major repercussions of their actions remain limited to that region. The notion of regional conflict does not imply that geographically defined regions are *ipso facto* regions in a political sense. By creating certain patterns of interaction, even if they are destructive, conflicts may create political regions, just as patterns of cooperation may do so. The creeping re-definition of the 'Middle East', as the area occupied by the major participants in the Arab–Israeli conflict, illustrates this point.

Fred Halliday makes the obvious but crucial distinction between regional conflicts in which the parties, be they state or non-state actors, were directly linked to the major protagonists of the Cold War, and other instances in which this was not the case. Put differently, de-escalation only occurred in conflicts in which one or all parties relied heavily on support from major Cold War protagonists. Although the end of the Cold War could lead to both superpowers withdrawing support from their respective clients – as occurred, for instance, in Afghanistan – the more common scenario was that Western support decreased far less than Soviet support, if at all. Consequently, balances of power in regional conflicts changed, so that Soviet clients were forced to move towards settlements which they would previously have rejected. An example was Syria's readiness to negotiate within the framework of the Madrid conference, and thus on a bilateral basis, whereas previously it had always insisted on the convening of an international peace conference to settle the Arab–Israeli conflict. At the same time, since the conflict between Israel and its Arab neighbours also has a logic uncoupled from that of the Cold War, and is fought with resources generated domestically, it has partly escaped pressures associated with the new world order. Though characterised by their own complexities, Ethiopia and Southern Africa supply additional examples, as Christopher Clapham explains.

Fred Halliday's proposal is supported by the continuation of tension and hostility in Sudan and in Kashmir. As Charles Tripp demonstrates, the former of these was predominantly fought out with local resources, and without much super-power involvement. Another aspect of the argument is illustrated by Graham Fuller's analysis of developments in Central Asia. In this case, the formal dissolution of the Soviet state encouraged opposition to Moscow and its allies, but the Western powers, and other local actors such as Turkey and Iran, have not been able or willing to back this up effectively. Hence, the post-Soviet regimes have largely been left to fend for themselves.

Generally, the end of the Cold War affected regional conflicts as a contributory factor, though sometimes a substantial one. Where regional conflicts had become determined by the Cold War, its end brought them closer to a solution, without necessarily resolving them. Conversely, where regional conflicts had been suppressed by the Cold War, its end exacerbated them without fully accounting for their eruption.

Among those conflicts which continue to escape solutions even after the end of the Cold War, Halliday pays special attention to so-called ethnic conflicts. Since the 1970s, these have grown in number and intensity, and arise between as well as within existing states in the third world. Again, Sudan and Kashmir are cases in point. The deepening and exacerbation of vertical cleavages within the societies of many states, whether analysed in terms of ethnicity or growing nationalism, forms the backdrop for Fuller's thesis that regional conflicts are on the rise generally in areas hitherto under Soviet control or influence. More than any other major power, the Soviet Union attempted to contain and suppress the emergence of rival groups, which contradicted existing state or administrative borders.

Fuller's thesis is borne out by the developments which he analyses in the context of Central Asia. However, similar divisions have also eroded most subsaharan African states. Here, as Michael Bratton and Christopher Clapham show, the end of the Cold War has deprived governments of resources, supplied externally, which so far had allowed them to maintain at least a semblance of domestic order. Ironically, as Clapham also points out, it was precisely such external support which, during the Cold War era, enabled African regimes to ignore internal demands, and thus exacerbated internal opposition. As Soviet resources dwindled, Moscow found it more and more difficult to maintain its Cold War role in allied or dependent states. In response, the winners of the Cold War in Western Europe and North America could divest themselves of burdensome areas such as Africa, thus contributing to the further weakening of these states. Thus, the balances of power in many intra-state conflicts were tipped against governments which had previously relied on superpower support. Conflict within increasingly state-less societies, or between groups in control of weakened states, escalated accordingly.

The former Soviet Union and large parts of Africa are not the only parts of the world where the stand-off of the Cold War maintained a precarious *status quo*. As David Shambaugh and Rosemary Foot argue, in East and South East Asia, the end of the Cold War has taken the lid off latent, simmering or suppressed conflicts, though between rather than within states, which may deteriorate in the future. This affects relations between the People's Republic of China, which for long has enjoyed a special status in global politics, and its neighbours. In line with part of Halliday's argument, such conflicts often involve states which, like South Korea and Japan in the days of the Cold War, were on the same side of the global divide, and under the influence of the same hegemonic force. At the same time, the virtual elimination of Moscow as a regional player, and its rapprochement with China, has inevitably enhanced Beijing's role.

The road towards collective regional security arrangements in East and Southeast Asia is therefore a long and stony one, though not necessarily an impasse, as there seems to be a growing awareness on the parts of governments of the benefits of such arrangements. The task, however, is not facilitated by the emphasis which most of these relatively self-confident governments put on sovereignty, and by their critical attitudes towards interdependence and globalisation. In a sense, such arrangements may, ironically, be more likely in the Middle East which in spite of being torn by greater conflict is more dependent on the winners of the Cold War.

Finally, the end of the *status quo* underpinned by the Cold War has already changed, and probably will continue to change the political map of the world, though not always through violent conflict. Among the states which the Cold War had divided, Germany and Yemen have already been reunited; Korea may follow. In these cases as in various regional conflicts the end of the Cold War did or may tip the balance of power against the allies of the losers in this global contest. In the former Soviet Union, the old central state, as the loser of the Cold War, has clearly lost power . In Africa not only the losers of the Cold War or their allies but also some allies of its winner have lost or are about to lose their strength. The Soviet Union has itself been fragmented, and in Africa states considered as illegitimate or artificial are fragmented or threatened by fragmentation, irrespective of their previous cold war alliances. In the former Soviet Union this process led to the emergence of new states or states of sorts. However, existing African states often seem to dissolve, to be replaced only by banditries and warlordism.

The empirical findings discussed so far have important implications for international relations theory. First of all, the classical notion of state sovereignty, much questioned and criticised in the field, is once more cast into serious doubt – especially in Africa, given the *de facto* dissolution of states in large parts of the continent. In the Middle East, the conditions forced on Saddam Hussein by the coalition powers after the Gulf War of 1991 had a similar, though more formalised effect, including the creation of a however precarious Kurdish entity in northern Iraq. The simultaneous emphasis on sovereignty by East and South East Asian governments fails to extinguish this trend. Such emphasis by governments is a political rather than an analytical statement. As Foot and Shambaugh themselves show, forces of inter-state integration are at work even between states which emphasise their sovereignty. Consequently, international agreements and international regimes, as well as the participation of non-state actors, become increasingly important in their mutual relations.

By implication, the assumption by traditional realists of the state as a unified actor can no longer be maintained. This applies to situations of growing interdependence, as in parts of Asia, but it is most obvious in those African cases where governments, at best, control no more than their own capital cities, and then perhaps only by daylight. The absence of internal sovereignty, together with the presence of non-state actors who escape a clearly fictitious state monopoly of the means of physical coercion, points to the holes in the third old hat on the international coat-rack – that of an international system purely consisting of states. As in the previous two cases, it would go beyond the scope of this introduction to dwell on the many criticisms which have been levelled against this assumption over the years. However, in the context of recent global change, it is noticeable that the relaxation of state controls in the former Soviet Union and eastern Europe has been paralleled in Africa, where the weakening of the state has multiplied the number and power of non-state actors.

A 'Free World' For All? Democracy and Human Rights after the End of the Cold War

The second part of this book addresses the spread of liberal institutions and values which has been commonly expected after the end of the Cold War, and partly materialised. The decline and eventual dissolution of the Soviet Union not only removed from the geographical and ideological map a state opposing 'Western' liberalism, but also ended the binary divide of opposing military alliances. In principle, this should have allowed all states, East and West, to ease security-related restrictions on political freedoms. The defeat of communism as an ideology and, more importantly, of the powers representing or advocating it, left liberalism triumphant. As Halliday suggests, Asian and African states were left without any convincing or serious alternative to political and economic liberalism, at least in the short and medium terms.

Besides turning the former Second World on its head, these developments deeply affected the Third World. Chronologically, the terminal phase of Soviet decline coincided with the beginning of a wave of elections striking the Third World, especially Africa. At the same time, emergency legislation in many states was relaxed, re-establishing the rule of law to a greater degree than previously. There were two major changes. First, there was a generally growing respect for human rights on the part of numerous (but not all) governments – even if this often remains far below the universally agreed standards to which these governments officially subscribe. Second are processes commonly designated as 'democratisation'. These should lead towards an increase in political participation, either by enfranchising new groups, or reinforcing existing channels. There are some losers from this process, however. For instance, it will work against the left, through the delegitimation of leftist models and the ossification of leftist movements. Hence, it should perhaps be described more cautiously as the redrawing of the boundaries of political participation.

Nonetheless, these changes, while similar to those simultaneously occurring in the former USSR and in Eastern Europe, did not come about in the same way. Developments in Asia and Africa differed much from the analysis developed for Eastern Europe. In the latter case, factors external to many of the states concerned were relevant, to the extent that the Soviet government under Gorbachev allowed other governments intent on liberalising to pursue such policies. In contrast to this situation, African and Asian governments were sufficiently independent from the Soviet Union to change track at their own behest. However, unlike Eastern European governments, they seldom harboured such intentions.

Coinciding as they do, the decline of the USSR and the end of the Cold War nonetheless seem to supply obvious explanations for these sorts of political change if/when they occured in Africa and Asia. The disappearance of the USSR as a source of moral or paradigmatic support created difficulties, not only for leftist movements and parties outside government, but also for governments pursuing some policies similar to those of the Soviet Union. Together with the decline in Soviet material support, whether economic or military, this meant for many states in the Third World an increased dependency on resources and models supplied by Western governments or financial institutions. Public sector-oriented development strategies had failed to generate the necessary resources. Politics of repression lost their legitimacy, since they had visibly failed to work. In terms of resources, the Western support institutions were thus in a better position to demand compliance with economic and political conditions of their choice.

The delegitimation of policies pursued by the declining USSR, it may be argued, influenced the choice of future policies by Third World states. It is at least interesting to note that when confronted with economic crisis, ruling elites in Syria and elsewhere opted not for a reform of the public sector but for economic liberalisation, the latter being more in line with successful cases elsewhere in the world (and, incidentally, more beneficial for the ruling elite personally). Worse, of course, was the loss of paradigmatic support for leftist movements and parties which saw their entire legitimacy thrown into question. In some cases, external pressures after the Cold War led to their marginalisation or fall from power. Elsewhere, under more democratic conditions, they may or need adapt to new conditions, so as to continue and participate in politics. It is in this light that Harihar Bhattacharyya studies the attempts by Indian communist parties to reform themselves, and the limits of these attempts.

While neither economic nor political conditionality are an invention of the post-Cold War era, they could now be applied to many more countries than previously. In many of the countries of Asia and Africa, the USSR had been able to forge alliances (of sorts) more easily than in Latin America. Thus, towards and after the close of the Cold War era, parts of Asia and Africa experienced pressures and transformations which Latin American states had experienced earlier, due to their greater dependency throughout on those forces which later won the Cold War. In this sense, Asia and Africa were catching up with Latin America.

Three types of pressures were exercised, which need to be analysed as to their political consequences for recipient states, one of them merely economic, the two others explicitly political. In the economic sphere, donor demands for stabilisation and structural adjustment obviously had distributional consequences. Hence, one may argue that they had more or less directly political results. Political conditionality, for its part, comprised demands for accountability, representation and participation as guarantees for good governance and, to underpin these, a greater respect for human and civil rights by governments. Though a standard caveat, it needs to be repeated that such conditionality has often remained verbal, that it has been applied selectively, and partly in bad faith – in some cases possibly even to cover disengagement by the donors.

From the side of the donors, the numerous aspects of economic and political conditionality have been discussed in a vast specialised literature, which cannot be analysed here. Nonetheless, three such points may be briefly highlighted, since contributors to this book make them more forcefully than other authors. First, whatever the impact or attraction of donor conditionality, it needs to be seen in the context of the lack of any credible alternative to liberalism. Secondly, as David Williams shows, the spread of liberalism is not only promoted through grand programmes such as structural adjustment or political conditionality, but also through more discreet and cheaper channels such as technical and financial support for elections. These reveal that, beyond capitalist self-interest, the major international financial institutions are also moved by deeply ingrained liberal values. Thirdly, liberal values may be used as a political weapon outside classical cases of dependency on international aid. Universal, but ultimately Western, concepts of human rights have become a weapon in new global economic contests – in particular, between Europe and North America on the one hand, and East and South East Asia on the other. Since the end of the Cold War, these have replaced the old geo-political or geo-military struggles.

If one shifts the focus to the impact of condionalities of whatever sort on individual recipients, the actual results may differ substantially from donor expectations. If the end of the Cold War has led to greater emphasis on conditionality, it has not always been effective or responsible for change. Hence, the contributions by Bratton, Kienle and Williams seek to assess the extent to which growing rhetorical emphasis on the donor side has actually been translated into reality by the recipients, and the degree to which external pressures account for relevant and actual changes. Alternative or additional determinants are the delegitimation of certain models or strategies which seemed to have failed elsewhere, and domestic developments, such as more spontaneous policies of economic liberalisation, which in many cases were started or gained momentum around the end of the Cold War.

While the theoretical devaluation of Soviet-style strategies is obviously linked to the dissolution of the USSR, the roughly simultaneous attempts at economic liberalisation may simply have been a response to sheer necessity, imposed by constraints rather than deliberately chosen. In the latter case, only the conditions which narrowed policy choices could be viewed as a result of the dilapidation of the USSR and the subsequent end of the Cold War. They could be treated as such to the extent that decreasing Soviet support prompted or contributed to economic difficulties in the state concerned. At any rate, under these circumstances the end of the Cold War would only be indirectly relevant as a factor of change.

Bratton and Kienle reach the conclusion that domestic transformations towards a greater degree of political liberalisation in the Middle East and Africa were helped, sometimes significantly, by the end of the Cold War and its various consequences. However, internal factors could be equally or more important. From a slightly different perspective, Williams confirms the importance of global change for the unleashing of the liberal transformation process. In his view, it was precisely the end of the Cold War divide which enabled the liberal orthodoxy of international financial institutions to become fully effective.

More specifically, Bratton and Kienle show that, towards and after the end of the Cold War, individual African and Arab governments introduced measures of political liberalisation (such as enlarged political participation and enhanced human rights) for one or more of the following reasons: first, to gain access to resources controlled by forces linking support to economic or political conditions; second, because the failure of certain types of policies in the USSR and in Eastern Europe invalidated them in the eyes of ruling elites; third, to preempt internal pressures for change from opposition groups, particularly when these were supported by simultaneous external pressures.

None of these motives were purely dependent on the end of the Cold War. As Halliday shows, public sector-oriented development models were already being questioned in the 1970s. Similarly, in the Jordanian case, Kienle points to attempts in the 1980s to preempt internal unrest through measures of political liberalisation. Nonetheless, with the end of the Cold War these factors could be expected to and – at least in Africa and in the Middle East – actually did grow in importance. Incidentally, as Bratton and Clapham point out, such policies were pursued not only by the United States but also by France, which continued to occupy an important position in Africa during the Cold War. Additionally, the notion of the 'winners of the Cold War' needs to be defined in very wide terms, including not only governments or state-actors, but also international or private financial institutions and other forces defending liberal capitalism.

As Bratton shows in the African case, the end of the Cold War also strengthened domestic pressures for change, and indeed contributed to their success. Conversely, in the Middle East, as Kienle suggests, domestic pressures, or government attempts to preempt them, seem to have led to certain types of political change, while external factors associated with the end of the Cold War, such as political conditionality, seem to have entailed other types of political change. The Syrian case underscores the independent role of domestic and external factors. For example, the new electoral law might be clearly linked to a perceived need to incorporate the increasingly important business community, while the release of certain prisoners equally unpopular with the regime and the private sector, followed external pressures. Many relevant domestic elements in the Middle East, particularly the growing weight of business communities with their own interests, could only be linked to the demise of the Soviet Union if their rise was viewed as a consequence of new government policies aiming to overcome economic crises which had been exacerbated by decreasing Soviet support. While a reduction of Soviet support certainly played its part in provoking economic crises – as, for instance, in Syria in the mid-1980s – such crises could hardly be reduced to this one factor. Hence, it seems safer to assume that, even towards and after the end of the Cold War, political transformations in Asian and African states were not only determined by factors related to the end of the Cold War.

Comparing Africa to the Middle East, an interesting difference emerges. In Africa, external pressures often reinforced internal demands. On the other hand, examples from the Arab world tend to show that domestic causes (though less so demands) led to certain political changes, while external pressures led to others, without these actually reinforcing each other. As Bratton points out, the extent to which external pressures influence domestic political transformation depends largely on the internal balance of power between government and opposition. In numerous African states, built on relatively precarious bases, the resources available to opposition forces matched closely those available to governments. This led to transformations which are largely absent from the Arab world, where states are more consolidated. The precarious nature of African states could also mean that external pressures, including the withdrawal of external resources, combined with internal opposition to produce the collapse of the state, rather than its transformation.

Finally, differences in the degree of external pressures also need to be taken into account. Returning to the selective nature of conditionality, Bratton argues for Africa that donor demands for political liberalisation come to an end when the political stability of the recipients is threatened. Conditionality may, therefore, collide with interest, in particular stability. A similar argument may be made for the Arab states in the Middle East where Western fears of Islamism have mitigated the eagerness to impose political liberalisation. As in the Cold War, *realpolitik* has come back into play, and some of the rules of the old game have remained unchanged.

PART ONE

Global Changes, Peace and Regional Conflict

1 ❧ The Third World and the End of the Cold War: An Interim Assessment

Fred Halliday

Introduction

For much of the Third World the end of the Cold War has not transformed the political or economic life, and the major new trends which Third World countries exhibit began well before the collapse of Soviet communism. Yet this latter process marks the end of an epoch in world history and has many implications for the countries of 'The South'. The earthquake that hit the international system at the end of the 1980s, conventionally summarised in one phrase, as 'the end of the Cold War', can more accurately be said to involve at least four distinct elements, three historical verdicts and one, as yet contested, trend: the end of the Cold War conflict which dates back to 1917 and, as a global phenomenon, to 1945; the break-up of the Soviet Union and its alliance system; the collapse of communism itself as a global challenge to the capitalist West; the 'triumph', in ideology if not in practice, of one single political and economic model, that of developed liberal capitalism. Interrelated as they are, the first three, historical, processes are developments with, amongst other things, distinct implications for the Third World. The fourth is more a postulate, and a potentiality, than a reality: it poses as many questions for the future of the Third World as it provides answers about the end of the Cold War.

First, let us examine in rather more detail what the conclusion of the Cold War has entailed. The end of the Cold War and the collapse of the Soviet Union have had wide-ranging consequences for the Third World the full import and variety of which it will take many years to assess fully. The end of the East–West conflict has removed the bipolar contest that fuelled, when it did not generate, most Third World conflicts and which served as the framework for many North–South financial and military flows. On the strategic side, while naive extrapolation would be misplaced, there is reason to accept a cautious version of the view that developed democracies do not go to war with each other: provided Russia consolidates a measure of democracy, and none of the other major powers regresses, at the moment an unlikely prospect, then it would seem that, for the first time in a century, war and the threat of war between developed countries is off the international agenda. This represents a momentous shift in world history, but it does not mean peace: new strategic issues have emerged, born of the break-up of the USSR and with regard to the regional impact of post-communist rivalries and to nuclear proliferation. One very important concomitant of the end of communist hegemony has been the break-up of multinational states, setting in train the end of the 'regime', the international understanding, that has prevailed with almost no exceptions since 1945, that the existing map of the world, unjust and arbitrary as it is, should prevail. Already, with the fragmentation of the USSR, Czechoslovakia, Yugoslavia and Ethiopia, more states have been added to the international system in one phase of fragmentation than at any time since the end of the middle ages. The demonstration effects on the Third World – Africa, India, Pakistan, the Kurdish regions of Turkey and potentially even parts of Latin America where a new ethnicity is emerging – are as yet incalculable. The breakdown of the post-1945 regime has also led to the erosion of state boundaries by fusion, first in Yemen and Germany, eventually, and almost inevitably, will lead to the merger of the two Koreas, and in time to that of the three Chinas.

Politically, the end of Cold War has removed the source of support for many states and movements who either received backing from one or other bloc, or who sought to play one off against the other. While it has strengthened the hand of the West in some respects, it has removed the model of an alternative path of development which, to varying degrees, provided inspiration and aid to radical forces in the Third World. The Cold War served to promote economic growth: communist states presented themselves as a model of economic development but, in the case of some Far Eastern capitalist countries, the strategic challenges of the Cold War also played a significant role in generating state-promoted growth. The sub-title of Rostow's *Stages of Growth* was 'A Non-Communist Manifesto'; the success of the NICs was based on *political economy*, not economics alone but the growth of these countries has long ceased to be reliant on such strategic rivalry and may now derive stimulus from its demise.

In the economic sphere the end of the Cold War initially raised the prospect of a significant redirection of financial and trade flows away from the Third World towards the newly emerging post-communist world, both because of the strategic threat which crisis in these countries may pose to the 'West', i.e. the developed, OECD countries and because, stripped of their communist carapace, these states re-emerge as what they were prior to the establishment of communism, namely semi-peripheral states, in competition with others, such as in Latin America, for trade and investment; the 'second', communist, world is disappearing, with the result that the countries formerly in it are being transferred to the 'semi-peripheral' branch of the Third World. As was graphically put by an international banker at debt rescheduling discussion in Paris in 1991, addressing his Soviet counterpart: 'I cannot understand it. A few months ago you were putting men into space. Now you are talking like the Sudan.' The Russian reply: 'you just do not understand what has happened.' And more has happened since. The implications of this for resource allocation may, however, be less dramatic than initially supposed.

Before assessing in more detail these changes a number of cautionary notes should be struck. On the one hand, while communism has ceased to be a global challenge, the 'end of communism', if by this is meant the end of communist party rule, is still far from complete and has, as yet, been confined to the European arena: of the 1.7 bn people ruled by communism at the end of 1988, over 1.3 bn remained so at the end of 1994 – in China, Korea, Vietnam and Cuba. Their economic system may be adjusting, in the Chinese case most obviously, and their political systems and ideologies may in the long run be doomed, but so far the 'end of communism' in terms of a system of political control has been a European affair, as has the 'triumph' of democracy. Secondly, it would be mistaken to see this as a unilinear process. In the strategic field the end of Cold War has been accompanied by an attempt to resolve around a dozen 'regional conflicts'; yet initial impressions suggest that in other respects the end of the Cold War will foster greater conflicts between and within states, while arms manufacturers, losing their East–West justifications, will be more eager to send arms to the Third World.

Table 1: Defence Expenditure of NATO Countries ($m at1985 prices)

	1985	1992	1995 (est.)
Belgium	2,428	1,866	1,397
Denmark	1,259	1,256	1,125[1]
France	20,780	21,893	17,987[1]
Germany	19,922	19,252	14,786[2]
Greece	2,331	1,903	n/a
Italy	9,733	10,690	7,456[4]
Luxembourg	38	57	65
Netherlands	3,884	3,818	3,837[3]
Norway	1,797	2,023	1,955[1]
Portugal	654	874	402
Spain	3,969	3,735	n/a
Turkey	1,649	3,423	6,866
United Kingdom	23,791	20,726	18,319[1]
Canada	7,566	7,790	6,926
United States	258,165	242,717	202,934

1 – by 1994; 2 – by 1996; 3 – by 1997; 4 – by 2003
Source: IISS, *The Military Balance*, 1993–94; NATO, *Facts and Figures*; NAA, *Military Trends within the Atlantic Alliance*, Rafael Estrella, October 1993 from Simon Lunn, 'A Reassessment of European Security' in Manfred Wörner et al., *What is European Security after the Cold War?*, (The Philip Morris Institute for Public Policy Research, December 1993) p. 53.

Most importantly, while this is undoubtedly a time of major change for the Third World, not all the changes are the result of the end of Cold War. The most important process affecting the Third World began two decades ago with the industrialisation of a group of Far Eastern countries followed by a number of both East Asian and Latin American states. In other respects too, the new international context of development long predates 1989 – as, for example, in regard to the 90 per cent fall between 1980 and 1989 in a form of resource transfer important a decade earlier – commercial bank lending to the Third World. Many of the other processes now affecting the Third World predate the collapse of Soviet communism in 1989: the 'Third World' itself had, over four decades, become more and more disaggregated as a result of the uneven spread of capitalist industrialisation; inter-state and inter-ethnic rivalries, separate from any East–West dimension were growing in many areas; there was a rising dissatisfaction with the project of the post-colonial modernising state, especially in the Islamic world; 'development' itself was in crisis, as a theoretical concept and as a policy, and earlier projects for global reform, articulated in the campaign for a New International Economic Order, had foundered. It did not take 1989 to cast doubt on the project for a non-capitalist, 'autocentred', 'self-reliant' or 'de-linked' project of economic development. In these, as in other respects, the end of the Cold War did not introduce a completely new situation; it compounded and added to a set of changes that were already underway and which had in some respects themselves contributed to the crisis of the communist project.

If its overall significance will take years to emerge, this multiple process has already confounded some of the expectations held before the events of 1989–91: not only did the end of communism come far more quickly and less bloodily than most had expected, but it has shown three suppositions, long held in the West at least, to be unfounded. One was the belief that, with the end of the Cold War, there would be a comprehensive reduction in international tension. While the overarching threat of great power war, and of nuclear war, has receded, that of localised inter-state and inter-ethnic war has nonetheless continued, particularly in the Far East and the Persian Gulf. Another belief apparently confounded was the hope that, with the end of an authoritarian and sanguinary socialism in the East, it would be easier for a 'democratic' socialism to develop in the West and South. The trend in most of the Third World remains away from all traditional forms of state ownership and social intervention. Also refuted has been the expectation that the development of the South, long inhibited by the diversion of resources to the arms race, can now be promoted by greater expenditure on development, by a global 'peace dividend': arms expenditures in the developed states will fall, but the resources saved are not, in large measure, going to be spent on development aid or foreign direct investment. In 1991, for example, as military budgets fell, total OECD aid to the Third World rose by a mere 1 per cent in real terms. As for the consequences for foreign direct investment in the Third World, no noticeable correlations can be made.

So mistaken have these assumptions turned out to be, at least in the medium term, that it is not necessary to discuss them further, but only to register that what were expected to be three positive consequences for the international system, and for the Third World in particular, have not come about. Thus the expectation of a global triumph of liberal, developed, capitalism may have some arguments in its favour, but it too may turn out to be another one of the illusions that are casualties of the post Cold War situation.

Consequences for the Third World

Provisional as any assessment of the import of these different changes in the international system must be, it is possible to identify a number of respects in which the end of the Cold War and the collapse of the USSR have had and/or may have consequences for the Third World. If it must be recalled that much of what was happening in the Third World had little to do with the end of the Cold War, there were a number of consequences, economic as well as political. The following, schematic, representation is designed to indicate some such general areas, with the evident proviso that in many ways these will overlap, whether in a reinforcing or contradictory way.

(i) Changes in great power competition

The Cold War, in the sense of Soviet–Western rivalry, ended in 1989–90 in the Third World as it did in Europe. Moscow ceased to be a strategic and ideological rival of Washington and abandoned its former 'internationalist' commitments, along with the idea that it could be strengthened by consolidating a rival bloc. The USSR, as much as the USA, rediscovered 'national interest'. The effect of this is evident in both diplomatic and strategic terms: former allies of the USSR's were forced to search for compromises with the adversaries against whom they were supported in the Cold War – be this Vietnam against China, the PDRY against North Yemen, Syria and the PLO against Israel, Nicaragua against the USA. In many cases the local states were reluctant to see the USSR abandon its previous role, and tried to forestall the process, Syria and Cuba being cases in point. In some other former Soviet allies the regimes objected strongly to changing priorities in Moscow – this was especially so in Pyongyang, Kabul and Tripoli. But the reality was that the USSR was not prepared to provide the kind of support it once did, and actively tried, within the resources of its waning international influence, to cooperate with the USA in resolving intractable Third World conflicts.

Although presented as a new era, a 'New World Order', in the period 1988–89 this ending of Soviet–US rivalry did not introduce a period of general peace in the Third World and was unlikely to do so. While the Cold War was over, differences of interest and opinion between major states were not necessarily a thing of the past. For all its pro-Soviet weakness, and the initial prospect of further fragmentation up to and including the secession of regions East of the Urals, Russia will at some point re-emerge as a significant actor in international affairs, with regard to Europe, the Middle East and Central Asia at least. It will not be easy about the increased influence of China or its old Islamic foe Turkey. In the Far East the most enduring conflict of the modern era, that between China and Japan, acquired a new vitality.

At the same time, as a result of the falling away of the Cold War disciplines, competition between advanced capitalist countries may well increase, first at the economic and then later at the political and strategic levels. The trade disputes focused on GATT and the WTO between the USA and the EEC, and the enduring Japanese–US economic competition, indicate how future rivalries could evolve, to include influence in the Third World: a century ago this rivalry took the form of competition for areas of formal, colonial, control; today such control is not acceptable or necessary, having been replaced by trading blocs, investment, access to raw materials and labour and other, relatively informal, means of control. Competition by developed countries in the Third World may, therefore, be seen as having passed through three historic phases: the quest for areas of formal colonial control (1870s–1945); Cold War rivalry between the Soviet and US blocs (1945–1990); and a phase of informal, predominantly economic, competition (1990 onwards). Economic competition was always there – evident, for example, in the oil industry – but has today become the predominant form, with the falling away of the Soviet challenge. What form this rivalry will take is impossible, as yet, to divine: it does appear that, as already indicated, and, for the first time in a century, i.e. since the outbreak of the Sino–Japanese wars of the 1890s, that armed conflict between major powers is improbable. But if the prospect, at the moment remote, of a division of the world into three major trading blocs – North American, European, Far Eastern – becomes reality then strategic and political issues will inevitably come to affect the Third World as well.

(ii) Regional conflicts and their resolution

The incalculable impact on the Third World of the breakdown of the post-1945 regime on frontiers is one further reason for scepticism about a new era of peace: whatever the changes in Soviet attitudes; as subsequent chapters indicate, many of the issues and enmities in the specific conflicts remain alive, and have in some cases been exacerbated or even created. Precisely because these – e.g. the Arab–Israeli, or Indo–Pakistani – conflicts were not the product of Cold War, however much they were fuelled by them, they did not disappear with the ending of Soviet–American rivalry. As we have noted, the desire to extricate itself from Third World conflicts that were diplomatically and economically costly was an important part of Gorbachev's 'new thinking'. As far as extrication is concerned, the former USSR was largely successful: for Moscow no significant and contentious Third World commitments remained by 1990, except in former republics of the USSR (Georgia, Tajikistan). Among other things, the USSR abandoned its previous policy of providing arms in return for political and strategic benefits, something that had dominated its arms supply policy to the Third World for the previous four decades. In common with the USA and other permanent members of the Security Council, Moscow now committed itself to an international register of arms transfers, effective from January 1993, and to restraint in situations of inter-state conflict.

More difficult was the achievement of political solutions: in this sense the end of the Cold War had its impact on these conflicts but did not automatically resolve them. In some success was evident: the independence of Namibia in March 1990 reflected a positive combination of diplomatic and strategic concerns. The evolving situation in South Africa itself owed something to the end of the Cold War: the Pretoria regime felt a little more able to open dialogue with the ANC because the broader strategic threat of 'communism' had receded. However, this was not the sole or even main reason for the regime's change: rather the regime's change of policy reflected the impact of other international factors – Soviet military backing for the ANC, US Senatorial pressure for tougher sanctions in 1986 – that were product of the Cold War itself, and of US and Soviet rivalry. Once these had their impact, especially from the mid-1980s onwards, the Afrikaaner regime was able to use the changed international circumstances to talk. On the ANC side, the shift in Soviet policy, and the attenuation of Moscow's military commitment, may also have made dialogue easier, although it has to be said that Mandela himself and those close to him had envisaged such a solution long before anyone in Moscow began to think of 'national reconciliation'. In two other Southern African states, Mozambique and Angola, the regimes, deprived of Soviet military backing and exhausted by a decade and a half of war, were forced to enter into negotiations with their right-wing guerrilla opponents, RENAMO and UNITA respectively, with both Soviet and US encouragement.

In Yemen, the USSR's longest-standing Arab ally, in Aden, exhausted by internecine conflict and sensing a waning of Soviet military and economic support, entered into negotiations with the larger North Yemen that culminated in the unification of May 1990. Here the ebbing of Cold War operated on both sides: both Yemeni states had long proclaimed their commitment to unity, but had been restrained by the fears of their Cold War patrons that this would mean engulfment by the other – North Yemen being restrained by Saudi Arabia, Egypt and the USA, South Yemen by the USSR. Moscow and Washington accepted that, with the Cold War over, Yemeni unity was not such a threat, leaving the Saudis to oppose it for regional reasons. A similar process of mutual adjustment could be observed in Cambodia where the willingness of both sides to find common ground was encouraged by the end of Cold War: China was less fearful of an independent, Vietnam-dominated, Cambodia, and Vietnam was more willing to allow a coalition government to come into place. As the Soviet Union's influence waned the Western powers, who had implicitly backed China's support for the Khmer Rouges, were also less committed to this strategy. This was far from meaning that all regional issues had been resolved. Some, with little or no Cold War dimension, continued to defy resolution: Cyprus, Western Sahara, Ireland, Burma, Kashmir, Punjab, Sudan, Somalia to name but a few. Even where international negotiating procedures had been set up, as in Afghanistan and the Arab–Israeli process, local animosities continued to rage.

Regional conflicts were, however, continuing to command

international attention for two other reasons, which appeared likely to offset whatever gains were brought by the end of the Cold War. One was that, from the 1970s onwards, there had been a growth of inter-ethnic and communal conflicts in the Third World, be this in Sri Lanka, various provinces of India, Burma, Pakistan, Lebanon, Somalia, Ethiopia or Yugoslavia. In other words the trend was for greater ethnic conflict, irrespective of the Cold War, and with the result that increasing areas of the Third World had become ungovernable, subject to forms of banditry and tribal violence.

To this had to be added a second trend, the specific contribution of the end of the Cold War itself, which, by releasing previously established forms of hegemony and coercive control, introduced new elements of inter-ethnic and inter-state rivalry. In Yugoslavia, Czechoslovakia, Georgia, Nagarno–Karabakh, Chechen–Ingush, Moldavia, Tajikistan and elsewhere, the collapse of communist authority meant not democracy but greater fragmentation and, in most cases, violence. Inter-state conflict and rivalry were also fomented by this collapse of Soviet rule. This was most obviously the case between former components of single multi-ethnic states – the USSR, Ethiopia, Yugoslavia – but it was also true of the opening up of new inter-state competitions for influence in formerly communist areas. In Central Asia the new rivalry between Iran and Turkey, with participating roles from Israel, Saudi Arabia, Pakistan and China, threatened to become a major focus of international concern, even if the actual importance of Central Asia was probably rather overstated. In the Balkans old alliances evident before the First World War were revived, with Germany and Turkey backing Croatia, while the countries of Orthodox Christianity, especially Greece and Russia, were sympathetic to Serbia.

It is in this context that the complex issue of the Gulf war of 1990–91 can be seen. Exactly how the end of the Cold War contributed to the Iraqi invasion of Kuwait is debatable: the invasion can be seen as a result of the end of the Cold War, a removal of pre-existing controls, but the opposite is also arguable – many observers, especially in the Arab world, believed it was because Saddam Hussein did *not* realise how far Soviet policy had changed, i.e. that it would not back him, that he invaded his neighbour. What seems most plausible is that the increased US commitment to 'democratic values', albeit selectively defined, combined with the evidence in Eastern Europe of Soviet willingness to allow its allies to be overthrown and even in some cases, as in Bulgaria and Rumania, to assist in the process, alarmed Saddam and led him to decide to act first, to boost his economic resources, before external pressure got greater. It is too simple to say that had the Cold War continued Saddam would not have invaded Kuwait, since Soviet allies had, in the past, committed rash acts that provoked international crises – Kim Il-sung in 1950, Nasser in 1967 to name but two. There did, however, exist a partial connection between the Gulf crisis and the end of the Cold War, both in regard to the Iraqi decision to invade and in regard to the manner of the US counter-attack and the international support it received.

(iii) Changes in Eastern bloc trade and aid

During the Cold War the Soviet bloc as a whole sought to organise international trade, and provide economic aid, on a basis substantially different from that of the West. To some extent it succeeded. Yet, in the end, it failed to provide a sufficient basis to boost economic growth in the countries concerned. During1980-87 Soviet aid represented only around 10 per cent of total aid to the Third World. At the same time, trade with the Soviet bloc trade was, in most cases, also a small part of overall trade involving the Third World. As Table 2 indicates, Soviet bloc imports from developing countries accounted for, on average, only around 5 per cent of Third World exports.

As far as exports were concerned, the main element in Soviet bloc exports, oil, was sold in the West, not the Third World, and no Soviet Third World ally was a major participant in international trade. On the other hand, the Soviet Union did have amongst its significant Third World commercial partners states that were not aligned with it politically but which, for a combination of strategic and economic reasons, developed substantial trade with the USSR: Turkey, Iraq, Iran and India amongst them.

The end of the Cold War and the collapse of the USSR has had serious implications for these trade and aid flows. At first, this involved an attempt by the Russians to put their trade with other countries, including members of COMECON, on a different, hard currency, basis. Thus from January 1991 all intra-COMECON trade was to be on the basis of world prices and demarcated in hard currency, and well before then the terms of agreements between members had started to change. But this reorganisation of intra-bloc trade was overtaken by the collapse of the bloc itself, including the dissolution of

COMECON. Information is still fragmentary; but it would seem that most trade of the former USSR has been curtailed as a result of the crisis. Eastern European countries now have to acquire most of their energy from the world market and find other outlets for their manufactured goods. A country such as Finland lost a third of its trade, and in part, because of this, acquired a 20 per cent unemployment level. In the Third World, Cuba saw its trade with the USSR fall by up to 80 per cent for a combination of political and technical reasons. India, which conducted substantial trade with the USSR, also suffered from the breakdown.

Table 2: Exports from Developing Countries,1980–1986 (percentage distribution)

	1980	1981	1982	1983	1984	1985	1986
Industrial Western Countries	63.6	60.9	59.1	59.7	60.2	60.1	60.2
Soviet Bloc	4.5	4.8	4.7	4.8	4.6	5.3	5.5

Source: IMF, *Direction of Trade*

What this all means in the longer run is still unclear. Some former trading partners of the USSR tried to maintain links with Moscow, on a new basis, and at the same time to negotiate new agreements with the former Soviet republics. Thus Cuba signed agreements on petroleum with Azerbaijan, while Iran signed a deal to provide energy to Ukraine. Pakistan, Turkey and Israel were all interested in finding partners in the former Soviet states. The least that can be said is that because of the triple disruption – renegotiated trading terms, disruption of production within the former USSR (the FSU), fragmentation of the Union itself – trade with the outside world was severely curtailed. It would take some years at least to re-establish itself in new patterns.

As already noted, Soviet aid was a significant factor in the development of some Third World states, notably Mongolia, Vietnam, Afghanistan, and Cuba. In all these cases the years 1985–89 saw a gradual reduction in the volume of aid, and increased criticism within the USSR of the way in which these states handled their affairs. In

1990–92 the cut-off became more absolute, in part because of disorder within the FSU itself. Yet there was a further, political, dimension to this, at both the domestic and international levels. Within the FSU and other Eastern European countries aid to the Third World became very unpopular, and was blamed, inaccurately, for many of the economic problems these countries had. There was resentment at the price it was believed had to be paid for sustaining dictatorial and ungrateful Third World allies, and at what was seen as a Western concern for development and human rights in the Third World, to the detriment of the communist countries. At a meeting held in 1991 of foreign policy experts from Eastern European countries the only thing they could readily agree on was that they had turned their backs on what they called 'internationalism', by which they meant economic and political support for Third World states. Equally, this change, especially with regard to revolutionary regimes, had an international dimension, in that the Russian government of Yeltsin, and even the Gorbachev regime in its later stages, wanted to make it demonstratively clear that they were not backing states regarded as dangerous by the USA. Hence the disparagement of Castro, Gaddafi and others by Soviet journalists and officials, many of whom were, only a while ago, mouthing the platitudes of socialist fraternity.

The consequences within these states were substantial. In Cuba the reduction and virtual cessation of economic links with the USSR led to the introduction of an austerity programme, named 'The Special Period in a Time of Peace': production was cut back, energy sparingly used, transport reduced, and the population prepared for a long phase of restricted goods and services. GDP fell by nearly 50 per cent in the years 1990–93. The expectation of Moscow, in liaison with the US, was that this would in time provoke such resentment amongst key sectors of the state, particularly the army, that the communist leadership would be ousted, thus reproducing the Eastern European scenario in the Caribbean. To counter this Castro resorted on the one hand to a spirited and patriotic defence of the Cuban commitment to socialism, and on the other to a greater reliance on tourism as a source of foreign exchange: the result of the latter was, however, to promote a two-tier economy, in which foreign visitors received high quality access to goods and services, while indigenous Cubans faced considerable hardship. The refusal of the Castro leadership to take the necessary initiative on the political front meant that there was a serious risk of the very substantial achievements of the revolution in the social sphere, health and education, being squandered in a complete and potentially bloody collapse.

In Nicaragua the economic and social situation had already begun to deteriorate after the mid-1980s, under the pressure of the Contra war, but worsened substantially with the change of government in 1990. In Mongolia the virtual cessation of Soviet economic aid led to dramatic disruptions in economic output, and a search for alternative sources of support, notably Japan. In Vietnam, where Soviet assistance was proportionately less significant, but still the main source of external aid, there was a gradual liberalisation of the economy, to allow domestic capitalists to flourish, while at the same time international business was invited to come in to share in the development of the country's oil resources. Prostitution now became rife in Vietnam again, as in Cuba. In Afghanistan, the cessation of Soviet aid after the August 1991 coup led to great hardship, inflation and misery in the government-held areas and contributed to the willingness of the Najibullah regime to find a compromise with the mujahidin opposition, one that the latter, internally fragmented, proved unable to honour.

The qualitative impact of this cut-off in Soviet aid was also significant. In certain respects, and for all its delays and inefficiencies, Soviet economic policy towards the Third World did meet the needs of some Third World states. Trade agreements, for five years and at fixed prices, enabled some countries to manage their economic policy with greater certainty. For some Third World capitalist states, such as India and Egypt, access to Soviet markets enabled them to exports goods that they would have found it difficult to sell in the more advanced countries. For others, such as Turkey, Soviet help with industrialisation of some sectors provided more appropriate assistance, and on better terms, than that provided from the West. In the case of Nicaragua, where Soviet bloc aid rose to account for over half of the total by the end of the Sandinista regime (included in this was cheap price oil), the ending of Soviet support was a further blow to the economy.

The impact of the end of Cold War on Third World economies was not, however, wholly negative, in at least two respects. First, while there was much exaggeration of this from Soviet and non-Soviet sources, it was evident that much of the Soviet aid was inefficient, distorting of the local economy and in quality and quantity inferior to that available from Western or multilateral sources. As such it contributed to the fossilisation and arresting of economic development in these states. Secondly, while aid from the FSU was probably something that could be expected only in the remote future, given Moscow's own economic needs and general lack of strategic interest in the Third World, positive changes in international trade resulting from the collapse of communism could be considerable. In some areas newly independent republics of the USSR have been keen to develop export agreements with Third World states: the links between Central Asian states and Pakistan or South Korea are an example. Figures for the early 1990s suggested no increases in Eastern European imports from Third World states but this may have been transitional, and Third World states may find new export opportunities, in Eastern Europe above all: first, in oil, since Russian supplies are likely to remain low in quantity and unreliable, and then in selected areas, such as textiles and tropical fruits, the latter an area of particular public demand in the post-communist regimes ('We want kiwis and nectarines' was one slogan of East Germans who came to the West when the wall came down). Insofar as, being semi-peripheral states, the post-communist countries were in competition with industrialising Third World states for the markets of the developed world the consequences were negative, but this could be countered by the longer-run, macroeconomic and product-specific, possibilities opening up, provided economic collapse was avoided.

An area of particularly contradictory consequences was migration. In the 1970s and 1980s there developed considerable labour migration from poorer to richer COMECON states, notably that of Vietnamese, but also Mozambiqueans, Cubans and others, to European communist countries, especially the USSR and East Germany. The collapse of communism was very hard for these people, who saw their jobs removed, their remittances blocked, and increasing racist abuse from the local inhabitants. For Vietnam, in particular, this was a serious blow. The broader migratory consequences concerned out-migration. Communism, once established, prevented out-migration, although the moment of revolutionary consolidation was often one involving large scale migration, from China to Cuba and Vietnam. The result of the breakdown of these controls was likely to be substantial out-migration to more developed countries, the level to be determined above all by political and economic conditions in the countries concerned. Here immigrants from the former communist states were likely to be direct competitors for the jobs of Third World immigrants. This was especially so in Western Europe, where anxiety about ethnic and religious diversity made the supply of white, more or less Christian, migrants from the East more attractive. In the case of Israel, and treating this issue in its purely economic dimensions, the flow of Soviet Jews reduced the need for a Palestinian labour force and may have made it easier to envisage withdrawal from territories occupied in 1967.

(iv) A model discredited

Beyond the flow of Soviet aid and arms, and the organisation of trade, the existence of the USSR acted as a model for Third World regimes committed to development, sustaining as it did the belief that some alternative to free market development was possible. Not all the responsibility for the widespread incidence of this model needs to be ascribed to communism, since the imperatives for planning, import substitution, protection, resources distribution, nationalisation and so forth were as much from within any country as they were externally inspired. The example of Kemalist Turkey, which, without communist influence, pursued a neo-Bismarckian path of what would later be called 'national democratic' development in the 1920s and 1930s shows how this was possible. Hence the policy pursued by India, Egypt, Peru and a range of other states in the 1960s was not simply a result of Moscow's influence. Nonetheless, the existence of the USSR and the inspiration provided by its apparent successes, including the industrialisation of the 1930s, the defeat of NaziGermany and the launching of the first man into space, gave to the USSR a prestige that affected development in Third World states. This often took the form of these states differentiating themselves from the communist model by particularist invocations – 'Arab socialism' of Nasser and the Ba'th, 'African socialism' of Nyerere, Kaunda and Nkrumah – or by proclaiming even more radical and revolutionary forms – as in China, Korea and Cuba. But all these were variants that claimed legitimacy from the central tenet of the Bolshevik revolution, that some alternative to capitalism was possible and, in some longer run scheme of things, inevitable.

Table 3: The Third World in Soviet Perspective, 1982

1. *Core Communist Party Ruled States*
   Afghanistan
   Cambodia
   Cuba
   Laos
   Mongolia
   Vietnam
2. *Leading States of Socialist Orientation*
   Angola
   Ethiopia
   Mozambique
   Nicaragua
   South Yemen
3. *Independent Communist Party-Ruled States*
   China
   North Korea
4. *Less Advanced States of Socialist Orientation*
   Algeria
   Benin
   Burma
   Cape Verde
   Congo–Brazzaville
   Guinea
   Guinea Bissau
   Iraq
   Libya
   Madagascar
   Sao Tome
   Syria
   Tanzania
   Zimbabwe
5. *Marginal States of Socialist Orientation*
   Upper Volta (later Burkina Faso)
   Ghana
   Seychelles
   Surinam

Source: Fred Halliday, *Cold War, Third World*, (Radius/Hutchinson, London, 1989) p. 99.

The collapse of the USSR did more than anything else to discredit this model, not only at the level of economic management, but also as a political project, a programme of revolutionary action designed to accelerate change and avoid the constraints of a system dominated by the West. It therefore weakened confidence in 'anti-imperialism' in general, as well as in state-run economic policy. It was, after 1991, much harder to claim that some 'alternative' path of economic development was possible: all now seemed to be condemned to accepting the dictates of the market, be this through the influence of multinationals and banks, or through the structural adjustment policies of the World Bank. Ideas of a 'third way', a nationalist, state-dominated but democratic model, common in the 1970s, had by then also been discredited. Acceptance of 'free market' policies became, along with political conditions such as respect for human rights and political pluralism, a condition not just for international economic support, but even for membership of international political bodies such as the OSCE and the new extension of NATO, the North Atlantic Council. The definition of what constituted acceptable political and economic policy was unambiguously the prerogative of the USA and its closest allies, or, on matters such as farm subsidies, of the US alone. Yet while these conditions were defined in the West, they were at first nowhere more spiritedly defended than in the former capitals of the communist East: here, in the immediate aftermath of the collapse of communism, the 'market' acquired the status of a new fetish and all that contradicted it was seen as representative of the now outmoded communist approach. Even such issues as concern for women's rights or for the welfare of the poor were regarded by much of the post-communist elites, and by significant sections of the population, as somehow part of the communist legacy.

Yet in several respects this process was a more complex one than it appeared. First, the discrediting of the orthodox state-centred approach to economic development had begun well before 1989, and went back to the first crises of this system in the 1960s. It was then that the first Soviet attempts at reform were made under Khrushchev; it was in the early 1970s that a number of Third World states began to move away from their versions of 'socialism' – Egypt being a prime example. The most important move was that of China, with the launching of the 'four modernisations' in 1978. Cuba had initiated a set of liberalising economic reforms in 1981, and throughout the 1980s Third World states, for reasons both domestic and international, had moderated their previous commitment to heavy industry, planning and state control of prices. Indeed the orthodox model of socialist development was being modified in the Third World before it became so in many

Table 4: Foreign Direct Investment: Selected Countries, 1990–91 US $ millions

	1990	1991
Third World		
Indonesia	964	1,482
Nigeria	588	712
Pakistan	249	257
Argentina	2,036	2,439
Chile	595	576
Malaysia	2,902	4,073
Philippines	530	544
Thailand	2,376	2,014
Singapore	4,808	3,584
Communist/ex-Communist		
China	3,489	4,366
Bulgaria	n.a.	4
Poland	89	291
Czechoslovakia	207	600
Hungary	n.a.	1,462
High Income		
Australia	7,086	4,833
France	12,733	15,235
Italy	6,413	2,403
Japan	1,760	1,370
UK	33,392	21,537
USA	37,190	11,500
Spain	13,841	10,502

Source: World Bank, *Global Economic Prospects and the Developing Countries*, 1991–92, 1992–9

of the main Soviet bloc countries. The difficulty with this modification process lay not so much in the problems generated by economic changes themselves as (a) in the inadequate, insufficiently supportive, response from the international system, especially at a time of falling commodity prices and (b) in the political risks which economic liberalisation involved. It was the latter which led to Cuba's catastrophic reverse into so-called 'rectification' in 1986 and to the Tien An Men crisis in China in 1989, as well as to the factional explosions that fragmented the regimes in both Grenada in 1983 and South Yemen in 1986. This contradiction between liberalisation in the economy and the attempt to retain political control was, of course, to prove the undoing of *perestroika.*

Table 5: Widening North–South Gap in Real GDP Per Capita (purchasing power parities in US$)
Index: North = 100

	1960	1990
All Developing Countries	17	15
Least Developed Countries	9	5
Sub-Saharan Africa	14	8
Algeria	28	21
Iran	39	23
India	11	7
Haiti	13	6
Mexico	46	41
China	15	14
Egypt	11	14
Thailand	15	28
Indonesia	10	15

Source: UNDP, *Human Development Report*, 1993, Table 7, 148–9.

Secondly, while the international trend throughout the 1980s was towards a Western definition of market economics, there were two strong, if divergent, counter-trends, in some countries a combative socialist backlash against the cautious liberalisation of the 1980s and, in others, a populist revolt against the whole project of state-led modernisation as such, which was seen as some kind of Western imposition. The collapse of *perestroika* only confirmed the socialist backlash, since it was seen to demonstrate the folly of Gorbachev's attempts to liberalised both economy and politics. In Cuba, for example, Castro resolutely set himself against the international trends and sought to defy the example of *perestroika*, for how long no-one knew. In China, there was a widespread sense after the collapse of the USSR and the attendant economic crisis, even amongst those who had supported the reforms of premier Zhao Ziyang in 1989 and the Tien An Men demonstrators, that economic reform had to precede political reform. In some countries revolutionary parties drew the lesson that they had to be even more orthodox and militant than before – Sendero Luminoso in Peru, the PKK in Turkey and for a time the EPRDF in Ethiopia were examples of this left backlash, something also present if not dominant within the ANC in South Africa, and amongst some of the Middle Eastern communist parties.

The alternative backlash was that of Islamic fundamentalism, a movement strong, and for a number of different reasons, in several Islamic countries: it attacked what it saw as capitalism, represented by in moral terms corruption and the dictates of the market, but it also consciously presented itself as an alternative to communism, both as a radical anti-imperialist movement and as a project for recasting state and society. Again, its rise in the 1970s was in part a result of the failures of the secular left, both as opposition forces (e.g. in Iran) and as secular modernising state (e.g. Egypt, Algeria). The fundamentalists claimed to have a distinctive economic policy based on Islam: what it amounted to was a radical social project (in law, family policy, gender relations, education) linked to a revived 1960s developmentalist project (state intervention, income redistribution, protection of infant industry, consumer austerity). Fundamentalism represented above all a new form of 'anti-imperialism', one that, mistakenly, believed it could resist the international pressures upon the societies concerned.

The difficulty with both these oppositions to the orthodoxy of the late 1980s was that, while they drew on a range of forces, from nationalism to religious populism, to dislike of the Western model, they offered no resolution of the problem that had long underlain Third World upheaval and which had also served more than anything else to discredit the Soviet model, namely living standards. The ability of revolutionary socialism to deliver on this front had appeared plausible in the 1950s and 1960s, but had disappeared by the 1980s.

On the one hand, the comparative performance of developed capitalist and communist states was evidently disparate; at the same time, the terms of the competition itself had changed, from rivalry in 'old' terms – heavy industry, gross output terms – to competition in 'new' terms, born of the consumerist revolution and the changes of the third industrial revolution. As I have argued elsewhere, the main reason for the collapse of the Soviet model was not so much military pressure from without, or political pressure from below, but the perceived failure to sustain competition in the economic domains valued both by the new elites, and by the increasingly informed populations. This was true for the USSR, where the key changes and decisions were taken, but it applied equally to a range of Third World countries – China, South Yemen, Vietnam amongst them.

(v) Redirection of economic resources

The greatest single anxiety expressed about the end of the Cold War and the Third World was that it would lead to a displacement of the developing world in terms of aid, investment and trade. This became known, in the mid-1990s, as 'capital crunch theory', the idea that between 2005 and 2010 there will be serious pressure on global capital markets and, hence, on interest rates. It was in the first place feared that aid to the Third World would be diverted to Eastern Europe, and that private sector and multilateral agency funding would also be so reallocated. The very fact of increased lending to ex-communist states, and their substantial debt repayment problems (Soviet debt in 1991 at $70 bn was comparable to that of some Latin American countries – e.g. Brazil's at $116 bn or Mexico at $102 bn) would, it was feared, put strains on world interest rates and on financial resources. It was also feared that with the decline in Cold War rivalries the political motive behind Third World aid would decrease, most obviously in the USA, where the foreign aid budget remained the object of considerable attack. On the trade front it was feared that improvements in the quality and volume of industrial output in former communist states would make it more difficult for Third World states to market goods in developed countries.

There was some validity in these fears. The sums of money involved in revitalising the East were enormous, and would continue to be so for years to come. The strain put on the Germany economy by reunification was eloquent enough in this respect. Economic considerations apart, the West had a political interest in ensuring stability and growth in the former communist world, to contain the dangers of war, refugee flows, nuclear proliferation, fundamentalist resurgence and the like. The European Bank for Reconstruction and Development, set up in April 1991 in London, had an initial capital of $13 bn, compared to a total of multilateral official lending to the Third World of $11.9 bn in 1989. The West committed itself to $8.9 bn worth of food aid to the former Soviet Union by the end of 1991, $2.8 bn of which came from the EEC. The successor states to the USSR joined the IMF and the World Bank and were expected to make claims on resources there as well. Arab states, notably Saudi Arabia and Kuwait, also began to loan to the FSU states. If, as anticipated, the difficulties of these countries lasted for years, if not decades, then competition for markets and funds would continue.

There are, however, some reasons for qualifying this picture. In the first place, the sum of finance available for lending or investment is not static, but depends on macroeconomic trends irrespective of what is happening in the post-communist world. The amounts of money diverted or not diverted are small compared to other outlays – an $18 bn US aid budget to the Third World, compared to a military budget of $300 bn, or a Savings and Loans loss of $500 bn or more. The turnaround in Japanese policy in 1991, when it went from a surplus in outward capital flows to a net inflow of around $35 bn, was of much greater significance for international liquidity than strains on the IMF or EEC.

A survey by *The Economist* of Third World finance in September 1993 indicated that despite a fall of total foreign direct investment between 1989 and 1991, the amount going to Third World states had risen from $29 to $40 billion. The rise in foreign direct investment as a percentage of total resource flows to the Third World, from 11 per cent in 1980 to 35 per cent in 1989, therefore indicates that underlying trends may offset current strains. If there were an upturn in the world economy then it would be possible to increase funds available to the World Bank and to individual donors, state or private, accordingly. Total FDI has recently been running at around $200 b per year, of which an average of around 75 per cent goes to developed countries (and the great majority of the remaining 36 b has in recent years gone to East Asian and Pacific countries). Ironically far more has gone in to (still officially communist) China than into the ex-Soviet bloc countries: in the years 1990–93 private FDI in China came to $45 billions, in contrast to $29 billions for the whole of eastern Europe and the Former Soviet Union.

Moreover, in the aid field, most donor states and agencies were careful to keep their financial operations vis-à-vis the post-communist world separate from their other aid programmes: separate lines, such as the UK's Know How Fund, a programme designed to transfer market skills, were established. The same thinking lay behind the EBRD: IMF and World Bank sources denied any pressure on Third World funds in the post-Cold War era. This did not, however, apply to the USA, and as time passed the distinction between traditional 'Third World' and 'post-communist' may well erode. A problem is, however, evident in the area of scholarships – post-communist countries themselves cut training programmes for Third World students, while Turkey for one shifted its educational assistance programme from the Third World to the Turkic peoples of Central Asia. In general, however, the main strain inside multilateral and bilateral aid agencies was not so much on funds as on personnel, those able to administer programmes and carry out missions in the relevant countries: here the East *was* diverting resources from the South. In addition, while the post-communist FSU states were facing great difficulties, they were not, with the possible exception of one or two Central Asian states, amongst the poorer countries of the world, and were not therefore eligible for soft, IDA, loans or for many forms of UN assistance. Where there was more likely to be competition was in regard to middle-income Third World states, not so much for aid, for which the latter were not eligible, but for private sector lending, and investment. Most FDI in the Third World went to middle-income countries, economies broadly similarly to the post-communist countries: but on available evidence, the eastern European economies remained very much second-best to the East Asian/Pacific states.

As of late 1995, there was little evidence of the post-communist world drawing funds off the Third World. Net resource flows to the Third World rose during the 1980s: official aid by 3 per cent per capita in real terms, private lending fell sharply (the figure for1989 being only 10 per cent of 1980) but there was a rise in FDI. If there were difficulties, it was as much as anything because the relations of donor states, agencies and private banks with the Third World had been under strain for a decade at least, evident in the debt crisis of 1982 and the switch to more demanding aid conditions by states and agencies alike. The collapse of communism may have added to, but certainly did not cause, this. Whether a decade or two further down the road the world would face a 'capital crunch' remained, however, an open question.

Conclusion: the Uncertainties of Capitalist Development

A longer-run answer to the question of how the end of the Cold War will affect the Third World rests upon assessing a set of underlying issues in the international system. At the political-strategic level, the question is how far a system of peaceful and co-operative relations between states can be maintained without hegemonic controls: if some hegemonic controls are necessary, the question is whether the developed capitalist countries, and in particular the USA, are willing or able to perform them, and in a way that meets the interests of the system as a whole. A world of inter-state and intra-state conflict will benefit no-one, and hurt the weaker states most. Moreover, there is the question of how the evident universalising trends in the world political and economic system will prevail in diffusing prosperity and in reducing the gap between richer and poorer states. This is an argument that has been much debated within liberal economic and Marxist camps for the past four decades, and which has received a notable reassertion in the interesting, if flawed, work of Francis Fukuyama: the least one can say is that the jury is still out – incomes in most states are rising, but the gap between rich and poor is widening, and new problems – ecological, demographic, inter-ethnic – threaten many states. A cursory reading of the *Human Development Report* reveals a disturbing picture as far as widening North–South gaps are concerned. As Giovanni Arrighi has pointed out, there appear to be very strong rigidities in the international hierarchy: there has been considerable alteration of position within the group of high income states, but over a century and a half none has left this group, and only one, Japan, has joined.

In broad terms, this was precisely the question that communism, in its seven decades of existence, sought to address – it was a crude, for a time quite successful but very costly, attempt at an alternative development project, a creation of semi-peripheral states. Now it has foundered in the face of some more successful developmental projects and the communist states have been returned, chastened and re-subjugated, like escaped labourers, to their place in the international capitalist hierarchy. Communism failed to come up with an answer that was either politically acceptable or economically competitive. If capitalism can do so for the majority of the world's population remains to be seen. The irony is that Karl Marx was one person who did believe that developed capitalism could transform the whole world in its image and that, *grosso modo*, it was doing a good job in the process. In this respect, at least, the new international environment of development looks very much like the old, not least because it has now been stripped of two diversions, both the artificial cover of colonialism and the chimera of a revolutionary alternative: this international environment turns out, in the fundamental issues it raises, i.e. peace, democracy and economic growth, to have varied remarkably little over the past century and a half.

Notes

An earlier version of this paper was published as 'The Third World and the End of the Cold War' in Barbara Stallings (ed.) *Global Change, Regional Response. The New International Context of Development* (Cambridge University Press, 1995). I am grateful to CUP for permission to publish this revised version in this volume. My thanks are due to Quentin Bach, Christopher Clapham, Bruce Cumings, Michael Donelan and Anna Matveeva for their most helpful comments.

1 'The End of the Cold War and International Relations: Some Analytic and Theoretical Conclusions' in Ken Booth and Steve Smith, (eds) *International Relations Theory Today* (Cambridge University Press, Cambridge, 1995).

2 The classic argument on this is Michael Doyle, 'Liberalism and World Politics', *American Political Science Review* ii/4 (1986). Doyle is theoretically right, but historically too trusting: his listings of which countries attained democracy, and when, is precipitate and gives a misleading overall picture. Fukuyama's argument on the same subject is equally jejeune – see note 24 below.

3 *OECD Letter,* vol. 2/8 October 1993, p. 7.

4 On Afghan communist resistance, see Diego Cordorez and Selig Harrison, *Out of Afghanistan, The Inside Story of the Soviet Withdrawal* (Oxford University Press, New York, 1995) Chs 5–6.

5 Fred Halliday, *Cold War, Third World* (London, Radius/Hutchinson, London, 1989).

6 Michael Ignatieff, *Blood and Belonging* (BBC Publications, London, 1993).

7 Of total aid of around $2.4–3bn in the early 1980s, the great majority, 70 per cent or over, went to the six communist allies.

8 Figures for 1991 show a 32 per cent fall in overall trade between the FSU and developing countries, this comprising a 29 per cent fall in exports and a 36 per cent fall in imports. G. W. Kolodko, 'Stabilisation, Recession and Growth in a Postsocialist Economy', *Moct-Most,* no. 1, 1993, p. 156.

9 In 1987 the USSR accounted for 90 per cent of India's imports and 19 per cent of its exports (*UN Monthly Bulletin of Statistics,* July–August 1988).

10 According to DAC figures Soviet aid disbursements fell from $3.0 bn in 1989 to $1.1 bn in 1991, and can be assumed to have stopped thereafter.

11 Compared to Eastern Europe, Western European 1989 *per capita* import levels of tropical products were twice as high for tea, four for coffee, five for bananas, 370 for tinned pineapple ('Eastern Europe and the Developing Countries', Overseas Development Institute, London, Briefing Paper, June 1991). In early 1992, the situation was in some ways reversed: East German levels of consumption were almost twice as high for bananas, oranges and tangerines than West German (*International Herald Tribune*, 26 March 1992).

12 On the political background, see Margot Light, *Troubled Friendships: Moscow's Third World Ventures* (British Academic Press, London, 1993).

13 For the re-thinking occasioned in Latin America see Jorge Castaneda, *Utopia Unarmed: the Latin American Left After the Cold War* (Knopf, New York, 1993).

14 I have gone into the Yemeni case in detail in Fred Halliday, *Revolution and Foreign Policy: The Case of South Yemen* (Cambridge University Press, Cambridge, 1990), ch. 2.

15 Fundamentalisms of all kind – Islamic, Hindu, Judaic, Christian – are above all movements for the acquisition or maintenance of political power, not theological or conversion trends: Juan Cole and Nikki Keddie, (eds) *Shi'ism and Social Protest* (Yale University Press, New Haven, 1986): Sami Zubaida, *Islam, the People and the State* (Routledge, London, 1989) and Fred Halliday and Hamza Alavi, (eds) *State and Ideology in the Middle East and Pakistan* (Macmillan, Basingstoke, 1988).

16 On Islamism see Olivier Roy, *The Failure of Political Islam* (I. B. Tauris, London, 1995); Fred Halliday, *Islam and the Myth of Confrontation* (I. B. Tauris, London, 1996).

17 'A Singular Collapse: the Soviet Union, Market Pressure and Inter-state Competition', *Contention* i/2 (1991).

18 *International Herald Tribune,* 2 April 1996. This cites an OECD study, *Future Global Capital Shortages: Real Threat or Pure Fiction?* that assesses the risk.

19 For Brazil and Mexico, World Bank, *World Development Report*

(Oxford University Press, New York, 1993) p. 279.

20 Figures from *Western Assistance to the Former Soviet Union,* (Background Brief, Foreign & Commonwealth Office, London, February 1992).

21 'New Ways to Grow: a survey of third world finance', *The Economist,* 25 September 1993.

22 FDI from OECD states stood at $196 billion in 1994, of which 37 per cent was invested outside the OECD. The ten biggest non-OECD recipients were China, Singapore, Argentina, Brazil, Malaysia, Thailand, Indonesia, Hungary, the Czech Republic and Poland (*International Herald Tribune*, 26 June 1995).

23 *Le Monde*, 30 April–2 May 1995, citing an OECD study. See also 'East Europe's Failure to "Emerge"', *International Herald Tribune*, February 4–5 1995.

24 Francis Fukuyama, *The End of History and the Last Man* (Hamish Hamilton, London, 1991). For critical discussion see Fred Halliday, 'An Encounter With Fukuyama', *New Left Review* 192, May–June, 1992 and Perry Anderson, *A Zone of Engagement* (London, Verso, 1992).

25 Giovanni Arrighi, 'World Income Inequalities and the Future of Socialism', *New Left Review* 189, September–October 1991.

26 For a critique of dependency theory and the Leninist underconsumptionist tradition, and a spirited defense of the classical Marxist position on capitalism's ability to transform the world, see Bill Warren, *Imperialism, Pioneer of Capitalism* (London, Verso, 1980).

2 ❧ The Sudanese Civil War in International Relations

Charles Tripp

Introduction

During the past thirteen years the mutiny of a Sudanese army garrison in 1983 at Bor on the White Nile has developed into a civil war which has engulfed much of Southern Sudan. In doing so, it has cost the lives of countless thousands of Sudanese, has driven thousands of others from their homes as refugees and has led to the direct or indirect destruction of much of the agricultural and economic infrastructure of the South. Meanwhile, the human and the economic costs have been felt throughout Sudan as a succession of governments has tried to prosecute the war whilst seeking to face up to agricultural failures, food shortages and a crippling foreign debt. This has intensified human misery in much of the North and has led to political instability, compounded by the repressive strategies of the regime that came to power in 1989. Unable to bring the war to a conclusion by negotiation or by military means, both sides seem to be locked in a destructive conflict, pursued at varying levels of intensity.

This depressing picture is worth bearing in mind while seeking to understand the significance of this war in international relations. Whatever the civil war may tell us about emerging trends in this sphere, it should be looked at primarily as a Sudanese phenomenon, generated by the particular histories, conflicts and insecurities of the peoples of Sudan. However, insofar as its features find an echo, if not necessarily any very exact parallel, elsewhere in Africa or Asia, the experience and development of the civil war may be instructive. It may throw some light on the kinds of forces working upon states such as Sudan in the aftermath of the Cold War. More importantly, for a general understanding of its significance within the larger sphere of international relations, the course it has taken and the international repercussions of the actions of the combatants may illuminate the emerging hierarchy of international rules and norms that characterise the larger environment in which it is being fought.

Before turning to these larger issues, it is worth asking two questions of the Sudanese civil war which may draw attention both to that which is specific to the Sudanese case as well as to those aspects of the Sudanese experience which may link it to that of others similarly situated. The first concerns the nature of Sudan as a state. It can be formulated simply by asking what it means to be Sudan in international relations during and after the Cold War. A number of characteristics suggest themselves which may not be exactly reproduced elsewhere, but which certainly have significant parallels in other parts of Asia and Africa.

Firstly, Sudan, upon coming to independence, was formally a sovereign territorial state, but it was clearly not a nation-state. Several fault lines of suspicion, mistrust and hostility ran through the population, produced by different groups' distinctive histories. These were responsible for the first civil war which broke out in 1956 and lasted until 1972. This, in turn, contributed to chronic political instability in the country, as military regimes alternated with short periods of civilian government. Their problems were compounded by equally chronic problems of underdevelopment, the consequences of misguided development schemes and the mounting size of the foreign debt. The scale of these problems eventually overwhelmed all governments, whether civilian or military.

Played out in an international order dominated by the preoccupations of the Cold War, successive Sudanese regimes sought either to disassociate themselves from the logic of that conflict, or else to exploit that logic for their own benefit and political survival. At the same time, it was clear that no Sudanese government was driven by any of the ideological impulses which characterised the spectrum of ideologies demarcated by the polar opposites of the Cold War.[1] Sudan's involvement in the Cold War largely depended upon outside powers' perceptions of its location in the context of their own geopolitical strategies. This led to forms of mutual exploitation by rulers and outside powers, which reached their greatest level of intensity under the rule of President Nimayri when the Horn of Africa, the

Indian Ocean and the Red Sea became areas of intense interest for both the USA and the USSR.

With the ending of the Cold War, these particular calculations and priorities may have faded from view, but the situational logic of Sudan remains the same. It is still riven by deep social divisions. The authority of its regime is continually contested. The civil war which began in 1983 still rages with little prospect of an imminent end. Under these circumstances, it is scarcely surprising that the country's economic situation has worsened and that, consequently, the present regime is likely to come to an end as abrupt as that of all its predecessors. It is against this background and with these impulses working upon it that the government must seek to order its relations with the outside world, whether in the shape of particular configurations of regional states, or with the dominant powers of international politics.

The second general question which should be asked is what it means to be fighting a civil war, not simply managing a domestic dispute. Just as there may be a situational logic to the condition and predicament of Sudan which will affect its place in international relations, so too there may be a logic stemming from the conduct of a war which will give a distinctive coloration to the place of Sudan in international relations. The hypothesis is that the prosecution of a war may construct a particular framework for regional and broader international action, shaped partly by considerations of strategic and tactical advantage by the belligerent parties and partly by the unpredictable outcome of military operations.

Firstly, there is the issue of the permeability of borders and the scale of cross-border movements, whether by refugees, by armed guerrillas or by government forces pursuing their enemy. This in turn raises the question of the sanctuary which may or may not be granted to the refugees and the guerrilla forces by neighbouring states, as well as the variety of motives which may affect decisions regarding the issue of sanctuary. Thirdly, the conduct of war obviously demands attention to the acquisition of the weapons needed to prosecute it, the terms on which either side may seek to acquire those weapons and the financial resources necessary for the supply of war matériel.

Lastly, the effects of war are such on both the regional and the international systems that the conduct of the fighting will almost always be accompanied by various attempts at mediation between the two sides to bring it to an end. The success or otherwise of these attempts, as well as the ulterior motives underlying them and the forms of persuasion or pressure which may characterise them, will mark in some form the relations between the combatants and various states or organisations in the international arena. The Cold War may have imposed a certain framework in which strategies appropriate to these concerns might have been pursued by the belligerents and the neighbouring states. In doing so, the correlation of powers, both regional and global, might have suggested more or less profitable avenues for the parties to the conflict to pursue. Nevertheless, the ultimate logic was that of the war itself and it is this which must determine the significance of that war in international relations.

The 'logic of the Sudanese state' and the 'logic of civil war' should, therefore, be borne in mind when trying to determine the significance of the war in international relations, whether during or after the Cold War. These are not constants, immune to reciprocal influence by the forces at work in the international system more generally; but they do constitute processes working out at their own distinctive paces which are not necessarily, or even at all the same, as those characterising the processes of world politics. It is, consequently, the intention of this chapter firstly to examine briefly how these different forms of 'logic' affected the place of Sudan in a world dominated by the preoccupations of the Cold War.

The second part of the chapter will look more particularly at some of the characteristic features in post-Cold War international relations which the Sudanese civil war has raised. Two such features or trends in particular will be highlighted. Firstly, there is the question of the significance and multiple repercussions of the assertion of ethnic identity and the consequent claim to self-determination, leading to the possible break-up of those states which have constituted the 'givens' of the international system for the past forty to fifty years. Secondly, there is the issue of humanitarian intervention, its principles and its practice insofar as these have been invoked and precipitated in relation to the civil war in Sudan.

These themes did not emerge with the ending of the Cold War. On the contrary, in various forms they have been visible for some decades past in the region. More realistically, they could be said to have achieved a new prominence, and sometimes a new form or coloration in the patterns of international relations emerging in the period following the Cold War. The task is therefore to understand the degree to which the combination of local dynamics in the Sudanese civil war with the forces at work in regional and international politics more generally could be said to reinforce such trends in the international system, with consequences both for international relations more generally and for the conduct of the civil war itself.

The Civil War 1983–89

The formation of the Sudanese People's Liberation Movement (SPLM) and its military wing, the Sudanese People's Liberation Army (SPLA) had its origins in a series of army mutinies in garrisons throughout the southern provinces of Bahr al-Ghazal, Upper Nile and – to a lesser extent – Western Equatoria during 1983. The wretched economic condition of the troops and the fear that these predominantly southern formations were about to be transferred to the North and replaced by northern soldiers led to the initial mutiny at Bor and to the subsequent mutinies elsewhere. However, these military incidents took place against a background of more general dissatisfaction, fear and resentment in the southern region.

Apart from the historical elements of distrust which are never far below the surface in relations between northerners and southerners in Sudan, there was a specific fear that President Nimayri was reneging on the Addis Ababa Accords which had ended the previous civil war in 1972. A number of factors contributed to a widespread belief that the government in Khartoum was preparing for a systematic assault on the limited degree of autonomy enjoyed by the southerners. In 1983, Nimayri issued a decree dividing the South into three separate regions. His move was viewed with intense suspicion by many since he made it at a time when two highly contentious issues were on the agenda of national politics. Firstly, there was growing alarm among the mainly non-Muslim southerners regarding the increasingly visible Islamic trend of Nimayri's government. Their fears focused on the 'September Laws' of 1983. These placed the Islamic *shari'a*, with its associated prohibitions and punishments, onto the statute book of the Sudanese state.

The second item of concern was the continued penury of the southern provinces. The broken promises of Addis Ababa over the economic reconstruction of the South, the tight control maintained by the Khartoum government over all expenditure and the clearly observable fact that the lion's share of development funds were diverted into schemes in the North added to southern resentments. During the late 1970s and early 1980s this resentment was compounded by the discovery of oil in the South and by the beginning of the construction of the Jonglei canal. The canal was seen to threaten the ecology and economy of the province of Bahr al-Ghazal for the benefit principally of major agricultural development projects in the North.

The discovery of oil was an even more contentious question. The Khartoum government attempted to redraw the boundaries between the northern and southern provinces to ensure that the major oil fields were located in the North. When thwarted, Nimayri made it clear that Khartoum would in any case be appropriating all the oil revenue, rather than granting a fixed percentage of them to the southern region.[2]

It was perhaps scarcely surprising that these moves should have provoked the formation of a resistance movement such as the SPLM/SPLA. Many southerners had clearly despaired of attempting to secure the interests of the South through the existing machinery of the Sudanese state. In their view, this was now the exclusive preserve of Nimayri and of the northern, Muslim establishment whose ideological preoccupations and economic interests would preclude any attention to the concerns of others in Sudan, let alone to the specific concerns of the South.

During late 1983 and early 1984, the nature of the SPLA and of the threat it represented to the central government became clear. Colonel John Garang, a prominent southerner and a member of the Dinka people in the Sudanese armed forces, was to emerge rapidly as the leader of the organisation. He had been sent initially by Nimayri to negotiate the surrender of the mutineers at Bor who were themselves largely of Dinka origin. When he arrived at his home town, however, he threw in his lot with the mutineers and proceeded to Ethiopia to negotiate a safe haven across the nearby frontier. Once this had been established, he led the mutineers into Ethiopia. The great majority of the rebels came from the dominant Dinka populations of Upper Nile and Bahr al-Ghazal. It was here that resentment over the redivision had been strongest and where the consequences of the Jonglei canal scheme and the discovery of oil had been most bitterly felt.

However, the origins of the SPLA and the very nature of its successes created problems for it elsewhere in the South, most notably in Equatoria. It was here that the SPLA met with stiff resistance, not so much from government troops as from the local people. At one level, the political leaders of Equatoria, against whom John Garang constantly inveighed, regarded the SPLA and its insistence on the re-unification of the South as typical of Dinka ambition to dominate the whole region. It was in order to escape being the target of such ambitions that many of them had overcome earlier inhibitions and had become supporters of the redivision of the South. At a more general level, the SPLA's close association with the Dinka was regarded with great suspicion by other peoples and communities which had historically been in competition with the Dinka for land and cattle.

The danger for Garang and the SPLA was that they would increasingly be seen as representative of little more than a specifically Dinka interest. This was far from being the intention of Garang. On the contrary, he was insistent in stressing the fact that the SPLM/SPLA was not even a specifically southern movement and indeed he denied that there was a 'southern problem' as such. In his first major public statement of policy, in March 1984, he attacked tribalism, ethnic politics and the southern political elite, just as he attacked what he termed the *awlad al-balad* of Khartoum (this might be loosely interpreted as the 'good old boys' of the northern establishment). He went on to stress that his was neither a racial, nor a religious conflict and that the SPLA was a vanguard for the liberation of all Sudan, seeking to create a unified, socialist Sudan in which the rights of all nationalities, beliefs and religions would be guaranteed.[3]

Nimayri sought to portray the SPLA as the vanguard of Marxist revolution in Africa and the Islamic world. In the hope of reviving the flagging fortunes of his regime, Nimayri attempted to use the rhetoric of the Cold War as a means of extracting more resources from the United States government, both financial and military. In labelling the SPLA as a Marxist organisation (due to its bases in Ethiopia and its rather anodyne socialist slogans) Nimayri was perhaps appealing to internal constituencies still fearful of the spectre of communism in the Sudan.[4] However, this portrayal seemed to be aimed chiefly at the USA and at some of the regional allies of Sudan, such as Egypt and Saudi Arabia, which shared Nimayri's concern for the security of the Red Sea and of the Horn of Africa. He had portrayed himself in the past as standing on the front line in containing alleged Soviet expansion in Africa and the Middle East, and had consequently extracted considerable assistance from these various sources.

However, in this instance it did not help him very greatly. It was certainly true that the regime of Mengistu in Ethiopia was providing both sanctuary and various forms of assistance to the SPLA. However, this had less to do with the Cold War, than with Ethiopia's own rebels in Eritrea, Tigre and among the Oromo, all of whom had found sanctuary in Sudan. Nor did the reference to Cold War themes produce the external aid that Nimayri desired. His regional and global patrons were mistrustful of the Islamist tone of his regime and tended to regard the civil war as a symptom of his own mismanagement and failing authority.

The SPLA's reaction to the coup which overthrew Nimayri in 1985 was one of deep suspicion. The ruling Transitional Military Council (TMC) attempted to persuade Ethiopia to reduce the level of its support for the SPLA, hinting at a reduction of Sudan's own assistance to the Eritreans and Tigreans. When this failed, the TMC tried equally unsuccessfully to persuade the USSR to bring pressure to bear on Ethiopia to the same end. In reaction to these failures, as well as to the military successes of the SPLA, Suwar al-Dhahab, the leader of the TMC, reverted to the same rhetorical ploys as Nimayri: he accused Garang of wanting to rule 'all Sudan under a Communist system' and appealed to the West for support in the name of Cold War values; meanwhile, he made an appeal to the rest of the Arab world based on the supposed anti-Islamic and anti-Arab character of Garang's movement.[5]

As far as the US government was concerned, this was as unconvincing as it had been when Nimayri had tried this ploy. In addition to which, there was some confidence that the TMC would really be a transitional regime and that a democratically elected civilian government would soon be ruling in Khartoum. It was on the eve of these elections that the process of negotiation between the SPLM/SPLA and the civilian alliance culminated in the meeting at the Koka Dam in Ethiopia. It was here, in March 1986, that a joint communiqué was issued which represented both the SPLA's conditions for ending the armed struggle and the northern parties' agreement on the necessary preconditions for the re-establishment of consensual, civilian politics in Sudan.[6]

The terms of the Koka Dam Declaration were principally the

convening of a Constitutional Conference to discuss all Sudan's problems – not simply the 'southern problem', but also the question of the future system of national government. In addition, it called for the immediate repeal of all *shari'a* legislation and the enforcement of the 1956 Constitution, with its 1964 amendments, guaranteeing the secular, democratic nature of the Sudanese state. Henceforth this was to form the core of the demands made by the SPLA of successive Sudanese governments. The problem for Garang was that he could not persuade those governments to implement them, even though a number of their members had been party to the Koka Dam Declaration.

This failure was most noticeable under Sadiq al-Mahdi who emerged as the leader of the largest party in the aftermath of the elections of 1986 and who led a succession of coalition governments until he was overthrown in a coup d'état in June 1989. Reluctant to act upon some of the provisions of the Koka Dam Declaration, Sadiq al-Mahdi's negotiations with Garang were doomed to failure. Initially, when he first came to power in 1986, he sought to pursue a conciliatory stance towards the SPLA and a non-aligned course both in the larger East–West configuration of the Cold War and in various regional conflicts and rivalries. This was a conscious reversal of the direction in which Nimayri had taken the Sudan, but it proved to be counter-productive. Al-Mahdi's close relationship with Libya succeeded in alienating Egypt and the United States. Nor did it make Ethiopia any more willing to make the kind of gesture which al-Mahdi was hoping for, namely curbing the activities of the SPLA. His careful attention to Sudan's relations with the USSR had as little effect on Ethiopia's attitude as had Suwar al-Dhahab's. Meanwhile, al-Mahdi's conciliatory attitude to Iran further alienated not simply the US, but also most of the Gulf states, terrified as they were at the time of the Iranian threat to themselves. Al-Mahdi discovered that claiming non-alignment, whether in global or in regional disputes was regarded with the utmost suspicion and ended in a degree of isolation for Sudan. Indeed, as his term of office proceeded, he used much the same language to denounce the SPLA as had been used by his predecessors – and with as little effect. On the one hand, he denounced the SPLA as Marxist–Leninists set on carrying out a communist revolution in Sudan at the behest of the Ethiopian regime. On the other, he claimed that the SPLA was the spearhead of an anti-Arab and anti-Islamic movement seeking to impose an 'African identity' upon all of Sudan.[7]

Elements of Sadiq al-Mahdi's government had meanwhile been conducting negotiations with Garang in Addis Ababa and this resulted in the agreement of November 1988 between Garang and Osman al-Mirghani, leader of the DUP. Essentially, this agreement restated the principles of the Koka Dam Declaration, notably the lifting of the state of emergency and the freezing of the *shari'a* legislation until the proposed Constitutional Conference was held.[8] Al-Mahdi was as dilatory in acting upon it as he had been about the original Koka Dam Declaration. It was only when senior officers of the armed forces faced him with an ultimatum that he agreed to negotiate directly with the SPLA on the basis of the 1988 agreement.[9] These negotiations were still proceeding when a military coup d'état, organised by the National Islamic Front (the Muslim Brotherhood), overthrew the government of al-Mahdi, dissolved parliament and banned all political parties.

The Sudanese civil war broke out in the final decade of the Cold War and gained momentum when the rivalries and tensions symbolised by that conflict were beginning to lose their force. In the changing circumstances of that decade, Nimayri discovered that the old certainties could no longer be relied upon to bolster his position as they had before. Furthermore, the outbreak of civil war was regarded by many as primarily a symptom of his declining authority and his misrule, rather than as proof of the attempt by the forces of Marxism–Leninism to break out of their containment in Africa. The Sudanese civil war could not easily be fitted into a paradigm of Cold War behaviour. Consequently, Nimayri, but more noticeably Suwar al-Dhahab and Sadiq al-Mahdi tried to portray it in a rather different light. Whilst it was true that they used the spectre of Marxism–Leninism to characterise the SPLA, this was intended to alarm a rather different, principally Islamic audience.

More persistent, therefore, was the use of another language to appeal to the same audience – a language in which the SPLA was portrayed in racial and religio-ethnic terms, respectively, as primarily 'African', as opposed to 'Arab', and as '*jahili*' [pagan or un-Islamic], as opposed to 'Islamic'. Insofar as these were attempts to drum up support not simply within Sudan, but also in the Middle East as a whole, they are pointers to a more explicit post-Cold War vocabulary of ethnic definition. These themes were to be developed with even greater intensity under the regime presided over by Omar Hassan al-Bashir, as the Cold War ended and some of the issues that were to characterise a post-Cold War world were to become more obvious. The subsequent section will be devoted therefore to an analysis of the ways in which the Sudanese civil war brought out some of these themes in international relations.

The Civil War 1989–96

For the past eight seven years, the government of Omar al-Bashir has tried a number of strategies, often deployed simultaneously and in apparent contradiction, to deal with the problem of the civil war. In doing so, it has reflected different ideas about the best practical means of ending the conflict, but has also reflected the ideological preoccupations of the National Islamic Front. The latter is the principal Sudanese version of the many radical Islamic groups visible in Middle Eastern politics during the past few decades, aiming at the creation of a distinctively Islamic state and intolerant of what they regard as the evil of secular forms of power, whether on a domestic or international level. They were the inspiration behind the coup d'état of June 1989 and have, since then, become more publicly visible and entrenched in all areas of public life in Sudan. Nevertheless, they must still depend on the officer corps of the armed forces to keep them in power. This creates a certain tension since not all the officers are enthusiasts for the NIF. Hitherto, this has been manageable, although at the price of repeated purges and severe repression. However, it is in this atmosphere and with these impulses behind them that the policies of the Sudanese state are formed, whether in the prosecution of the civil war or in the kinds of relations marking Sudan's links with the rest of the world. It is in this regard and, bearing in mind their significance for international relations, that two issues in particular have marked the ways in which the civil war has interacted with the imagination and interests of the rest of the world.

Ethnicity and Ethnic Self-determination

As in many independent states in Africa and elsewhere the question of ethnic definition and self-determination has traditionally been a question of extreme sensitivity in Sudan. The daunting consequences for this state with its heterogeneous population, as well as for the political map of the African continent should states be recast to suit specific constructions of ethnic identity have tended to inhibit attempts to incorporate secessionist aims into the political programmes of rebel movements such as the SPLA. This does not mean that such sentiments and aspirations have not existed. Rather, they have tended to exist on the margins, among such groups in southern Sudan, for instance, as the Imatong Liberation Front, or the Anyanya II organisation, both of which emerged in the late 1970s.

As is the case with many such ideas, however, it took a combination of events, both at the local and at the international levels, for the feasibility and thus the credibility of such a goal to emerge as an aspiration of many within SPLA by the mid-1990s. Although John Garang, the leader of the SPLA, has been an opponent of secession, he was obliged to make increasing reference to the possibility of 'self-determination' in order to retain the support of the growing numbers of southerners who came to believe that this would be both a desirable and necessary outcome of their struggle. However, it became clear that the questions of ethnic self-definition and thus of possible future political self-determination were considerably more complex and potentially divisive within the South than some of the chief protagonists were willing to admit.

The SPLM/SPLA was initially portrayed by its leadership as constituting a movement for the liberation of all Sudan. This was never very convincing, given the origins of the vast majority of the members of the movement, the site of its military operations and the identity of the populations among which it moved with relative ease. These were all distinctly of the 'South'. This can be defined administratively as applying to the three southern provinces of the country, Bahr al-Ghazal, Upper Nile and Equatoria (although, during the war, the question of the future administrative boundaries of the northern provinces of Kordofan and Blue Nile has been raised). In terms of religious identity, very few of its members were Muslim and most were either Christians or adherents of more local southern religions. Linguistically, scarcely any spoke Arabic as their mother tongue and the great majority spoke one or other of the Nilotic languages. This also helped to define what has sometimes misleadingly been called the 'tribal' identity of southerners, belonging as most do to self-consciously distinct peoples, such as the Dinka, the Nuer, the Latoka, the Acholi, the Lokoro, the Bari, the Mandari, and so on.

As the war developed, the distinctively southern nature of the SPLA – as defined by all the above criteria – remained as marked as ever. Nevertheless, its leader, John Garang, was fierce in his denunciation of those who were pressing for secession and insisted that the SPLA was aiming for radical reform within the framework of the unitary state of the Sudan. There is no reason to suppose that he did not genuinely believe that the best way forward for the South as a whole lay within a significantly reformed Sudanese state in which power and access to resources had been radically decentralised. However, during much of the 1980s, this was also a pragmatic line to pursue both within the context of Sudanese politics and internationally.

Under the governments of Nimayri, of the TMC and of Sadiq al-Mahdi this was the only basis on which Garang could forge an alliance with the predominantly northern civilian parties and organisations. First in opposition and then in the government, groups such as the Umma Party, the DUP and the associations of professional and trades unions would only negotiate with the SPLA if they were convinced it shared their ideal of a unitary Sudanese state. Indeed, it was on this basis that the two significant accords of the Koka Dam in 1986 and of Addis Ababa in 1988 were signed.

Internationally, it was equally clear that the label 'secessionist' would have done the SPLA little good, either in the region or in the world at large. For the neighbouring African states on which Garang had to rely for the supply and sanctuary they could provide for the SPLA, secessionist goals, based on ethnic difference, would have been ill received. Whilst it was true that Mengistu in Ethiopia had his own reasons for wanting to get back at Khartoum and was probably not overly concerned about the precise programme of the SPLA, the subject of ethnic secessionism was clearly a sensitive one in Ethiopian politics. Nor would the Kenyan or the Ugandan governments at the time have been very enthusiastic about the reshaping of the Sudanese state along these lines, given their local preoccupations, reflected in their adherence to the charter of the OAU.

Equally, in the international community at large and more especially in the USA and Europe, the SPLA was more likely to have gained a sympathetic hearing at the time if it confined itself to criticising the shortcomings of the current regime and of the way power was structured within Sudan than if it had called for the break up of the Sudanese state. In the view of the US government at the time, there were too many dangerously inimical regional interests, ranging from Libya on one side to Ethiopia on the other – and possibly the USSR, often cited as standing behind them – which might have sought to profit from the dismemberment of Sudan.[10]

This situation began to undergo a distinct change with the seizure of power by Omar al-Bashir and the NIF in 1989. Controversially, members of the NIF had always been among those in the North who had been willing to contemplate the possibility of the secession of the South as a whole. They had been unwilling to enter into either of the accords signed with the SPLA in 1986 or 1988 precisely because they believed that the price the northern parties seemed to be prepared to pay for the ending of the war – the removal of the *shari'a* from the statute book and the reaffirmation of the secular nature of the Sudanese state – was too great.

When the NIF achieved power and the possibility of establishing a distinctively Islamic state in Sudan was now before them, the SPLA was militarily at the height of its power. Thanks to the success of its military operations in the preceding years, by 1989 it controlled most of the territory of the South. Furthermore, all attempts at negotiating an end to the war collapsed on the SPLA's repeated insistence that the *shari'a* be removed from the statute book of the Sudanese state. The NIF based government was equally adamant in refusing to contemplate this, since the reinforcement of the Islamic character of the Sudanese state through the introduction and implementation of the *shari'a* was its raison d'être. It did not take long, therefore, before the idea of possibly sundering the North and the South of the country began to be aired in public.[11] The reasoning was that if the SPLA refused to accept the validity of the *shari'a* as the framework for the Sudanese state and if Khartoum lacked the resources to conquer the South, then it might be preferable to let the South go, since that appeared to be the only way in which an Islamic Sudanese state could be constructed.

Officially, Sudanese government policy has been to exempt the three southern provinces from some, at least, of the provisions of the *shari'a*, thereby recognising the cultural and religious differences between those areas and the north of the country. However, these exemptions do not apply to the estimated two million or so southerners living in the north.[12] Nor, controversially, are they to be allowed to apply to the two thirds of the Nuba people whose lands are in southern

Kordofan – a traditionally northern province – but who are not Muslims. This has been unacceptable to the SPLA (which includes the Nuba rebel forces) and has tended to reinforce those in the NIF who believe that some kind of ethno-religious refounding of the Sudanese state may be necessary.

These northern sentiments have provided indirect reinforcement for a re-examination of ethnicity and its proper objects in the South itself. There were always those in the South who believed that Khartoum could never be trusted and that 'northern' interests would always be antithetical to the identity and interests of the southerners. Thus, the idea of secession from an untrustworthy and unstable northern political establishment was an attractive one for some. Nevertheless, this was regarded as an extreme position, difficult to sustain within the given realities of regional and domestic politics. In the 1990s, however, the idea of self-determination for the South, leading almost inevitably to thoughts of secession and of the establishment of a separate state, has gained ground.

Initially, this trend was encouraged by the very success of the SPLA and the determined Islamism of the NIF based government in Khartoum. It also became intertwined with power struggles within the SPLA which, in turn, derived some of their momentum from the ethnic differences which exist among the southerners themselves. During the years 1987–92, the SPLA exercised effective control over much of the three southern provinces. Government forces were confined to the major towns and even a number of these fell into the hands of the SPLA, giving it an increasing air of permanence. This success and the nature of the regime produced by the 1989 coup gave rise to questions in the South about why the SPLA should not simply cut all links with the North and make a bid for independence.

However, talk of the independence of a distinctive southern Sudan brought two reactions in its train. The first was the raising of the question of what it was that bound the southern Sudanese together as a distinct community, other than the negatives which had hitherto distinguished them from the northerners – i.e., as non-Muslims and non-Arabs. For many in the South, the SPLA's administration had been somewhat disillusioning since its members were often seen to be acting not in the interests of the 'southerners', but rather to favour members of their own particular community, however defined. Because of their preponderance within the movement, this was often perceived as being largely a Dinka interest, although, at a local level, more particular loyalties and networks seemed to be operating. This seemed to be compounded by the second reaction which took shape in John Garang's intolerance of dissent and the apparently heavy-handed, authoritarian manner with which he treated those who disagreed with his vision of a united Sudan.

In the summer of 1991 these tensions and the resentments associated with them erupted with the public split in the SPLA between John Garang and a number of senior commanders, most notably Riek Machar Teny-Dhurgon and Gordon Koang Chol. Accusing Garang of human rights abuses and of instituting a reign of terror, they denounced his leadership. They became known as the 'Nasir' faction (the name of the town which became their headquarters near the Ethiopian border) and subsequently styled themselves SPLA-United.[13] Riek Machar and Gordon Chol are both from different branches of the Nuer people and were thus able to capitalise upon ethnic resentments of the Dinka in the Nuer territories of the Upper Nile province.[14] The significance of these developments for the future of the SPLA programme and for the course of the civil war were various.

Firstly, it was not long before this new faction, SPLA-United, had dropped the demand that Sudan remain a united state in its communiqués. Increasingly, this faction became associated with the demand that the southern Sudanese be allowed to exercise the right of self-determination, with the ultimate objective of forming their own state should they so desire it. Secondly, in giving voice to this aspiration, SPLA-United began to attract others within the SPLA who had begun to feel uneasy at the continuing demand that the movement work within a unified Sudanese state when the aims of the government in Khartoum seemed to be so much at odds with their own interests. They also attracted the increasing number of SPLA members who resented Garang's leadership and methods, regardless of programme. Thirdly, SPLA-United came in for cultivation by the Khartoum government, precisely because they were seen to represent a potential lever against what came to be known as SPLA-Mainstream, led by Garang. This led to accusations of collaboration and to a certain closing of ranks in the SPLA-Mainstream, particularly when the Khartoum government launched its first serious offensive in the South in March 1992.

SPLA-United's control of around 35 per cent of the rebel-held South at the time made it a useful ally for the Khartoum government. The association was one which was denied at the time by Riek Machar, but there was little doubt that the Nuer regions of Upper Nile controlled by his faction emerged from the 1992 offensive remarkably unscathed, whereas those held by Garang's forces experienced the most severe fighting for five years. Periodic attempts at reconciliation between the two factions broke down and led eventually to the emergence of a third SPLA faction headed by William Nyuon Bany, Garang's deputy commander in chief and deputy chairman of the SPLA. By 1993, clashes between the various factions were becoming intense, leading to great loss of life and encouraging a degree of explicit ethnic conflict within the South. Ominously for the future of any distinctively southern political order, the terms 'Nuer' and 'Dinka' were taking on a particularity and political significance associated with ethnic conflict everywhere.[15]

The need both to establish trust between the SPLA forces and the peoples of the South, as well as to agree on the final outcome of the war if successful, sharpened ideas of identity and interest. One outcome was the emergence of sections of the SPLA associated with particular localities, recruited from the linguistically distinct peoples who inhabit those localities and led by local personalities. This made sense strategically in prosecuting a guerrilla war against the government forces. The danger, however, was that such units could become the power bases of individuals on which they could fall back should they disagree with the overall leadership of the SPLA. In addition, the inevitable frictions with local people which occurred when these units had to operate outside their own specific regions could fuel the belief on both sides that the interests of the groups concerned were fundamentally opposed because of their different linguistic identities. During the 1990s, these developments have been all too apparent in the South, weakening the unity of the South and providing an opportunity for the forces of the Khartoum government to seize the military initiative at various times.

An awareness of the damage which the factions of the SPLA were inflicting on each other led to a number of efforts at reconciliation. Most notably these produced the Washington Declaration of October 1993, in which the two principal factions of the SPLA agreed on a number of articles outlining their joint position vis-a-vis the future and the Khartoum government. Significantly, amongst these were those articles which called for the 'right to self-determination for the people of southern Sudan, the Nuba mountains and the marginalised areas' and the pledge to oppose any Khartoum government which denies them that right.[16]

This agreement did not put an end to the rivalry, but it was important in a number of ways. Firstly, it included amongst those with a right to self-determination – and thus, in principle, a right to secede from the Sudanese state – all those who felt in some sense alienated from prevailing ethno-religious order of the northern Sudan. Thus, the Nuba people were included. They inhabit the Nuba mountains in the northern province of Kordofan, but have been subjected to a particularly violent campaign of ethno-religious persecution by the present Khartoum government, determined to eradicate this outpost of non-Arab culture in the North.[17]

Secondly, the Declaration was significant in that the civil war in the Sudan was now quite expressly about the question of self-determination and thus potentially about the aspiration towards independent statehood by the major southern political and military factions. In order to preserve the movement intact and at the risk of alienating the northern opposition forces, Garang had apparently bowed to the growing sentiment in southern Sudan that only independent statehood would guarantee for all southerners the rights that he had been hoping to achieve within the framework of a unified Sudan.[18]

Part of the reason for this growing feeling may have been due to the third significant development: the fact that this was an agreement reached in Washington, brokered reportedly by US Assistant Secretary of State for African Affairs, George Moose, and the House Africa Subcommittee Chair, Harry Johnson. In other words, in the world of the 1990s it appeared that the US no longer looked with trepidation at the prospect of ethnic redivision of the political map of Africa. Whether that could be said to constitute American policy is debatable, but it was certainly the impression created – although clearly there was also, and perhaps principally, an American warning here for the Sudanese government. Only a few months before, the behaviour of that government had led the US to brand the Sudan officially as 'a nation sponsoring terrorism'.[19]

Irrespective of the particular animosity that existed between

Washington and Khartoum, developments in the region during the preceding few years had indicated that some changes had occurred in attitudes towards secessionism on the grounds of ethnic self-determination. The most obvious was the 1991 overthrow of the Mengistu regime in Addis Ababa by the combined forces of the Eritrean and Tigrean liberation movements, leading to the emergence of Eritrea as an independent sovereign state. Although a logistical blow to SPLA operations at the time, these developments undoubtedly encouraged those in the SPLA who had favoured taking the road to independence. The rapid international recognition accorded to the new state had also appeared to soften the OAU's attitude to the redrawing of frontiers in Africa, although it could be argued that Eritrea had experienced a separate existence under colonial rule. In fact, the OAU, through its chairmen, still held to the principle of working through the existing framework of states. Hence the successive, but finally fruitless attempts first by Uganda and then by Nigeria to organise negotiations between Khartoum and the SPLA in 1992 and 1993.

At the same time, a number of regional states, brought together in the Inter-Governmental Authority on Drought and Development (IGADD) consisting of Kenya, Eritrea, Ethiopia and Uganda began to offer their services as mediators. Initially and ostensibly, this was aimed at mediation between Khartoum and the SPLA. Taking heart from the Frankfurt Agreement in 1992 between Ali al-Haj (then deputy minister for foreign affairs) for the Sudanese government and the representatives of SPLA-United which seemed to commit both parties to a referendum on self-determination, the IGADD states organised a meeting in Nairobi in September 1994 between the Sudanese government and the SPLA factions.[20]

However, the talks broke down over the two key principles which the IGADD states and the SPLA expected would form the substance of the discussion: the question of self-determination for the South and the institution of a secular constitution for the Sudanese state. The SPLA and the IGADD states, as well as the special US envoy, Melissa Wells, who had been instrumental in bringing the meeting about, found the representatives of the Khartoum government in no mood to discuss such radical options. A considerably more hard-line member of the NIF, Ghazi Salah al-Din, had replaced Ali al-Haj and refused to discuss the issues of self-determination or that of a secular constitution. Encouraged by the recent military successes of the government forces in the South and by the internecine conflicts within the SPLA, as well as by the relative weakness of those in the NIF who had been advocating the separation of North and South as a price worth paying for the establishment of an Islamic state in the north of Sudan, the Khartoum government delegation saw no reason to make concessions. Indeed it claimed already to have made two significant concessions: the proposed establishment of a federal system of government, as outlined in the Juba conference of 1947 and the exemption of those states with non-Muslim majorities from the application of the *shari'a.*[21]

Subsequently, relations between the Sudan government and most of the members of IGADD deteriorated sharply. In December 1994, Eritrea broke off diplomatic relations with Sudan, accusing the Khartoum government of encouraging and arming Islamist groups active in Eritrea, such as the Eritrean Islamic Jihad. Eritrea then became the meeting place for the combined forces of the Sudanese opposition (the National Democratic Alliance), as well as the base of operations for the Sudanese Allied Forces led by Brigadier Abd al-Aziz Khalid Osman.[22] In April 1995, Uganda broke off relations with Sudan after a series of clashes along their common border and accusations by both parties of assistance to rebel forces operating in the territory of the other. Although relations were restored in June of the same year, the mutual accusations and recriminations continued.[23]

By that stage, relations between Sudan and Ethiopia had gone into a sharp decline following the attempted assassination of President Mubarak of Egypt in the Ethiopian capital and the belief that Sudan had given shelter to the would-be assassins, if it had not actually encouraged them. These suspicions led to the formal Ethiopian complaint against Sudan at the UN Security Council which in turn led to the unanimous condemnation of Sudan by the UN Security Council in January 1996, followed by the threat of sanctions.[24] Sudan sought to retaliate by complaining to the UN Security Council of Ethiopian armed incursions into its territory in early 1996 and it was certainly true that the SPLA seemed to have no difficulty crossing the Ethiopian frontier, regaining the sanctuary it had lost in 1991.[25] Only relations between Sudan and Kenya remained more or less amicable, resulting in mutual visits between Arap Moi and Omar al-Bashir at which the commitment of both countries to the IGADD peace initiative was reiterated.[26] However, since the IGADD peace initiative is premised on the discussion of two key issues – the possibility of self-determination for the South and the secular constitution of the Sudanese state – which the Khartoum government finds unacceptable and since Sudan is at loggerheads with most of the IGADD states, the commitment of Khartoum to such a process must remain doubtful.

The issue of self-determination for the South is thus very much on the agenda, although the motives of those parties apparently advocating it need to be examined carefully. For the IGADD states which have fallen out with the government of Khartoum, the reiteration of the need for self-determination for the southern Sudanese may say more about their intention to up the stakes in their respective conflicts with the present Sudanese government, than about their determination to bring an independent state of southern Sudan into being. This may also apply to the US and to the grouping of states calling itself the 'Friends of IGADD' which has been formed as a pressure group to help advance the peace process.[27]

For these countries, the preferred solution would be the acceptance by Khartoum of the second principle of the IGADD peace initiative, namely the removal of the Islamic *shari'a* from the statute book of the Sudanese state and the constitutional reaffirmation of the secular character of that state. They hope, thereby, that the unity of the Sudan may be retained since the fears and the sensibilities of the southerners regarding the Islamic character of the Sudanese state would be allayed. In addition, they might hope that this would spell the end of the NIF's domination of Sudanese politics and with it the end of Sudan's association with radical Islamist organisations and their activities in the Middle East and beyond. There has even been some suggestion that the US administration in 1995 was seeking to persuade both IGADD and the SPLA to abandon the principle of self-determination in the hope of persuading the Sudanese government to abandon its goal of an Islamic state in Sudan.[28]

In internal Sudanese politics as well, both among northerners and southerners, the issue of self-determination is very much alive, but in a contested and sometimes ambivalent way. In December 1994, the 'Declaration of Political Agreement' issued in Asmara by the combined forces of the Sudanese opposition (calling itself the National Democratic Alliance, and consisting of the Umma Party, the DUP,

SPLA-Mainstream and the SAF) stressed national unity and affirmed that the civil war was not simply a southern issue, but a national one. At the same time, however, it appeared to leave the way open for the possibility of southern independence by stating that should the principles of a multi-racial, multi-ethnic and multi-cultural society be violated in the future, 'a referendum which would include all options' could be held. Nevertheless, all reference to a secular constitution for the future Sudanese state was carefully avoided.[29]

The ambivalence of all the signatories was evident. However, it was clear that the NDA was seeking to accommodate the SPLA's apparent advocacy of southern autonomy since the 1993 Washington Agreement. Garang, in turn, was responding to the growing feeling in the South that some form of self-determination was necessary, whether or not it would lead to independent statehood. In September 1994, Riek Machar had renamed his faction of the SPLA the Southern Sudan Independence Movement/Army (SSIM/A) and had declared that he was now demanding full independence for southern Sudan.[30] Under pressure from the leaders of the IGADD states, Garang and Machar were persuaded to cease their hostilities and in February 1995 Machar could declare that the objectives of the SPLA and the SSIA were now identical.[31] It was by no means clear that this was really the case, but it seemed to push Garang further down the path of self-determination for the South in order not to be outflanked by Machar.[32]

This became more evident in the June 1995 meeting of the NDA in Asmara. Garang ensured that he and the SPLA-Mainstream were the only southern forces invited. The resolutions adopted were more specific than those of the December declaration, even if the issues of southern independence and of the secular constitution were not spelled out. There was a joint commitment to a referendum on self-determination during the period of transitional government (following the presumed overthrow of the NIF regime) both for the South as a whole and for the Abyei area (part of southern Kordofan inhabited primarily by Ngok Dinka). This right was specifically not accorded either to the people of the Nuba mountains in Kordofan, or to the Igessana Dinka of Blue Nile province who were to be given the possibility of a referendum on their administrative future in order to 'remove disadvantage'.[33] The fact that a distinction was made suggests that the NDA had agreed that more radical options, including possible independence, might be open to the peoples of the South and of

Abyei.[34]

Nevertheless, there was nothing permanent about such an agreement and the vagueness of the language, as well as the ambivalence of the parties involved, allowed Garang to backtrack to some degree when he felt that the pressure from Machar's pro-independence SSIA had eased. During 1995 Machar was beset by problems within his organisation, leading to numerous defections and the fragmenting of the group that had initially set up the SSIM/A.[35] Garang was able to block the application of the SSIM/A for affiliation to the NDA in January 1996, perhaps by playing on the fears of the dominant northern parties about the determination of the SSIM/A to win independence for southern Sudan. Despite all the talk of referenda and self-determination, this goal was still too radical for the NDA to accept as part of their platform. Instead, they preferred Garang's articulation of the SPLM/A's position as 'part and parcel of the NDA, in support of the unity of the country, based on the philosophy of justice, equality and freedom from the old politics', reiterating that the right to self-determination did not necessarily imply secession, as long as the conditions for a just unity existed.[36]

Disconcertingly for those who saw Machar as a champion of southern Sudanese independence, he reacted to the NDA's rejection of his application for membership by opening up a dialogue with the Khartoum government. This resulted in the signing in April 1996 of a 'Political Charter' in Khartoum by the Sudanese government, Riek Machar and Kerubino Bol (a former associate of Garang and then of Machar who had fallen out with the latter in 1995 and formed his own armed grouping in the Gogrial area). The Charter reiterated the 'unity of the Sudan with its known boundaries', but promised a referendum 'after full establishment of peace, stability and a reasonable level of social development'. The options for the voters in this referendum were not spelled out. Furthermore, the Charter stated that Islamic *shari'a* and traditions would be the basis of legislation, although the southern states would retain the right to enact special legislation to complement the federal law. In accepting what amounted to the stance of the Khartoum government as first enunciated in 1989, Machar nevertheless claimed that the Charter guaranteed people's basic rights and 'provided a framework for a peaceful resolution of issues of national unity'.[37] Whether this represents a change of heart by Machar is doubtful. It is more likely to reflect the weakness of his position and the fact that he has felt ever more marginalised by the increasingly successful Garang and the resurgent SPLA.

From these developments it is possible to conclude that the issues raised by the civil war have caused self-determination to enter the debate in a way which would not have been possible some years ago. To some degree, this has been due to the nature of the successive governments which have conducted the war from Khartoum, particularly that which came to power in 1989. To some degree, also this has been due to the processes of the war itself, in which the self-definition and interests of the various parties have become more marked as *de facto* administrative control over large areas of the South has fallen into the hands of southern guerrilla groups.

In addition, the willingness of regional states and of outside powers to encourage the notion of self-determination in the aftermath of the Cold War has also been a factor lending credibility to this aspiration. In this regard, however, any initial enthusiasm for such a project by interested outside powers has been tempered by an awareness of the risks and the fragmentation that may be associated with efforts at ethnic self-definition. This is particularly the case when the ethnic identity of the inhabitants of the region in question is unclear and when the prospect of independent statehood may intensify competition among a number ethnic groups for control of the new state. The idea that the southerners are jointly fighting against 'the Arab fascist and Islamist enemy', may express one of the major ethno-religious fault lines in the Sudan.[38] However, within the South itself, fragmentation within the SPLA, along lines of more particular ethnic self-identification, has been all too evident at various times and remains a threat with which the present leadership must cope. So far from being the solution to their problems, the actualisation of self-determination and the imminence of independent statehood may bring new problems in its train. Experiences in the former Yugoslavia and the former USSR have driven home to many the fact that ethnic self-determination may not be the answer that some may have hoped to the problems of a post-Cold War world.

Humanitarian Issues and Intervention

Ethnicity and the ethnic rationale for self-determination have not been the only issues raised by the Sudanese civil war and given a new significance in the period following the end of the Cold War. Of equal salience was the question of humanitarian issues and, particularly, of intervention by the United Nations and by Western powers to enforce the human rights criteria by which the Sudanese government was increasingly judged. In the context of the civil war, the various aid and relief organisations had never had an easy task, since they tended to find themselves caught between the Sudanese government and the SPLA. During the 1980s and particularly under the government of Sadiq al-Mahdi there had been a good deal of tension between Sudanese officials and the various NGOs working in the South. On the one hand, the NGOs were accused by the government of acting in support of the SPLA and this led to the expulsion of a large number of them in 1987.[39] On the other hand, in those cases where they accepted the conditions imposed upon them by the government for working in the South, they found that they were often obliged to supply not simply government held towns, but also the government's own soldiers. This led to hostility and threats against them from the SPLA.

However, with the initiation of the massive UN Operation Lifeline Sudan in 1989 for famine relief, in the South as well as the West, the relationship between the SPLA and the relief organisations appeared to undergo a marked change. Seeing cooperation with the UN agencies as a means of gaining international credibility and of proving to the world the extent of its *de facto* control of much of the South, the SPLA assisted the UN agencies involved and the many NGOs operating under the Lifeline umbrella. Declaring a cease-fire unilaterally in certain key areas and opening up others for use by the famine relief agencies, the SPLA role in the operation was said to have been in marked contrast to the disorganisation and suspicion which the agencies encountered in Khartoum.[40]

The new regime in Khartoum in June 1989 did little to alter this situation, despite early protestations of good will. In fact, as soon as the long cease-fire between government forces and the SPLA broke down and fighting resumed in November 1989, the Khartoum government banned relief flights by both the UN and the ICRC, suspicious that the aid would be falling into the hands of the SPLA.[41] This was followed within six months by strong criticism of the Sudanese government by the then US Assistant Secretary of State for African Affairs, Herman Cohen. Stating that the USA wanted above everything peace and a continuation of the relief effort in Sudan, the Sudanese government was condemned for failing to promote these objectives and for human rights abuses. Despite the strength of the criticism, there was some attempt to be even-handed and the SPLA was also criticised for the obstacles it seemed to be putting in the path of relief operations and of peace.[42] The ambiguity of this message could be seen as a symptom of the difficulty faced by the US administration in working out a new policy in the Horn of Africa. The Cold War rivalry with the USSR had faded out and Washington was obliged instead to deal with the local, often unstable and 'unreadable' regimes and rebel forces of the area on their own merits.

The Sudanese government responded by rejecting an American plan for ending the civil war which would have involved disengagement of the two sides and the deployment of a multi-national force between the opposing forces.[43] This was scarcely surprising since the proposals would have involved both the internationalisation of the conflict and the treatment of Sudanese territory more or less as if it were territory of separate or disputed sovereignty. As the Sudanese government was to discover, however, these were to be themes which recurred with increasing force during the coming years. On the one hand, the record and behaviour of Sudan as a state was held up for ever more intensive and critical scrutiny in various international fora. On the other hand, this development, combined with the circumstances of the civil war seemed to some to be setting the scene for a more thoroughgoing intervention in Sudan by forces justifying their activities with reference to humanitarian principles.

The strategic miscalculation of the Sudanese government in appearing to support Iraq during the conflict over Kuwait in 1990/1991 had the effect of bringing much of the Sudanese government's behaviour under close and hostile scrutiny by the states of the victorious allied coalition. It was in this light that a number of countries began to reappraise their aid projects and to question the restrictions which the Sudanese government placed on relief operations.[44] In addition, the dismal human rights record of the Sudanese government, both in the South and in other parts of the country, was increasingly invoked as a reason for the reduction in official aid schemes. Hoping to capitalise upon the very evident international isolation of the government in Khartoum following the Iraqi defeat in 1991, John Garang went on a tour of Western capitals, seeking humanitarian aid.

Apart from putting the cause of the SPLM/SPLA before officials in London and Washington, he urged aid agencies to deal directly with his movement, rather than with Khartoum.[45] Some may have been tempted to do so, but at this stage, there was little official encouragement for such a course of action. Wary as many governments might have been of the regime in Khartoum, it was still regarded as the proper agency through which to deal, even though its *de facto* control over large parts of the South no longer existed.

By 1992, however, a rather different note was being struck. This was most loudly heard in October 1992 when the US Congress passed a strongly worded resolution condemning the Sudan government's human rights abuses and its prosecution of the war. Although it also condemned human rights abuses perpetrated by the SPLA, it demanded of the Khartoum government the right of unconditional and unrestricted access for the ICRC, for UN officials and for other relief organisations to all parts of the country. At the same time, it opened up the path towards the internationalisation of these issues by calling on the UN Secretary General to convene a Security Council meeting on the human rights situation and to consider 'further international means, including within the UN system, to ameliorate the humanitarian situation'.[46]

A few months later, the US Assistant Secretary of State for African Affairs was reported to have given a more explicit warning to the Sudanese government not to complicate the planned US operations in Somalia. The analogy was not lost on the Sudanese government. Although the situation was scarcely identical, there were evidently fears in Khartoum at the time that a similar pretext of humanitarian relief operations might be used to justify more direct, military intervention in Sudan. This might have explained the Sudanese government's abrupt agreement with the SPLA in December 1992 concerning the creation of demilitarised corridors through the war zones for relief supplies to be delivered to the various relief centres in the South.[47]

Ominously for Khartoum, that same month the 47th Session of the UN General Assembly adopted a resolution on the human rights situation in the Sudan. The states which moved this resolution included most of the EU states, all of the G7 states and many of the African and Latin American states. The resolution provided for continuous monitoring of the human rights situation in Sudan and called upon the UN Commission on Human Rights to make this a priority at its forthcoming meeting. The resolution further called on all parties to the civil war to respect the rights of civilians and permit 'international agencies, humanitarian organisations and donor governments' to deliver humanitarian assistance to the civilian population. The question of the sanction that might be used if, for instance, the government in Khartoum failed to comply was left unanswered. However, despite the significant differences between the situation of Sudan and that of Somalia there was clearly some fear of future military action in the light of the Somali experience.[48]

During 1993, these trends became more clear cut. On the one hand, at the behest of the USA and most of the European states, the UN pursued its investigations into the human rights record of the Sudanese government by appointing a special rapporteur to investigate human rights abuses in Sudan.[49] On the other hand, John Garang called for international support for the creation of 'safe havens' both in the South and in the Nuba mountains. He was supported in this by Youssef Kuwa, the leader of the Nuba rebel forces within the SPLA, who called for arrangements similar to those set up in the Kurdish areas of Iraq by the Western allies in 1991.[50] In agreement with the rival factions of the SPLA, Garang's forces created unilaterally a number of 'demilitarised zones' for the delivery of UN supplies through Operation Lifeline. For its part, the UN appointed a new director of the operation in Nairobi who evidently had a more pro-active attitude to the provision of relief supplies, if necessary disregarding the government entirely. The Khartoum government cannot have been reassured either by the extensive transport equipment which he acquired, or by his sentiments when he said that 'traditional UN people are saying that sovereignty is paramount. But there are also the beginnings of a new ethic which says a government has a duty and an obligation to protect its people – and the UN has a commensurate duty'.[51]

The Sudanese government evidently saw the dangers looming of this 'new ethic' which seemed to them to be setting the stage for extensive international intervention. It donated enough sorghum to the World Food Programme to cover the South's emergency needs in 1993 and furthermore reversed its policy in March 1993 and allowed UN relief agencies to operate in the South once again.[52] It also hired a well-known PR firm in Washington to improve its public image and to represent Sudan before Congress and in the media.[53] After initially denouncing the idea of a UN rapporteur in furious terms as anti-Muslim and anti-Third World, Khartoum eventually said that it would cooperate with him, even though the USA and its allies had manipulated the system.[54] Such cooperation was not much facilitated in the meantime by the Sudan being placed on the US list of sponsors of terrorism. For many in the Sudanese regime this seemed to be yet another indicator of imminent US intervention.[55]

Given these anxieties, it was perhaps scarcely surprising that the Sudanese government's reaction to the report of the Special Rapporteur on Human Rights should have been so vehement. Professor Biro's report to the UN Commission on Human Rights gave a grim account of human rights abuses by both sides in the civil war. However, it was not this which so infuriated the Sudanese government. The section of the report which earned him denunciation as 'satanic', as 'an enemy of Islam', and held him to be guilty of blasphemy consisted of a number of paragraphs in which he had pointed out that there were severe inconsistencies between the Islamic legislation in force in Sudan and the human rights standards embodied in such international conventions as the Covenant on Civil and Political Rights and the Convention on the Rights of the Child to which the Sudan was a signatory. As he observed, the fact that the legislation was derived from the Qur'an was irrelevant, since the key question was whether the laws in question contradicted Sudan's international commitments to human rights. So vehement was the Sudanese government's reaction that for the first time all the members of the UN Commission voted for a motion in support of Professor Biro and called upon the Secretary General of the UN to ensure that Sudan did not repeat its threats against him.[56]

The debate moved later in the year to the UN General Assembly where a vote was taken which overwhelmingly condemned the government of Sudan on the basis of a report drawn up by Professor Biro concerning human rights abuses in the North and the South of the country. This, in turn, led to calls for more concrete action to be taken against Sudan, in the shape of trade embargoes of various kinds.[57] The Sudanese government rejected Professor Biro's allegations of human rights violations and 'his affront to the Islamic faith' and, indeed, sought to portray the international scrutiny of the government's human rights record as an attack on Islam in general. The Sudanese attorney general argued at the UN in Geneva that there were severe dangers of 'discrepancies' between religious faith and the UN Charters. He called for the establishment of a committee to discuss the place of religion in international charters, claiming that any criticism of Sudan's application of the *shahari'a* was a violation of Sudan's sovereign right to institute whatever it saw fit.[58] However, it was clear that many of the human rights violations of which Sudan stood accused had nothing to do with Islam and much to do with the repressive and discriminatory policies of the Sudanese government. Some of these had their origin in the tensions and conflicts of the civil war, but others seemed to be due simply to its intolerance of all forms of dissent.[59]

By this stage, however, there was little talk of direct intervention for humanitarian or other reasons by the USA itself, or through the UN. The experience of the intervention in Somalia had proved decidedly discouraging and the experience in Iraqi Kurdistan, although more easily sustainable, had been disappointing, given the violent internecine strife amongst the Kurds themselves. Instead, direct humanitarian assistance was provided in some of the southern regions through the UN Nairobi office, but the US government fell back on a more traditional policy and concentrated on seeking to 'contain' the Islamist government in Sudan by providing assistance to some of its African neighbours. Eritrea in particular, but also Uganda, Ethiopia and Kenya were in receipt of substantial US military assistance and there was some speculation that a proportion of this equipment was finding its way into the hands of the SPLA.[60]

In a significant admission during 1995 a senior American official[61] acknowledged that Sudan was 'a tragedy and difficult for US policy'. From his testimony, it was clear that the US administration did not have a very high opinion of either the Sudanese government or its opponents. Significantly, in this post-Cold War world, he lamented the fact that neither Khartoum nor the various factions of southern rebels were in the least responsive to US concerns about human rights or international terrorism. He ended by spelling out the US intention to maintain bilateral and international pressure on Khartoum to bring about changes in its behaviour, adding with thinly veiled menace that 'these policies which we find threatening and objectionable will eventually cause the regime's downfall'.[62] However, this seemed to be giving voice to a desired, rather than to a planned outcome. The sentiment that comes over most strongly in this testimony is the difficulty for the US government of 'reading' the politics of Sudan in the post-Cold War world. Instead, the intention seemed to be to place it within the paradigms established by human rights criteria and by its designation as a 'terrorist state'.

These themes were highlighted during 1995 and 1996 by the dispute between Ethiopia and Sudan concerning the would-be assassins of President Mubarak. This resulted eventually in the unusually unanimous UN Security Council's condemnation of Sudan in UN Security Council Resolution 1044 of January 1996. It required Sudan to hand over the three men suspected of having perpetrated the act who had then allegedly fled to Sudan. In addition, it called on Sudan to 'desist from engaging in activities of assisting, supporting and facilitating terrorist activities and from giving shelter and sanctuary to terrorist elements.' The Secretary General was to report to the UN Security Council on the progress of Sudan in the implementation of these desiderata after sixty days. The clear implication was that sanctions of some kind would be considered should a positive report not be forthcoming at the end of March. Given the lack of progress in this case, the report was inevitably negative and it then fell to the UN Security Council to discuss possible sanctions against Sudan in the hope of putting pressure on the government.

However, when it came to the question of sanctions or of action other than of a rhetorical kind, there was considerably less unity within the UN Security Council than there had been on the original resolution. A number of countries, including Egypt (which should in theory have been the most aggrieved party) were not in favour of harsh economic sanctions which would have harmed the population of Sudan in general. Rather they favoured such measures as the limitation of the numbers of Sudanese diplomatic personnel, restrictions on visas for Sudanese and a ban on the operation of Sudanese airlines. It was reported that one of the considerations which had influenced the Egyptian government's rejection of a possible arms embargo against Sudan, had been the military advantage this would have given to the SPLA in the civil war, bringing closer the possible break up of the Sudanese state – an outcome the Egyptian government wished to avoid at all costs.[63]

These developments illustrate vividly some of the trends in post-Cold War international relations. The first is the question of sovereignty when humanitarian issues come onto the agenda. A situation such as the civil war, creating as it does widespread misery and obscuring the extent to which the government's or its opponents' writ runs in any given area lends itself in this international environment to the possibility of external intervention. Clearly, if such intervention is to be conducted under the auspices of the UN, principles must be invoked which enjoy a large, if not necessarily a universal degree of support. It was not surprising, therefore, that the Sudanese government should have felt increasingly nervous about the possibility of foreign intervention when it saw the spotlight of international scrutiny turned upon it and its indictment according to the principles of the universal declaration of human rights.

This raises the second issue which revolves around the question of local norms versus universal norms and the choice which governments may have to make in order to achieve respectability or approval. In the past, Sudan's government saw some purpose in making Sudan a signatory to the various international conventions on human rights. With the emergence of the distinctively Islamist regime of the NIF, the present government evidently has other preoccupations and these may be incompatible with the norms and values embodied in those conventions. The question that arises therefore concerns the circumstances under which the UN, or those with the power to move the UN, might find it profitable or desirable to enforce compliance with these criteria – and the reaction which that might provoke in many countries where particular cultural values are not necessarily compatible with those embodied in these universal declarations. This, in turn, raises the question of who is interpreting what the obligations emanating from these various 'collections of equally valid official norms' [to quote Professor Biro] might be and to what end.[64]

The question of human rights has thus come to the fore in the relationship between Sudan and the rest of the world. To some degree, international attention was drawn to this aspect of the Sudanese government's behaviour through the scale of the human suffering caused by the civil war. Although the human rights record of the Sudanese government has been roundly condemned whether in the North or the South, Professor Biro's latest excoriating report focused attention once again on the abuses of human rights perpetrated in the war zones of the South and the Nuba mountains.[65] Humanitarian concerns have already led to forms of unilateral intervention on the ground in the South by UN and other humanitarian agencies, regardless of the wishes of the sovereign Sudanese government. In the North, as the case of the Nuba mountains has demonstrated, outside parties seem to be more circumspect.

However, in the formal international arena of the UN Security Council, there have been greater reservations about officially endorsing unilateral intervention against a member of the UN on humanitarian grounds, despite the fact that its government may be ill regarded by most of the other members. After the first flush of post-Cold war excitement wore off, the US administration found that direct intervention was as costly as it had ever been, far more complex and potentially counter-productive. For its part, the Sudanese government discovered that it could rally some support in two areas: among those governments which were uneasy about the ways in which international agreements might be used to impose liberal values at variance with their own normative beliefs, especially those associated with Islamic precepts; among those governments which were anxious that their own records on human rights should not be held up to international scrutiny, let alone used as a pretext for UN sanctions.

Conclusion

The causes and the progress of the Sudanese civil war have been due chiefly to internal and regional dynamics which had little, if anything to do with the Cold War. Nor did successive Sudanese governments' attempts to invoke 'Cold War values' to justify their conduct of the war have much effect on the course it took or on their capacity to direct that course. Consequently, it is difficult to sustain the argument that the Sudanese civil war has been significantly affected by the ending of the Cold War. An argument could, of course, be made that the fall of the Mengistu regime in Ethiopia was an indirect result of the Soviet disengagement from the Horn of Africa which presaged the ending of the Cold War itself, although it would appear that other dynamics in domestic and regional politics would better explain this collapse. If the former interpretation of events in Ethiopia were admitted, then one might say that there was a knock-on effect in the logistical set-back this represented for the SPLA. However, this would seem relatively insignificant compared to the other forces or factors at work and it has proved to have been only a temporary set-back, in any case.

As far as the significance of the Sudanese civil war in international relations is concerned, it is less the absence or otherwise of Cold War influences which is important, than the ways in which the conflict has had resonance for two issues of considerable and perhaps growing salience in international relations following the end of the Cold War. The first is the way in which it has raised an array of questions revolving around the issues of ethnicity and self-determination. In particular, the issues of the redrawing of state boundaries, the refounding of states and the establishment of new states on the basis of various markers of ethnicity have emerged in ways which might suggest changing attitudes to the potential and the dangers of these projects in the post-Cold War world. Secondly, the suffering inflicted by the civil war on the populations of southern Sudan, as well as the general condition of the Sudanese as a whole, have raised the question of external intervention – whether by international agencies or by great powers – on the basis of humanitarian principles.

In both areas, the issues raised have been affected in their capacity to develop through their complex interplay with the realities of power. In the first place, the SPLA's capacity to defeat or to thwart the intentions of the Khartoum government in their efforts to establish control over the whole of the South by force will clearly influence the credibility of the project of self-determination. The attitudes of the NIF government, of elements within the South itself and of external powers to the idea of secession will all be affected by the degree of lasting *de facto* control which the SPLA can exercise in large areas of the South. Conversely, of course, the power of the SPLA will also be affected by the severity of internal domestic conflict, based on disparate forms of ethnic self-definition within the South itself. The uncertainty which these processes may generate will shape the attitudes of external powers, in the region especially, towards the key question of self-determination.

As far as the second issue is concerned, the question of invoking humanitarian principles to justify sanctions or even intervention has been raised in the case of Sudan, not simply because of the poor human rights record of its government and the misery of the civil war. It has also been closely connected to the perception of Sudan as a weak and relatively isolated state whose pattern of alliances – Libya, Iraq and Iran – are more likely to provoke than to deter thoughts of retribution by the dominant powers in the international hierarchy. The nature of the civil war and the weakness it may demonstrate in the Sudanese government's ability to control its territory have clearly been important in these calculations. The question which can only be answered in a larger setting – and probably over a longer time-span – is whether these considerations and perhaps the *de facto* practices emerging in connection with the civil war may indeed be tending to establish a 'new ethic' of humanitarian intervention in international relations, with a corresponding diminution of respect for the sovereignty of certain states, which may have real consequences in terms of the deployment of power.

As always perhaps in international relations, as in politics more generally, the interesting object of study is the interplay between principles which justify the uses of power and the practices which come to shape the norms themselves. The ending of the Cold War has clearly affected the ways in which it is possible to imagine that power can be used effectively, just as, at an earlier stage, the internal transformations within the Cold War itself affected the principles whereby the uses of power could be – or rather needed to be – justified. Consequently, in the post-Cold War world other principles are invoked to signify the concerns of the dominant powers in international politics. These have not yet suggested a distinct course or way forward. Indeed, action based upon them has been a tentative and sometimes contradictory process. Nevertheless, insofar as Sudan's civil war has been a conflict which has resonated internationally in the two senses outlined above, it could be said to constitute one among many of the testing grounds for the principles of international behaviour likely to characterise the post-Cold War world.

Notes

1 The many changes of direction which this caused in Sudanese foreign policy are well captured in Muhammad Bashir Hamid, *Aspects of Sudanese Foreign Policy: 'Splendid isolation', Radicalisation and 'Finlandisation'* (Paper presented to the Fourth International Conference on the Nile Valley: 'Continuity and Change', Institute of African and Asian Studies, University of Khartoum, 24–28 November 1981).

2 For a good account of the debate in Sudan about the proposed redivision of the South and the fears to which this gave rise, see Raphael K. Badal, 'Political Cleavages within the Southern Sudan – an empirical analysis of the re-division debate', in S. Harir and T. Tvedt (eds), *Short-Cut to Decay: the case of the Sudan* (The Scandinavian Institute of African Studies, Uppsala, 1994) pp. 105–25. This contains a useful description of the differences of

opinion among Southerners about the merits and disadvantages of the redivision.

3 John Garang, *The Call for Democracy in Sudan*, edited and introduced by Mansour Khalid (Kegan Paul International, London, 1992) pp. 19–25.

4 *Le Monde*, 27 April 1984; *Africa Confidential* xxv/7 (28 March 1984) p. 6.

5 Ann Mosley Lesch, 'Sudan's Foreign Policy: in Search of Arms, Aid and Allies' in John O. Voll (ed.), *Sudan – State and Society in Crisis* (Indiana University Press, Bloomington, in association with the Middle East Institute, Washington, 1991) pp. 55–6.

6 *Sudanow*, April 1986, pp. 33–4.

7 Lesch 'Sudan's Foreign Policy' pp. 58–62; *Le Monde*, 20 June 1987.

8 *The Guardian*, 15 November 1988.

9 *The Independent*, 14 December 1988, 6 March 1989, 17 June 1989; *The Guardian*, 27 December 1988, 29 December 1988, 10 June 1989; *The Times*, 23 February 1989, 27 March 1989.

10 *International Herald Tribune*, 18 February 1985.

11 See General Omar al-Bashir's comment, as reported in *The Guardian*, 29 September 1989; *Africa Confidential* xxx/22 (3 November 1989) pp. 3–4.

12 The great majority of these people are of Dinka origin and their future status is obviously a major concern for John Garang and the dominant Dinka faction of the SPLA.

13 *Africa Confidential* xxxii/18 (13 September 1991) pp. 2–3; *The Independent*, 3 September 1991; *Financial Times*, 10 September 1991.

14 *The Independent*, 27 December 1991.

15 This was reflected in comments by members of SPLA-United that they had 'pushed the Dinka enemy right beyond the frontiers of Nuer country' and by graffiti reportedly seen in the town of Ayod shortly after its capture by SPLA-Mainstream stating that 'Nuers will be eliminated this year'; *Le Monde*, 29 April 1993.

16 *Africa Confidential* xxxiv/22 (5 November 1993) p. 5.

17 For further details of this campaign see the publication by African Rights, *Facing Genocide: the Nuba of Sudan* (African Rights, London, 1995).

18 This came as something of a shock to the northern opposition parties who were reportedly stunned by the SPLA's apparent abandonment of Sudanse unity in favour of the unity and self-determination of the South. *Africa Confidential* xxxiv/22 (5 November 1993) p. 6.

19 *The Independent*, 19 August 1993; Abdel Salam Sidahmed, 'Sudan on US "terrorist" list', *Middle East International*, 8 October 1993, pp. 18–19.

20 At this stage, these numbered three: SPLA-Mainstream, led by John Garang; the Southern Sudan Independence Movement/Army (SSIM/A), led by Riek Machar (by the beginning of 1995, this was to fragment, leaving Machar in command of the SSIM/A but leading to the creation of two further factions, confusingly going under the same name: SPLA-United, led by Lam Akol; SPLA-United, led by Kerubino Bol) and a grouping, led by the late

William Nyuon Bany (who was to ally himself with Machar in 1994, but to break with him in 1995, rejoining Garang. He was killed in January 1996 in an ambush by Machar's forces). Despite mutual suspicions and hostilities they agreed to adopt a joint negotiating position in Nairobi which appeared to revolve around the two issues of self-determination and separation of religion and state. *The Times*, 5 September 1994; for details of the SPLA factions, see *Africa Confidential* xxxvi/5 (3 March 1995) pp. 2–3.

21 *Africa Confidential* xxxvi/5 (3 March 1995) p. 2; *Sudan Update* v/17 (13 October 1994) p. 1.

22 *Africa Confidential* xxxv/25 (16 December 1994) p. 6; *Africa Confidential* xxxvi/3 (3 February 1995) p. 8.

23 *Africa Research Bulletin* xxxii/2 (1–28 February 1995) pp. 11744–5, xxxii/4 (1–30 April 1995) p. 11813, xxxii/6 (1–30 June 1995) p. 11876.

24 *Africa Confidential* xxxvii/1 (5 January 1996) pp. 1–2; G. Lusk, 'Foes go to the UN', *Middle East International*, 5 January 1996 pp. 15–16.

25 *Africa Confidential* xxxvii/8 (12 April 1996) p. 2.

26 *Africa Research Bulletin* xxxii/5 (1–31 May 1995) (11862); *Sudan Update* vii/4 (7 March 1996) p. 3.

27 In 1995, this included the United Kingdom, the Netherlands, Canada and Norway – as well as potentially, Morocco and Sweden. *Sudan Update* vi/6 (17 April 1995) p. 2.

28 See the article by Baroness Cox and John Eibner in *International Herald Tribune*, 14 August 1995.

29 *Africa Confidential* xxxvi/3 (3 February 1995) p. 8.

30 *Sudan Update* vi/2 (6 February 1995) pp. 1–2.

31 *Sudan Update* vi/3 (20 February 1995) p. 2.

32 *Africa Confidential* xxxvi/5 (6 March 1995) p. 2; G. Lusk, 'Time for the ballot box', *Middle East International*, 17 March 1995 pp. 14–15.

33 *Africa Confidential* xxxvi/14 (7 July 1995) p. 3.

34 An indication of this had been given a few months earlier when Sadiq al-Mahdi (leader of the Umma Party) had made a public speech at the mosque in Omdurman, endorsing the right of the people of southern Sudan to self-determination: 'Southern Sudan should decide in a free and fair referendum whether to remain part of a united Sudan'. If they voted for independence, he continued, there was no point in trying to maintain unity by force. *Sudan Update* vi/6 (17 April 1995) pp. 2–3. This, of course, went contrary to everything he had tried to achieve during his various terms as Prime Minister and may have been simply a means of upping the stakes in his ambivalent and troubled relationship with the NIF government.

35 *Sudan Update* vi/16 (20 October 1995) p. 3.

36 *Sudan Update* vii/2 (5 February 1996) p. 3.

37 *Africa Confidential* xxxvii/8 (12 April 1996) pp. 2–3; Republic of Sudan Radio, Omdurman 10 April and 11 April 1996 in BBC SWB ME/2585 MED/30–31, 13 April 1996.

38 A description used by an SPLA-United spokesman, Peter Sule in

Southern Sudan Vision, 10 February 1996, cited in *Sudan Update* vii/3 (22 February 1996) p. 3.

39 *The Guardian*, 22 April 1987 and 10 July 1987.

40 *The Guardian*, 31 May 1989.

41 G. Lusk, 'Pressures Mount', *Middle East International*, 17 November 1989, p. 13.

42 G. Lusk,'Sudan and the US', *Middle East International*, 13 April 1990, p. 12.

43 *Le Monde*, 7 June 1990.

44 *The Independent*, 27 October 1990, 14 November 1990; *The Times*, 6 November 1990, 6 May 1991; *The Guardian*, 18 January 1991.

45 *The Guardian*, 29 June 1991.

46 G. Lusk, 'Harsh Condemnations', *Middle East International*, 23 October 1992, pp. 13–14.

47 *The Guardian*, 10 December 1992.

48 Abdel Salam Sidahmed, 'Sudan falls foul of the UN', *Middle East International*, 8 January 1993, pp. 18–19.

49 G. Lusk, 'Back to Abuja', *Middle East International*, 5 May 1993, pp. 11–12; *Le Monde*, 13 March 1993.

50 *The Guardian*, 24 May 1993, 25 August 1993. Kuwa felt particularly aggrieved since it appeared that the UN and relief agencies treated the area of the Nuba mountains as part of Sudan into which they would not venture without the permission of the Sudanese government. This was in marked contrast to their activities in the three southern provinces of the Sudan.

51 *The Guardian*, 19 March 1993.

52 *The Economist*, 6 March 1993.

53 *Africa Confidential* xxxiv/6 (19 March 1993) p. 8. It did not seem to be particularly effective since the US government placed Sudan on the list of states 'sponsoring terrorism' a few months later.

54 *Africa Confidential* xxxiv/7 (2 April 1993) pp. 1–2.

55 Abdel Salam Sidahmed, 'Sudan on US "terrorist" list', *Middle East International*, 8 October 1993, pp. 18–19.

56 *International Herald Tribune*, 9 March 1994; *Le Monde*, 7 June 1994.

57 *Sudan Update* v/21 (16 December 1994) p. 4.

58 Radio National Unity, Omdurman, 3 March 1995 in BBC SWB ME/2244 MED/18, 6 March 1995.

59 *Sudan Update* vi/4 (5 March 1995) pp. 3–4; *International Herald Tribune*, (9 March 1995) p. 6.

60 *Africa Confidential* xxxvi/5 (3 March 1995) pp. 2–3.

61 Edward Brynn, Acting Assistant Secretary of State for African Affairs in testimony to the House Committee on International Relations concerning US policy towards Sudan.

62 *Sudan Update* vi/9 (1 June 1995) pp. 2–3.

63 *Africa Confidential* xxxvii/8 (12 April 1996) p. 1. As the debate about possible sanctions proceeded, the US government chose this moment to expel

a Sudanese diplomat allegedly involved in a plot in 1993 to blow up the UN building itself. A couple of months earlier, in a public gesture of no confidence in the government of Sudan, all US diplomatic personnel had been withdrawn from Sudan since, according to the US State Department, the Khartoum government had refused to guarantee their safety. *International Herald Tribune*, 2 February 1996.

64 *Le Monde*, 7 June 1994.

65 *Africa Confidential* xxxvii/8 (12 April 1996) p. 3.

3 Central Asia and Transcaucasia after the Cold War: Conflict Unleashed

Graham E. Fuller

The collapse of the Soviet Union and the end of the Cold War – one of the most astonishing events of the entire twentieth century – has left an uncertain legacy in the world. On the one hand the fading of the nuclear balance of terror is an immense relief for the world. A globe artificially polarised into two camps has now broken down and is returning to a more 'normal' state of multi-centred international politics with a wide range of movements and ideologies at work.

Regional conflicts too, have been severely affected. First, with the end of global ideological struggle, it is now seemingly less fashionable or acceptable to maintain ideological conflict on the local level. Furthermore, many conflicts that have been sustained by the Cold War now find themselves without patrons and forced to reach rapprochement of some kind: South Africa, Nicaragua, Angola, Ethiopia, Cambodia, and even the Arab–Israeli conflict have been sharply affected by the removal of the 'global factor' from aspects of local struggle. There is now an opportunity to return to 'politics as usual', to get on with the 'real issues' as opposed to Cold War constructs that often dominated and perpetuated local conflict. In this sense, the end of the Cold War has brought welcome change; the world now seems open to new possibilities never before thought possible during the geopolitically relatively frozen era of East–West conflict.

But with the euphoria of fading nuclear confrontation, a grim new realism has also set in. It is becoming clearer that a return to 'politics as usual' is now marked by a reopening of visceral national and religious hatreds and conflicts that had often been suppressed during the Cold War as impermissibly dangerous to the superpowers and to their domestic interests. The Soviet Union in particular – an island of stability in the world, until one day it suddenly was not anymore – had frozen virtually all political evolution throughout the region stretching from Eastern Europe, through the Balkans, into the Caucasus and Central Asia; much of East Asia was similarly frozen in a communist ice-age under communist domination or communist influence.

World conflicts with the end of the Cold War perhaps now fall into two categories: those taking place outside the former communist bloc, and those taking place within the confines of the old bloc. Of those outside the bloc, some are freer to move towards international solution than ever before; other conflicts, in non-communist areas of Africa, Asia, and the Middle East, are emerging more strongly once again. But these non-communist struggles have long existed, even in a more open world: the existence of these frictions had never been denied, but had just been kept relatively quiescent and allowed to evolve only slowly in the international discipline of Cold War years. But within the former communist regions, the situation is very different. Here the very existence of problems have been denied: ethnic and religious conflict were ideologically viewed as remnants of the past, of imperial structures, of bourgeois or feudal political orders on the way to extinction. By the Brezhnev era the Soviet Union had announced that ethnic problems within the USSR had been all but solved – they were regarded as relics of the past.

Although most scholars were perhaps inclined to believe at that time that perhaps seventy years of Soviet socialism had indeed tamed if not eliminated 'archaic' ethnic and religious differences, other scholars were not so sure that these conflicts were anything other than put on hold.[1] Indeed, with the collapse of the Soviet Union and its Eastern European satrapies, it has become abundantly clear that not only had these problems merely been frozen during the Soviet period, but that their very freezing had denied them the opportunity of normal evolution for the better part of a century. In many circumstances, the only way to understand the nature and virulence of the current problems was to return to the history books of the early twentieth century to examine the characteristics of that period when 'history ended' with the onset of Soviet power. In many cases the Soviet era had not only not solved long-standing frictions, but had actually exacerbated hatreds and created new ones.[2] These traditional problems have now been rendered yet more virulent in the post-communist period by the traumatic process of political, economic, and social *perestroika* throughout the area that tends to accentuate differences yet further; the demanding privatisation process produces winners and losers that directly affects all ethnic groups in differing ways. In many senses then, the end of the communist era has intensified ethnic and religious problems more than ever before: these societies are among the most troubled of any in today's world.

Ethnicity in the Soviet Era

Ethnicity and nationalism in the areas of the Transcaucasus and Central Asia present special problems in themselves. In Central Asia in particular, nationalism never had a chance to develop organically, as it were, compared to most other countries where the political system and the peoples themselves had allowed a nationalist process to emerge. Nationalism, after all, is a process of self-definition, usually against a foil of surrounding events and forces. In the case of Soviet Central Asia, however, specific national identities were foisted upon ethnic groupings in a process in which the peoples themselves did not really participate. Soviet republics, peoples, and languages were created for them, largely at the political and administrative convenience of a Bolshevik leadership whose primary goal was to seize and retain all power. There were, to be sure, Uzbeks, Turkmen, Kazakhs, Kyrgyz and Tajiks, but they were often tribal names, with very poorly delimited geographical, linguistic, and tribal boundaries. Most of them had never had a state, certainly never in their name. The region had long been well aware of itself as a culture, and it had possessed 'nationalist' feelings, but these feelings were expressed in terms of an Islamic or overall Turkic identity rather than as Uzbeks, Tajiks, and so on. Nomadic peoples – Kazakh, Kyrgyz, Turkmen – did have clearer identities but had never linked that idea to a sense of political community or state.

Great khanates had also existed during the history of Central Asia, but within them the concept of ethnicity had been quite vague, usually involving various hierarchical relationships of subordination to a ruling tribal clan. The great khanates of the nineteenth century, Khiva, Bokhara, and Qoqand, all operated on what is primarily Uzbek soil today, but the term 'Uzbek' had been irrelevant to their public political identity. 'Muslim', or the more ethnically generic term 'Turki' were the common defining terms for most of the population, amidst a welter of clan and tribal names that included Uzbek, Tajik, Kazakh, and the like. It was the Bolsheviks who established the new republics, their borders, and even their languages and histories.[3] Languages that often bore close affinity to each other such as Kazakh and Kyrgyz, possibly close enough to be called dialects if desired, were proclaimed as languages of the republic. Alphabets, grammars, ethnographies and histories were designed to highlight differences among the various groups rather than to stress similarities and unifying features. The last thing the Soviet leadership wanted was anything that might serve to unify the Central Asian people against Moscow's dominance.

Thus Soviet rule of Central Asia for seventy years perpetuated the existence of the five new republics of the region, instilling into them some sense of boundaries and distinctiveness one from the other – perhaps in a somewhat artificial and arbitrary fashion, but one that nevertheless finally took root in many ways. If these states had operated truly independently throughout the seventy years of Soviet power, the evolution of their identity might have been more definitive; but they were not, of course, independent. They spoke from a common communist liturgy, took orders from Moscow, had limited bilateral dealings with each other, and in one sense represented little more than administrative convenience with a little folkloric colouration mixed in to distinguish them merely from being, as it were, 'the northern republic, the southern republic, the eastern republic' and so on.

If their internal bilateral relations were almost non-existent, their external relations were virtually nil. All dealings with the outside world were carefully controlled and channelled through Moscow. As a result, a clear sense of nationhood was only poorly developed in these republics. In many cases, such as between Uzbeks and Tajiks, nationality was often arbitrarily assigned. Local communist rulers were 'loyal' to Moscow as long as Moscow gave them a long enough leash to pursue their independent domestic politics in a kind of 'feudal communism'.

As a result, when the empire came to an end in 1991, none of the Central Asian republics had genuinely evolved classic Third World precursor liberation movements with clear national independence agendas supported by the broad backing of the population. While independence was not unwelcome to the populations, it still represented a shock for which few were prepared. Nationalist leaders, to be sure, did exist, but they represented only a tiny fraction of the population and had to emerge virtually from the underground. The communist *nomenklatura* itself saw independence (and its predecessor movement, *perestroika*) primarily as a threat to its own grasp on power. Local 'unofficial organisations', latent nationalist movements, had evolved a series of nationalist demands that were fairly quickly coopted by the ex-communist leadership, but they were designed to provide a patina of nationalist independence. In no case had any of the Central Asian republics been able to develop a coherent nationalist movement with a vision of the nation, its character, goals, and future – and particularly one which would enable genuine political reform to take place that would break the hold of the old *nomenklatura*.

The Transcaucasus differed somewhat from Central Asia. The three states of Transcaucasus – Georgia, Armenia, and Azerbaijan – were slightly more 'real' than those in Central Asia. The Georgians and Armenians had both enjoyed a long and distinctive history as distinct peoples with a full sense of national self-consciousness and political community.[4] The Azerbaijanis came to a sense of individual ethnic nationhood much later – only in the latter part of the nineteenth century; Muslim and Turkic, or mixed Perso–Turkic, identity had predominated before then.[5] All three peoples had been subjugated by the Tsarist Empire in the nineteenth century. But all three declared independence from Russia after the Russian revolution and enjoyed several years of self-rule until the Bolshevik reconquest in 1920. Despite subordination within the Bolshevik Russian empire, all three of these states did have a clear sense of nationhood, and were ready and eager to declare independence as soon as feasible once the Soviet empire collapsed. This did not mean that they did not suffer from problems of sub-nationalism within each republic (with the exception of Armenia which is the single most ethnically homogeneous republic of the former USSR) but their desire to move quickly to independence was strong, and nationalist leadership rapidly came to the fore – at least for a while – in each of the Caucasian republics.

Post-Communist Tribulations of Identity

The end of communist rule in the Central Asian states thus exposed a major set of problems relating to national identity. First, the states had to determine who they really were. Were they Soviets – and hence 'Western', or Muslims, or Central Asians, or Turkestanis, or more narrowly defined Uzbeks, Tajiks, etc.? Apart from their own identities, what was the identity of their neighbours, many of whom contained ethnic population similar to their own? (For example, every republic in Central Asia has a larger or smaller Uzbek minority, as well as other minorities. Uzbekistan contains a culturally very important Tajik minority. Kazakhs are a minority within their own state with 41 per cent of the population. All have larger or smaller Russian populations – up to 37 per cent in Kazakhstan).[6] How would each state handle the question of large internal minorities? Under Soviet rule, minorities existed all over the multiethnic empire, posing no special problems. But with independence and the emergence of new 'nation-states,' where do minorities now fit in?

With newly assumed statehood (*gosudarstvennost'*), geopolitical problems immediately emerged as well. What was to be the relationship towards neighbours? Who were potential friends and allies, who were potential rivals and adversaries? Most nations of the world have lived in a long-established geopolitical environment of known and tested relationships with other peoples and borders. Not only were the borders new in Central Asia, but their citizens had never exercised statehood in that form before. Major question marks thus emerged in all these respects.

Ethnic conflict broke out on several levels shortly after independence, and even before as the republics moved towards autonomy under Gorbachev's *perestroika*. The Armenian autonomous enclave inside Azerbaijan declared independence several years before Azerbaijani independence and unleashed a war that has still not ended, with major loss of life on both sides and economies prostrate. Hundreds of Meskheti Turks were slaughtered in Uzbekistan. The Abkhaz region of north-west Georgia has also undergone civil war with thousands dead and a key tourist region ravaged. Ossetians in Georgia seek separation to join their brethren in the Russian federation. Many hundreds of Uzbeks and Kyrgyz died in clashes in the southern Kyrgyz city of Osh over land rights. A disastrous civil war broke out in Tajikistan encompassing conflicting religious, ideological, regional and ethnic differences that is far from solved despite Uzbek and Russian armed intervention. The Russian populations in all Central Asian republics have felt a growing nervousness as the nationalist mood has grown, causing many of them to depart of their own volition.[7]

At the centre of the problem is an inherent contradiction in nation-building: on the one hand, the nationalist imperative exists to build new ethnic 'homelands' (*rodiny*) for the dominant ethnic national group – where else can Kazakhs preserve their language, culture and future if not in charge of their own state? On the other hand, there is also a liberal imperative to build tolerant, multiethnic, liberal democratic societies – a solution that probably requires dominant ethnic groups to forgo nationalist expression and nation building in acquiescence to the needs of multiethnic society. While the second approach is by far the more attractive to Western liberals, it is not realistic in this era of increased search for identity to expect that the dominant nationality (or indeed any nationality) with willingly cede the opportunity for dominant voice over its own cultural and political destiny – especially when they have been consistently denied it in the past. This is the first contradiction that will haunt the former Central Asian and Muslim republics for a long period to come, almost certainly ensuring greater ethnic conflict, and possibly even some revision of arbitrary Soviet-drawn borders.

A second problem relates to the national minorities within each of the states, as noted earlier. How will these minorities be treated, especially since most of them are potential citizens of the neighbouring state? Will they be viewed as fifth columns within each state, should relations deteriorate on the interstate level? There remains a great deal of sorting out to take place in the future. Given the patchwork quilt-like character of ethnicity scattered across Central Asia, it is possible that nothing less than some kind of future federalism will be able to ensure the rights of individual peoples to live in an environment that is not strongly dominated by the dominant, or 'titular' nationality.

Sub-nationalism is no less a problem in the Caucasus. Georgia and Azerbaijan are both afflicted with a variety of minorities . This reality presents two serious problems. First, ethnic separatist movements seriously affect the territorial integrity of the state as we have already seen. Second, and perhaps more seriously, these separatist movements and clashes are grist for external manipulation, now an immediate Russian agenda; Moscow, at a minimum, seeks to restore some kind of theoretically voluntary union within the old borders in which it would take primary responsibility for security, and dominate economic relations as well. Russia has already played on these subnationalisms – either through encouragement, support, or acquiescence – to force wayward nationalist regimes in Georgia, Azerbaijan, Moldova, and Tajikistan to return to full membership in the CIS fold, thus assuring Russian paramountcy and thereby denial of the region to the political influence of other states.

Separatism, of course, afflicts not only the new independent republics, but is a prime fear of Russia itself within its own Russian Federation. The declaration of independence by the Chechens in the northern Caucasus in 1991 was an early salvo in a call for greater autonomy or 'sovereignty' by many ethnically distinct regions within Russia itself, including Tatarstan, Bashkortistan, and Sakha (Yakutia). The exceptional violence to which Moscow was willing to resort to attempt to crush Chechen claims – possibly involving itself in a running guerrilla war for a long period of time – will give pause for thought to other ethnic groups in the Russian Federation and in the CIS more broadly: is this the kind of Russia to which these peoples wish to attach their future? The affliction of sub-nationalism is widespread and no region is immune; the story of these interrelationships has hardly played itself out.

The Outside World Intrudes

But whatever kind of union or federation Russia creates on the territory of the old Soviet Union, the clock can never again be turned back to the old Iron Curtain days where the external world was literally sealed off from access to the republics. The external world is inevitably intruding everywhere with new economic, political, cultural, and even limited military relationships. Thus, the problem of identity and place in the geopolitical sun is no longer limited to merely sorting out the complex interrelationships among the Central Asian states themselves. A strong external factor now exists as well, involving the more powerful states that surround them.

Indeed, classic Central Asia was never limited to what we know today as the Central Asian states of the former Soviet Union; Iran, Afghanistan, northern Pakistan, and Western China have all been part of the old Central Asia, and form a part of the even broader geographical unit of Inner Asia that also includes Mongolia, Tibet, and Kashmir. These cultures were closely linked, especially the Islamic ones. With the fall of the Iron Curtain that divided Soviet Central Asia from its southern neighbours, the old meaning of 'Central Asia' has returned, involving new geopolitical relations that sharply influence the identities and orientations of the new Central Asian republics.[8]

Turkey is the first state to affect the region. The modern Turkish state under Mustafa Kemal Atatürk had firmly eschewed any relationship with the Turkic peoples of the Soviet Union; he had rightly perceived that any such pan-Turkist adventure would lead to a dangerous clash with the new Bolshevik state that came into being simultaneously with Turkey. As long as the Soviet Union existed, Turkey acted as if the Turkic republics to the East did not exist. Today, however, the Kemalist ideology in this particular has lost its relevance: the Turkic republics are now independent and open to relations with Turkey. Turkey has responded cautiously but with great interest. Turkey has not wanted to blatantly offend Moscow and has publicly eschewed any kind of pan-Turkish impulses and ambitions. But despite ideological protestations to the contrary, pan-Turkish impulses do inherently lie behind Turkey's rapid efforts to develop political, economic and cultural relations with the Central Asian republics; there is no other reason why Turkey – not even remotely contiguous to these new states – should otherwise seek close ties, open air routes to the region and so on, particularly when the economic prize there is otherwise not that great. It is the common ethnic and cultural linkage – pan-Turkish – that provides the impetus.

As a result, these new opportunities in Central Asia and the Caucasus have revolutionised Turkey's own foreign policy; Ankara now faces unprecedented new opportunities for influence in regions closed to Turkey ever since the birth of the Turkish republic in the 1920s. But the size of the Turkish economy automatically puts realistic limits on what Turkey can do in Central Asia – about which Ankara is realistic. Turkey can greatly broaden Central Asia's options, but it cannot single-handedly replace Russian influence in the region – even over the longer run. The Central Asian states themselves, too, do not seek to replace one Russian 'older brother' with a Turkish one; the new leaderships want to diversify their options to the maximum extent possible.[9]

One of the broader identity questions Central Asia must face is whether they are to remain as individual states, or are to seek links among themselves of some kind. And are those links to be cultural, ethnic-linguistic, or simply regional? Central Asia was once viewed as a common cultural region by the Muslims of Central Asia in the late days of the Tsarist Empire; the term 'Turkistan' (originally created by Russia) was widely adopted in the region. Today, as a result, the Central Asian states are now confronted with the issue of how deeply they wish to follow a pan-Turkish – or regional unification – agenda, with or without Turkey. In Central Asia, however, unification takes on other connotations.

Uzbekistan – as heir to the great centres of civilisation and the territory of the great historical Khanates, and with the largest population in the region – is the most likely state to pursue regional unification – and without Turkey. It has already taken a few tentative steps in that direction, again without reference *per se* to pan-Turkism, a term deeply anathematised by Soviet ideology for long years. Because of Uzbekistan's size and traditional heavy-handedness in the region, however, the other states are wary of what is known as 'Uzbek chauvinism'.[10] The question of regional unification under the flag of ethnicity thus remains an ambiguous question. A further problem for a pan-Turkish ideology uniting these states is that it excludes the Persian-speaking Tajiks.

The role of Turkey in the region then, presents many new options and dilemmas. Not the least of these is Russian resentment. While Russia is aware that it can no longer maintain a total monopoly over the politics and economics of the region, it sees Turkey as potentially the single greatest rival over the long run. It has already dislodged in 1993 the pro-Turkish anti-Russian elected president of Azerbaijan, Abulfaz Elchibey, in favour of a more malleable candidate (who is also proving somewhat more fractious than hoped). Turkey represents an alternative path to the West that also weakens Russian influence. Thus there will be a permanent rivalry between these two states for sway in the region. While the economic and military power of the two states is highly disproportionate, Turkey is aiming at long term cultural influence through linguistic, cultural, and economic ties that in the end will probably prove significant. Russian psychology, too, is aware that a struggle between Turko–Mongol and Slavic peoples has been a prominent feature of Russian history for well over a thousand years – including the period of the 'Mongol yoke' over young Russia.

A second external force is Iran. Iran was long the dominant cultural, and sometimes even political, power in the region – until the Tsarist take-over. Iran, like Turkey, thus has new options for political, economic, and even cultural influence to the north that has not been feasible for centuries. In addition, Iran now sees a rival in Turkey – something that had never been true ever since the formation of the two new national states in the 1920s – under the modernising and Westernising leadership of Atatürk and Reza Shah that gave the two countries a broad and shared outlook on the world. With the foundation of the Islamic Republic of Iran in 1979, ideological frictions emerged for the first time since World War I that have been sharply exacerbated by the fall of the Soviet Empire that left Turkey and Iran rivals once again in this newly opened region. Iran views both the Caucasus – especially Azerbaijan – and Central Asia, as areas of Persian influence. Turkey's attempt to gain a foothold in the region is seen as directly threatening to Iran.[11]

In Azerbaijan in particular a deadly long-term rivalry has emerged: the six million population of Azerbaijan is more than matched by the perhaps ten million Azeris who live in northern Iran, or Iranian Azerbaijan. Azeri nationalists in Baku, who consider themselves to be a Turkic people, have talked of eventual unification of the two Azerbaijans – in what would be a huge loss of important territory to Iran. Azeri ethnic separatism in Iran, however, is by no means a foregone conclusion since the population there is uncertain about their conflicting Persian and Turkic identities. While Turkey has not been involved in this issue, Ankara would be the potential beneficiary from a weakened Iran and a strengthened and augmented Azerbaijan closely linked to Turkey. Iran thus perceives a potentially vital pan-Turkish threat to the north, coupled with concern for the spread of Turkey's influence and broader currents of pan-Turkism in Central Asia itself. This rivalry is serious and would seem to represent a continuation of a 'permanent' tug of war for over a millennium between 'Iran' and 'Turan' – enshrined even in Persian epics.[12]

Iran, of course, has its own cultural extension to the East. Northern Afghanistan has long been part of the cradle of Persian culture; the Tajik language spoken there, closely related to Persian, extends across the north on into Tajikstan and even into the small Tajik population of China. The Tajik population of Afghanistan is double that of the three million Tajiks of Tajikistan itself. In geopolitical terms then, the outlines of a double ethnic belt stretches across the centre of Asia – a Turkic one to the north and an Iranian one to the south. Both were negligible factors in the Russian-dominated politics of the last century; today the belts are more real concepts. It would, of course, be a mistake to see regional politics as driven strictly by these considerations. All the states involved have other interests and priorities as well, especially in the very difficult post-Soviet transition period. But the new ethnic elements that have emerged in the region are likely to be constant sub-themes in the political evolution of the area that can take on particular salience if seized upon by regional politicians or conflicting interests.

Iran thus has new opportunities, but faces far greater threats. It may have been one of the losers in the new geopolitical legacy of the Soviet break-up while Turkey was a winner – in the sense that it has now opened up potential separatist risks from Iran's Azeri and Turkmen minorities, and a new role for Turkey now east of Iran where none existed before. But Iran will always enjoy an important position by dint of geography alone: it represents the sole alternative land route to the West apart from the Russian route. Central Asian states seeking access to the Persian Gulf for oil, gas, and commercial shipping must go through Iran. This alternative route is extremely important to Central Asia states who find Russia intent on trying to monopolise all such land and pipeline routes through the region. Iran must always be a major factor then, and Russia may see it as a counterweight to Turkish power.

Afghanistan too, has vividly reworked itself back into the classic politics of greater Central Asia. Afghanistan was the recipient of many millions of Tajiks, Uzbeks and Turkmen who fled Soviet troops in the 1920s as the Red Army put down the massive Basmachi uprising against Soviet power. Northern Afghanistan still contains a million Uzbeks, several hundred thousand Turkmen, and several million Tajiks, many of whom are native to the area. The civil war and invasion of Afghanistan by Soviet troops has torn the country asunder, even after the withdrawal of Soviet forces in 1987. Afghan warlords have been unable to agree on a settlement or to rule the country ever since the Soviet departure. The Pashtuns in the south, who once dominated Afghanistan, have lost their dominant position for now. The country thus runs the risk of separating into a Pashtun south and a non-Pashtun north, unless some kind of reconciliation can be found that involves a formula of reduced Pashtun power.

At the same time, civil war in Tajikistan itself – a struggle that pits ideological, regional, ethnic and religious differences against each other – has spilled over into Afghanistan. An Uzbek–Tajik struggle for power, that is at least a part of what the Tajikistan war is about, has crossed the border; Uzbekistan firmly supported the Uzbek warlord Dostam in northern Afghanistan against the Tajik political refugees there, many of whom are being recruited into fundamentalist cadres to go back and do battle against the neo-communist regime in Dushanbe – that is supported by both Uzbekistan and Russia.

The future of the region has thus been considerably unsettled by potential and actual conflict that emerges from the south. Turkey, Iran, Afghanistan, and even Pakistan are involved directly or indirectly as forces that are contesting the identity and allegiances of the new states in Central Asia. India, too, cannot be excluded, for it has basically been dismayed at the emergence of five new Muslim states in a region where pro-Indian Russian power was long dominant. The appearance of these states on the international stage has strengthened and heartened Pakistan which desperately seeks 'Islamic strategic depth' in its confrontation with the colossus of Hindu power along its eastern borders. Pakistan sees a major role for itself in Central Asia – an access that has been delayed only by continuing conflict in Afghanistan. The Indian and Pakistani factor has thus also extended itself into Central Asia and will figure more prominently in the future.

The Chinese Factor

China too, counts heavily in the Central Asian equation. Some eight million Muslim Uighur Turks live in Xinjiang province in Western China, also known as 'Chinese Turkistan'.[13] They are linguistically closely related to the Uzbeks and possess a distinctive written culture and civilisation going back over a thousand years. They have enjoyed periods of independence, most notably in the years before Communist Chinese troops moved into the region in 1949. They basically aspire at the very least to a full-blooded autonomy today in China, and most likely seek full independence similar to their Turkic brethren on the Soviet side of the border. They have no opportunity to gain such independence until Chinese communist power founders in Beijing – an unpredictable date, but likely in the next five years. The Uighurs are likely to take advantage of any future Beijing weakness to declare independence, supported by numerous Uighur liberation groups outside the country in Central Asia, Turkey and the West. They are in close coordination with the independent movement of Tibet.

Uighur aspirations thus represent another area of conflict which has implications for Central Asia. What position will the Central Asian states take when Uighurs move for independence and call for external support? Will some of the Central Asian republics – especially Kazakhstan which has the greatest number of Uighurs – stand aside, or assist the Uighurs? Will they value the not inconsiderable trade ties they have with China more than ethnic ties? The Kazakhs actually have a far stronger interest in the repatriation of the 300,000 Kazakhs that also live in the Uighur regions, but whom the Chinese have not yet released. And how will Russia itself react to this potential turmoil in the region; will it not welcome Chinese loss of empire paralleling its own losses? However the Chinese situation evolves, there is no doubt that China will be a major influence in Central Asia, potentially in conflict with Russia. This region historically has been a cockpit of conflict between the two great states.

Russia itself, of course, is the most important regional state of all. As mentioned earlier, Russia seeks to re-establish some kind of federal state in the region, in principle on a voluntary and more equal basis than in the past. While both Russia and the Central Asian and Caucasian states have interest in mutually beneficial economic ties with Russia, none of them are willing to grant Russia a monopoly over their futures.[14] The chances are, then, that the Commonwealth of Independent States (CIS) will never attain the level of a federation. The present neo-communist leadership in most of the republics today is basically not representative of the future leadership in the area which will be much more strongly nationalist, and more inclined to avoid binding ties with Russia. Thus, although Russia will always remain a great power in the region, it will gradually find its relative weight in the region declining in proportion to the growth of external influences, many of which we have already described.

There is one area where Russia could become involved in serious conflict: in Kazakhstan. The Kazakhs are a minority in their own republic, and deeply anguished by this fact. Russians make up almost as much of the population as Kazakhs themselves, some 37 per cent compared to perhaps 41 per cent for Kazakhs.[15] Northern Kazakhstan, furthermore, is populated predominantly by Russians who may decide to secede – taking with them valuable agricultural land, resources and industry – and rejoin Russia. Kazakh nationalists are concerned at how to build a truly Kazakh state while the Russians are present.

Because of conflicting ethnic aspirations, conflict in Kazakhstan is quite likely; the secession of the north cannot at all be excluded. This issue will be the single most burning issue in Central Asia in the future. Outsiders conceivably could join in the struggle, thus broadening its dimensions – at least on the ideological plane. Apart from Kazakhstan, the region is involved in a long and complex process of decolonisation, with much attendant stress and friction. It is uncertain how much Russia will acquiesce to a gradual loss of influence in the region; yet its is quite conceivable that English may even come to replace Russian as the second language of the region after a generation or so; Russian – a great cultural vehicle – simply is no longer as useful an international language for dealing with the outside world for Central Asian states that seek to enter the world more actively.

Conclusion

In the post-Cold War world, then, the former areas of the Soviet Union present special problems. Decolonisation is always painful for all involved. Russia is already resisting parts of the process. Ethnic conflicts from the past that have been submerged and left unattended are now emerging with greater virulence. New 'nations' have been created that never before existed as independent players on the international scene; their orientation, allies and rivals are not yet clearly understood. So many new states added to the international stage will have a complicating effect on the region. All the major states around their periphery have now also become engaged in the area, affecting relationships among themselves as well. Because of the relative newness of these states, growing pains are likely to be severe. Their internal struggle for leadership has barely begun to sort itself out, creating yet other unforeseeable consequences. Ethnic conflict and disorder is thus likely to be a major aspect of the scene for some time to come.

Fortunately, however, these problems should not take on the characteristics of a global chess game as it would have done during the Cold War years. The West in particular, is not likely to contest Russian influence in the area, although signs of a recrudescence of Russian nationalist or imperialist expansionism will without doubt draw sharp response from the West as a harbinger of a broader return to Cold War polarisation.

Notes

1 Indeed, one of the early proponents of the fact that the Muslim peoples of the Soviet Union had retained their Islamic, anti-Russian identity intact was Alexandre Bennigsen: see his 'Mullahs, Mujahidin, and Soviet Muslims', *Problems of Communism*, November –December 1984, as well as Alexandre Bennigsen and S. Enders Wimbush, *Muslims of the Soviet Empire* (Indiana University Press, Bloomington, 1986).

2 See, for example the excellent set of essays published before the break-up of the Soviet Union in Robert Conquest, *The Last Empire: Nationality and the Soviet Future* (Hoover Institution, Stanford University Press, Stanford, 1986).

3 The definitive work on this process of Soviet national formation remains Richard Pipes, *The Formation of the Soviet Union* (Harvard University Press, Cambridge Mass., 1954).

4 For further information on the Georgian experience, see the excellent book by Ronald Grigor Suny, *The Making of the Georgian Nation* (Indiana University Press, Bloomington, 1988). Suny has also written one of the best general histories of modern Armenia: *Looking Toward Ararat: Armenia in Modern History* (Indiana University Press, Bloomington 1993).

5 Two excellent volumes on Azerbaijan are Tadeusz Swietochowski, *Russian Azerbaijan, 1905–1920* (Cambridge University Press, New York, 1985) and Audrey L. Alstadt, *The Azerbaijani Turks: Power and Identity under Russian Rule* (The Hoover Press, Stanford, 1992).

6 For good statistics on nationality breakdown see the appendices in Ian Bremmer and Ray Taras, (eds), *Nations and Politics in the Soviet Successor States* (Cambridge University Press, New York, 1993).

7 For details, see the excellent essays in Bremmer and Taras, *Nations and Politics.*

8 For a first class conceptual discussion of Central Asia in the grander geopolitical/historical picture see S. A. M. Adshead, *Central Asia in World History* (St Martins Press, New York 1993).

9 For a broader discussion of Turkey and its new policies towards Central Asia and the Caucasus, see Graham E. Fuller and Ian O. Lesser, *Turkey's New Geopolitics: From the Balkans to Western China* (Westview Press, Boulder, 1993).

10 For an analysis of Uzbek political culture and history, see Edward A. Allworth, *The Modern Uzbeks* (Hoover Press, Stanford, 1990).

11 For a broad discussion of Turkish–Iranian relations and Iran's outlook on Russia and Central Asia see Graham E. Fuller, *The Center of the Universe: The Geopolitics of Iran* (Westview Press, Boulder, Col., 1990).

12 For a series of illuminating essays on the historical relationships of an earlier period see Beatrice F. Manz, (ed.), *Central Asia in Historical Perspective* (Westview Press, Boulder, Col., 1994).

13 For a discussion of Islam in China – though not focused on the Uighurs

themselves, see Dru C. Gladney, *Muslim Chinese: Ethnic Nationalism in the People's Republic* (Harvard University Press, Cambridge Mass., 1991).

14 For a thorough discussion of the economic dilemmas of earlier Soviet economic relations with Central Asia see Boris Z. Rumer, *Soviet Central Asia: A Tragic Experiment* (Unwin Hyman, New York, 1989).

15 For historical background on Kazakhstan, see Martha B. Olcott, *The Kazakhs* (Hoover Press, Stanford, 1987).

4 ◆ International Relations in Africa after the Cold War

Christopher Clapham

Introduction

The significance of the end of the Cold War for sub-Saharan Africa lies in the fact that this transformation in the international system coincided with a profound internal crisis of the African state. The origins of this crisis, certainly, can not be entirely divorced from the impact of the Cold War on Africa, any more than the outbreak of many of its specific manifestations in the late 1980s and early 1990s can be separated from the effects of changes in the global system. Insofar as the end of the Cold War has had distinctive consequences in Africa, however, these essentially derive from the internal problems of the continent itself.

The clearest indicator of crisis is the 1.2 per cent annual average decline in *per capita* Gross National Product, as measured by the World Bank, over the period from 1980 to 1991; this contrasts with annual average growth rates of 3.1 per cent for South Asia and 6.1 per cent for East Asia over the same period.[1] Whatever the statistical problems associated with gross figures of this kind, they accurately reflect the misery which has afflicted very large numbers of Africans. It is also worth noting that, unlike the situation in East Asia or even Latin America, figures for economic growth or decline in Africa bear little evident relationship to the willingness of national governments to espouse development strategies geared to domestic capitalism and production for international markets; ostensibly capitalist states such as Côte d'Ivoire and Gabon have had the fastest declining economies in Africa. Nor have attempts at rehabilitation mounted from the early 1980s in the form of structural adjustment programmes sponsored by international financial institutions had any clear-cut success.[2]

The continent's political record has been no better. The monopoly states established after independence, by rulers who sought to subject any actual or potential source of dissent to their own control, had proved by the late 1980s to be unsustainable. Whether in their single-party or their military form, or indeed in the personalist regimes of rulers like Doe or Mobutu, monopoly states had failed not only to meet the minimal legitimate political demands of African peoples, but even to supply the basic conditions of peaceful and effective government. Though there were certainly important differences in the political record between African regimes, there was again no substantial distinction between those which sided with one alliance or the other in the global bipolar order.

The Cold War and Africa

This harsh prelude is essential if we are to appreciate either the impact of the Cold War on Africa, or the effects of its sudden disappearance. In many respects, this impact was relatively slight. Africa was rarely if ever of critical importance to the superpowers, and did not excite anything remotely resembling the level of commitment assigned either to the Middle East or to south-east Asia. In much of the continent, the former colonial powers – notably, of course, France – continued to take the major role as patrons or protectors to newly independent regimes, and it was only under exceptional circumstances that either the United States or the Soviet Union became deeply involved. The region most evidently involved in Cold War rivalries was the Horn, where geographical proximity to the Middle East, the absence of effective linkages between the African states of the region and former colonial powers, and the intense conflicts both between and within states led to a set of alliances between African states seeking external (and notably military) protection, and superpowers seeking regional allies. A secondary arena of superpower confrontation was created in southern Africa by support for rival sides in the Angolan civil war of 1975–76, and by subsequent United States backing for the Unita opposition, and continued Soviet and Cuban support for the MPLA government.

Despite the dire effects of conflicts in both the Horn and Southern Africa on local populations, the relative detachment of sub-Saharan Africa from the major centres of superpower rivalry meant that the Cold War could be regarded by African rulers in largely instrumental terms.[3] Despite ritual condemnation, they could afford to treat it as a resource on which they could draw, and which enhanced more than it threatened their own security, and the role which they could play in world affairs. The most basic element in this positive evaluation of the bipolar system was that both superpowers generally supported the conventions of African state maintenance which were upheld both by African governments themselves and by the former colonial powers. The United States, obviously enough, was constrained by its alliance with the former colonisers, but the Soviet Union also swiftly recognised the advantages of dealing with governments, rather than seeking to provoke any upheaval in the continental order. Soviet support for the federal government in the Nigerian civil war of 1967–70 established both the pattern of support for existing governments, and the USSR's usefulness as an alternative (and generally much more efficient) source of armaments for regimes which could not obtain them from the West. Unlike the United States, moreover, the Soviet Union suffered from no inhibitions in its aid to liberation movements fighting against colonial or white minority regimes.

African states also benefited during the Cold War from the paradox of impotence: since they did not matter very much, it was not necessary for the superpowers to control them, and this enabled African rulers to play off the superpowers against one another, in a way that would scarcely have been permissible in, for example, South east Asia or the Caribbean. This in turn reinforced the impression of the Cold War as a resource, since the aid that the superpowers had to offer, however slight it may have been on their own scale of operations, was nonetheless significant within the reduced circumstances of generally small and poor African states.

The impact of the Cold War on Africa was greatly intensified by – and may even be reckoned to have started with – the 'Second Cold War' which lasted from the mid-1970s to the mid-1980s. The Angolan civil war of 1975–76 and the Ogaden war between Ethiopia and Somalia in 1977–78, coupled with the invasions of the Shaba region of Zaire by opposition forces based in Angola, also in 1977 and 1978, marked the only period when it appeared, not only that the Cold War might become critically important to Africa, but even that Africa might affect the Cold War; the comment by President Carter's National Security Adviser, Zbigniew Brzezinski, that 'SALT lies buried in the sands of the Ogaden', exaggerated though it was, was to my knowledge the one occasion when any significant development in global relations was ascribed to events in Sub-Saharan Africa.[4] This period was also associated with the emergence in Africa of a number of major states – notably Angola, Ethiopia and Mozambique – which appeared to have a genuine commitment to pursuing Marxist–Leninist trajectories of economic and political development, and aroused comparison with other Soviet clients in the Third World, such as Cuba or Vietnam. Unlike these, however, there was no question of admitting them to the CMEA.

The incorporation of parts of Africa into Cold War alliance structures from the mid-1970s was most evidently reflected in a dramatic increase in arms supplies to the continent, the greater part of which came from the Soviet Union.[5] In some degree, this helped to protect African states from one another, as with Soviet military aid to Ethiopia to fend off the Somali invasion of 1977, or to Angola to protect it against South African destabilisation. To a very large extent, nonetheless, it provided African regimes with a means of trying to control their own peoples, and in turn encouraged such regimes to believe that external military backing would provide an effective substitute for domestic political support. Ethiopia under the Mengistu regime is the classic case, but Somalia under Siyad Barre, Zaire under Mobutu, or Liberia under Doe, equally provide examples. Though armaments also flowed to some African states outside the context of Cold War alliances, notably through post-colonial connections and in some cases through Islamic ones, the Cold War from the mid-1970s thus played an important role in exacerbating the levels of misgovernment which in turn prompted not only the demands for democratisation which erupted from the late 1980s onwards, but also an increasing level of domestic insurgency directed against African regimes.

The most notable conclusion to be drawn about external arms supplies to African regimes was, however, how counterproductive they turned out to be. Recent analyses of state capabilities in the 'Third World' have usefully distinguished between the 'hardware' available to states in terms of variables such as military power, and the 'software' indicated by the effectiveness of their political institutions.[6] In practice, military equipment could be no more effective than the mechanisms of social control available to those who wanted to use it, and in many African cases these were entirely inadequate. The manipulation of

Somali clan loyalties by Siyad was no better as a means of keeping the regime in power than the highly selective ethnic recruitment into the supposedly national armed forces by Doe in Liberia. In each case, the collapse of the techniques of military control entailed the total collapse of the state itself. In Mengistu's Ethiopia, one of the more organisationally effective African armies was eventually defeated with the very weapons which the Soviet Union had supplied in such massive quantities, but which rapidly found their way into the hands of the opposition. Only in a very limited and temporary sense did the military aid supplied by the superpowers to their African clients enable these regimes to survive; its inadequacy had become all too evident, even before the collapse of the bipolar order that produced it.

The End of the Cold War

The sudden ending of the Cold War thus left African states in an extremely vulnerable position. On the one hand, their opportunities for manipulating the global order were instantly whisked away, and in place of the familiar geography of balancing and alignment, they were left with a bare international landscape which exposed them all too visibly to the influence of a dominant and newly triumphant West. On the other hand, the mechanisms which they had used to retain control over their own populations were simultaneously removed. Not only were the Soviet Union's former clients left suddenly high and dry;[7] even devoted clients of the West, such as Moi in Kenya or Mobutu in Zaire, found that anti-communism was no longer the talisman that it once had been for gaining United States support. African peoples – often led by previously excluded politicians with a keen eye for changing market conditions – were quick to take advantage of the opportunities which their rulers' new uncertainty had given them.

The inability of the Soviet Union and its allies to provide any meaningful economic aid to African states had become evident even during the period when Soviet military assistance was at its peak, with the result that Africa's economic subordination to the West became apparent, in the form of structural adjustment programmes, a decade or so before its political equivalent in the form of political conditionalities concerned with democracy and human rights.[8] The end of the Cold War nonetheless brought about a further economic marginalisation of Africa, as aid programmes were diverted to Eastern Europe. From the viewpoint of the aid donors, this made a great deal of sense: not only was the fate of Eastern European states much more important to the Western alliance than that of African ones; aid also offered a plausible prospect of kick-starting moribund but industrialised Eastern European economies into self-sustaining capitalist development, whereas in Africa it all too often looked like pouring money into an ever-deepening hole. From an African viewpoint, it looked as though 'their' aid was being sent to someone else.

At one level, the new political terms of trade left African rulers and would-be rulers with a greatly enhanced need to gain the support – and hence, with any luck, seek the welfare – of their own peoples; and in view of the detrimental impact of the monopoly state, this could only be regarded as welcome. But given the frequent fragility of African states themselves, they also presented an extremely unwelcome threat to the maintenance of the whole African international order. Precisely because of their weakness and artificiality, African states had placed a special emphasis on the formal principles of state sovereignty which were built into the charters of the United Nations and, still more stringently, the Organisation of African Unity. In the new order, the value of these principles – which turned whatever government was in power into the sole valid intermediary between the domestic political system and the international order – was drastically reduced. At one extreme, the principle of 'territorial integrity', which assured overwhelming international support for the central government against any attempt at secession, and which had served the Nigerian federal government so well at the time of the civil war, no longer carried anything resembling the clout that it had once done. With the mighty Soviet Union breaking up into fifteen separate states, Western states could scarcely be expected to intervene in order to prevent secession in some weak and divided state in Africa. Even if the threat of disintegration was averted, it soon became clear that African states were no longer protected against levels of external involvement (or interference) in their 'internal' affairs that would previously have been unthinkable. Nowhere was this clearer than in the very public way in which the US ambassador to Kenya, Smith Hempstone, encouraged multi-party elections and the formation of opposition parties, to the intense annoyance of President Moi.

The 'New African Order' and its Failure

Even if the old sovereignty regime was a thing of the past, it was nonetheless possible to envisage a new African continental order which would rectify the all too evident deficiencies of the old one, and rest on a different relationship between domestic statehood and the international system. This would have to depend on reasonably democratic structures of government within African states, of the kind that the wave of democratisation in the early 1990s appeared to be bringing into existence. If, in a relatively small number of cases, the election of governments by African peoples meant that existing states were split apart into separate political units corresponding to the demands of their populations, that was a price that would have to be accepted. Once internal democracy had removed the need for African governments to gain access to external sources of weapons to control their own populations, it should also be possible to resolve disputes between African states, which almost invariably derived from internal conflicts in at least one of the states concerned and often both. Such local settlements could then be guaranteed by regional organisations at sub-continental level, which themselves generally depended on the leadership of the major state within each region. The Organisation of African Unity would then serve as the continental umbrella body, ratifying solutions reached at regional level, serving as a court of appeal against states dissatisfied with the role of the regional leader, and mediating between the continent and the global order represented by the United Nations. Though direct extra-continental intervention in African affairs would have to be avoided, outside states and global institutions would be needed, to provide the external pressures and inducements needed to establish and maintain fragile African democracies, to uphold and reinforce the security structure through the new world order, and to furnish financial and logistic support for African peace-keeping missions which could not be met from the continent's own resources. Once both African states and their external aid donors were democratic, and guided by a similar respect for human rights, this relationship could however be managed in a way that was more open and less subject to abuse than the old connections between African clients and superpower patrons.

Utopian though it might seem, this scenario at least appeared at times in the late 1980s and very early 1990s to have some prospect of realisation. The first success, dating from just before the end of the

Cold War in December 1988, was the signing of the Angola–Namibia accords, which assured Namibia's passage to independence and led to the withdrawal of Cuban troops from Angola, and the subsequently unsuccessful attempt to resolve the internal conflict in Angola by democratic means. These accords, formally negotiated by the United States but with the Soviet government in close attendance, marked the one major influence on Africa of the Gorbachev period in the Soviet Union. A second and still greater success, though one on which the end of the Cold War had a less direct impact, was the transition to majority rule in South Africa, which opened with the de Klerk reforms in early 1990. However difficult and tortuous the path which eventually led to the April 1994 elections, it promised to remove the single most important source of conflict in the continent, and to replace destabilisation by a new southern African order, in which a democratic South Africa would take its inevitable place as the regional leader.

A further success, this time only marginally affected by the end of the Cold War, was the eventual resolution of the seemingly endless civil wars in Ethiopia, with the ousting of the Mengistu regime and the victory of the EPLF in Eritrea and the EPRDF in the rest of Ethiopia in May 1991. This instantly led to the *de facto* independence of Eritrea, which was formally achieved two years later; this breach in the previously sacrosanct principle of 'territory integrity' was nonetheless amicably negotiated by the two regimes, and led to none of the predicted domino effect on the rest of the continent, though the rulers of the former British Somaliland announced (to global indifference) its secession from the Somali Republic. And even though the Liberian civil war which broke out in December 1989 could not conceivably be regarded as anything but horrific, it did at least prompt the formation of a regional peacekeeping force, ECOMOG, which marked a first attempt at conflict resolution in West Africa under the auspices of the major regional organisation, the Economic Community of West African States, and the leadership of the regional hegemon, Nigeria.

These developments were accompanied by an attempt to create a more effective continental organisation, following the election as OAU Secretary-General in 1989 of the former Tanzanian foreign minister, Salim Ahmed Salim. The contrast between Salim and the succession of frankly uninspiring francophone West African diplomats who had preceded him could scarcely have been more marked; Salim was not only a diplomat of global reputation who had been a serious contender for the secretary-generalship of the United Nations, but was also the long-serving foreign minister of the state which had, more consistently than any other, challenged the OAU's rigid insistence on national sovereignty. The OAU at least started to discuss the formation of a mechanism for conflict resolution, and a small section concerned with attempting to resolve internal conflicts was established within the secretariat. It is also worth noting the setting up (by General Obasanjo, the only Nigerian leader to have left power voluntarily) of an informal body, the African Leadership Forum, designed to create an authoritative continental political climate for conflict resolution.

It scarcely needs pointing out, however, that this 'new African order' failed to materialise. Despite some continuing successes, notably in the installation of at least a number of African governments with evident popular support, and the marked improvement in regional relations in southern Africa, it failed moreover at each of its constituent levels – national, regional, continental, and global.

The most evident problems, horrifyingly exemplified by the Rwandan genocide, arose at the level of the African state itself. Some states, notably Somalia, Liberia and Zaire, effectively ceased to exist as recognisable units in anything but a cartographical sense. In others, such as Sudan and Angola, civil war resumed as a result of the refusal of established groups with access to weapons – in Sudan the central army, in Angola the leading opposition movement – to accept any negotiated political compromise. The once apparently irresistible movement towards multi-party electoral democracy was subverted by the ability of a number of deeply flawed regimes, like those of Biya in Cameroon and Moi in Kenya, to cling on to power through a mixture of electoral fraud, political manipulation, and opposition inadequacy. In Sierra Leone, The Gambia and Nigeria, the military coup resurfaced as a means of gaining power – in the first two cases with some popular support against long-established regimes, in the last as a transparent device to annul the results of the election.

All these cases reflected the extraordinary difficulty of bringing about deep-seated changes in the structure of African government, through constitutionalist means which – despite undoubted internal support – ultimately needed external pressures in order to make them effective.[9] The problems of African democratisation – and indeed its successes, in states such as Benin, Zambia, and Malawi – lie beyond the scope of this paper, but the point does at least need to be made that any viable post-Cold War continental order had to rest on a structure of domestic statehood which was both internally effective and externally accepted. This was most evident of all in southern Africa, where the installation of just such a structure in South Africa went at least some way towards transforming the regional order. South African-led mediation in Lesotho provided the first example – albeit a low-key one, in a particularly dependent state – of intervention by the regional hegemon in order to lay down conditions not simply for relations between states, but for an acceptable domestic political order.

The other major attempt to establish a regional security structure, through the Nigerian-led ECOMOG force in Liberia, was however deeply flawed, not only by the entanglement of the force on the ground in domestic political conflicts – a fate virtually unavoidable for any external force intervening in an on-going civil war – but by the abortion of the democratic process within Nigeria itself. Effective regional leadership depends, not only on the size and power of the would-be leader vis-à-vis its neighbours, but on its ability to embody the principles on which the regional order is to be based within its own domestic structure. The failure of democratisation in Nigeria fatally undermined the credentials of the entire ECOMOG operation in Liberia. Though a fragile peace settlement was eventually implemented in Liberia in September 1995, this depended not on any political settlement that commanded legitimacy in either Liberia or the West African region as a whole, but simply on a division of the spoils among the contending warlords; its collapse in April 1996 was unsurprising.

In central and eastern Africa, there was no viable basis for a regional security structure anyhow, since there was no effective regional leader or core alliance around which such a structure could be built. Zaire, the potential core state of central Africa, was removed from contention by its state of internal collapse and the personalist nature of its regime; Ethiopia, which in population terms was substantially the largest state in eastern Africa, was likewise disqualified from any position of regional leadership by its peculiar historical origins and domestic political structure, its desperate poverty, and its devastating civil wars. Sudan was similarly excluded by its internal divisions (which were vastly exacerbated by the seizure of power by an Islamist regime), while the three Commonwealth East African states were prevented by diverging political trajectories dating back to the time of independence from exercising the stabilising role that their combined size and central location might otherwise have enabled them to take on. The Rwandan horror, though internal in origin, was also at least in part the result of the failure of any regional constellation of states to exercise any restraining role.

It scarcely needed Nelson Mandela to point out the reproach which Rwanda, like Somalia before it, presented to the OAU's pretensions to continental management. The OAU, irreparably bound up in its original obsessions with state sovereignty, was incapable of generating any approach to conflict resolution appropriate to an era in which the myth of the sovereign independent territorial state has collapsed. Salim Salim's modest and watered down proposals for some kind of African Security Council – to be called, in deliberately self-effacing terms, the Bureau of the Summit – were eventually implemented early in 1995, and created a mechanism through which the OAU could become involved in conflict resolution within African states, though only with the consent of the regime in power in the state concerned. The OAU was however unable to lay down minimal conditions for any acceptable form of domestic government; Nelson Mandela's public outrage at the Saro-Wiwa executions in Nigeria, enhanced by personal pique at the Nigerian military regime's contempt for his efforts at mediation, had to be toned down once it became clear that other African states would not support him. And while some leaders like Museveni in Uganda and Isaias Afewerki in Eritrea, who had come to power after long struggles against regimes upheld by the OAU, castigated it for its failings, there was no indication at all of a willingness to make the changes in the organisation's structure and ethos that continental conflict management would require.

The capacity of non-African states and global institutions to make up for the deficiencies of continental structures was always limited – and in the view of many, rightly so. In the first flush of post-Cold War enthusiasm, it may have appeared possible to establish an alliance between the newly triumphant Western states, with their rediscovered commitment to liberal democracy and human rights as universally applicable values, and emergent democratic forces within Africa. This combination certainly accounted for the wave of popular demands, and the readiness of African governments to succumb (at least formally) to them, which swept through the continent from 1989 onwards. Western powers also retained a willingness to intervene (from whatever motives), in Somalia and Rwanda if not in Liberia. But even though the weakness of United States foreign policy management under the Clinton administration could scarcely have been predicted, Western states could not in any event have been expected to maintain an active commitment to democratisation and conflict resolution in Africa, once the first wave of enthusiasm had passed, and the costs of involvement – in a continent where their economic interests were negligible – had become apparent. It remains an open question whether the US intervention in Somalia could, with greater political skill, have produced at least some impression of success, and in my view at least it could; but both in the United States and in France, intervention in Africa was more closely geared to fleeting domestic political priorities than to long-term involvement in a complex process of political reconstruction that would require skill, patience and commitment to have any reasonable chance of success.[10]

New Patterns of African International Relations

If, therefore, we want to assess Africa's international relations after the end of the Cold War, we need to shift our attention from these idealised scenarios – which, whether they were plausible or not, have simply not been realised – and ask ourselves what has actually been happening in the continent, and what alternative scenarios might follow from it.

The main development has been a continued decline in the presence of the state, and in the political and economic resources which state power conferred on those who held it. This power was most directly challenged by the growth of insurgent movements which, over large areas of Africa, denied governments even nominal control over the territory ascribed to them on maps. Not only in the Horn of Africa and lusophone southern Africa, the two long-established foci of African insurgency, but over a virtually continuous swathe of territory stretching from Djibouti on the Red Sea to Angola on the South Atlantic Ocean, territorial control was contested by groups which varied from reasonably coherent guerrilla movements to the followings of individual warlords. In West Africa, generally the most stable area of the continent in terms of effective government (if not in the tenure of power at the centre), the collapse of Liberia into a congeries of personal and ethnic fiefdoms seriously affected Sierra Leone, and had repercussions as far afield as the Gambia. Widespread violence occurred even in northern Ghana, while the political failure in Nigeria raised at least the possibility that the centre there might fail to hold.

This failure of statehood obviously derived, most basically, from the economic and political failures which were noted at the very start of this paper. Equally, the measures promoted by external agencies in order to resolve them, had at least in the short term the effect of further reducing the resources available to governments, and hence the authority which – in a continent where patronage has been at the centre of political power – those governments were able to command. The capacity of governments to extract a surplus from the export of primary commodities was affected both by the dismantling, under the aegis of the World Bank and IMF, of the structures (such as produce marketing boards and inconvertible currencies) which were previously used for the purpose, and by the growth of what might once have been called smuggling, but might better be described as free trade which ignored decreasingly relevant national frontiers. This process encompassed a rapid increase in African involvement in the international drugs trade, and a kind of booty mercantilism which consisted in exporting anything that could be sold and carried away.

In this context, attempts by established governments to stay in office through the manipulation of multi-party elections, or the seizure of power by the military, represented little more than a desperate clinging to the wreckage by state-centred elites who could see nowhere else to turn. While occasionally, leaders such as Rawlings in Ghana or Museveni in Uganda appeared to have some project of state reconstitution, for the most part African politicians were preoccupied with personal survival, under circumstances which offered little prospect of developing effective mechanisms for conflict resolution or political management, either domestically or internationally.

The international response to these developments largely consisted in the attempts at external management represented by structural adjustment programmes and democratisation schemes, in the despatch of humanitarian aid (which in countries such as Mozambique and Somalia represented well over half of recorded GNP), and occasional ill-considered cases of military intervention. All these measures, while regarded externally as attempts to resolve the problems of African statehood (or to ease the sufferings of African peoples), were treated internally as providing resources through which, following the processes of extraversion made familiar by Bayart, local actors could find some means to keep themselves going.[11] The US intervention in Somalia, for instance, created a set of tactical opportunities through which each of the local factions sought to increase its access to money, weapons or food. The concern of Western aid agencies to find counterpart African non-governmental organisations through which to manage their relief programmes immediately spawned a set of NGOs designed to meet the purpose. External actors readily found their presence perpetuating the very conditions which had prompted their intervention in the first place.

It must be apparent that we are now entering territory to which the end of the Cold War has only a marginal relevance. Once this had ceased to hold any plausible prospect of bringing forth a new world order in which Africa might be able to find a part, the continent was left pretty much on its own, removed (except perhaps for South Africa) from any significant role in the rapidly changing international economy which must provide the basic underpinning for whatever new structure of global politics may now be emerging. It must equally be apparent that continued external interest in a part of the world which excites attention largely on humanitarian grounds is liable to be precarious.

In these circumstances, any prognosis as to the future form of international relations in Africa must be uncertain, depending as it does on an assessment of the political forces emerging within the continent. Some of these forces, certainly, favoured the maintenance of existing state authorities, especially where states were economically viable, administratively efficient, and held together by a sense of common identity among their peoples. And whatever the record of a number of African states over the last three decades or so, there is nothing in the experience of failed or collapsed states to suggest that any form of non-state entity provides a preferable alternative. Much of Africa, nonetheless, does not now form part of a state, for anything but purposes of cartographical convenience, and this condition is likely to continue and even increase.

This in turn means that much of Africa's external relations will – as is already happening – escape from the confines of formal diplomacy. In place of ritualised relationships derived from the mutual recognition of sovereign statehood, connections both within the continent and with the outside world are likely to depend on the actual balance of political power and economic interest, reverting in the process to something approximating to the situation in the pre-colonial era. Where there are effective governments, other governments will continue to do business with them. Where there are not, other means will have to be found. The workings of this 'new diplomacy' have already been illustrated by the way in which 'warlords' such as Charles Taylor and Jonas Savimbi have inserted themselves into the international system: partly through informal contacts with the official representatives of states, both in Africa and outside; partly through the mediation of non-governmental or quasi-governmental agencies, like the Heritage Foundation or the Carter Center; partly through contacts with media institutions like CNN or the BBC World Service, or through access to aid agencies which help to bring in both food and convertible currencies; and partly through deals with businessmen who can turn a ready profit on the export of drugs, diamonds, timber or anything else through unofficial channels.

The idea that what we describe as 'international relations' is essentially concerned with relationships between states which encompass the whole inhabited territory of the globe, and which are in turn bureaucratised through a world-wide grid of diplomatic representation and international institutions, has become so universally accepted that it is easy to forget how recently it has become established. It is essentially the result of the nineteenth century carve-up of the globe by the European empires (including the land-based Russian Empire), and the admission of the states which resulted from subsequent decolonisation into the international order established by the colonisers. In many cases, these states have established a political coherence and economic viability that have enabled them to become normal and seemingly permanent members of an expanded international order. In others, including not only parts of Africa but Yugoslavia, Afghanistan, and parts of the former Soviet Union, the basis of statehood has effectively disappeared. In this light, the Cold War may now be seen as a mechanism which, among other things, facilitated the survival of a state-based international order which started to crumble at the edges as soon as the overarching structure of bipolarity was removed. In this respect, however marginalised Sub-Saharan Africa may be within the new world order (or disorder), it exemplifies an aspect of post-Cold War international politics which is of much wider concern.

Notes

1 World Bank, *World Development Report 1993*, Table 1, pp. 238–9; the decline for the Middle East and North Africa region, at 2.4 per cent, was even greater than for Africa, but operated from a base figure some six times as great, and was heavily influenced by prices for a single commodity, oil. The World Bank figures exclude a number of states, notably Angola, Somalia and Zaire, for which figures were unobtainable, and which are likely to depress the continental total even further.

2 There is a massive literature on structural adjustment programmes. See, for example, Thomas M. Callaghy and John Ravenhill, (eds), *Hemmed In: Responses to Africa's Economic Decline* (Columbia University Press, New York, 1993) and Rolph van der Hoeven and Fred van der Kraaij, (eds), *Structural Adjustment and Beyond in Sub-Saharan Africa* (Currey, London, 1994).

3 See Christopher Clapham, *Africa and the International System: the Politics of State Survival* (Cambridge University Press, Cambridge 1996) ch. 6.

4 Z. Brzezinski, *Power and Principle* (Weidenfeld and Nicholson, London, 1983) p.189.

5 *SIPRI Yearbook 1988: World Armaments and Disarmament* (Oxford University Press, Oxford, 1988) Appendix 7A.

6 See, for example, Mohammed Ayoob, *The Third World Security Predicament* (Rienner, Boulder, 1995) p.11; Ayoob in turn derives this distinction from Edward Azar and Chung-in Moon, *National Security in the Third World* (Elgar, Aldershot, 1988) ch. 4.

7 For a piece which clearly looks back with some nostalgia to the comforting presence of the USSR, see Mohamed El-Doufani, 'Regional revisionist client states under unipolarity', *Third World Quarterly* xii/2 (1992) pp. 255–65.

8 See Clapham, *Africa and the International System*, ch. 8.

9 There is now a substantial literature on democratisation in Africa. See, for example, John Wiseman, (ed.), *Democracy and Political Change in Sub-Saharan Africa* (Routledge, London, 1995).

10 I have examined the failure of hegemony in the Horn, in Christopher Clapham, 'The Horn of Africa: International Politics in the Post-Cold War Era, *Oxford International Review* v/1 (1993) pp. 16–19.

11 See J. F. Bayart, *The State in Africa: the Politics of the Belly* (Longman, London, 1993) pp. 20–32.

5 ❧ Prospects for Asian Security after the Cold War

David Shambaugh

Peace appears to have broken out in Asia. The current lull in more than a century and a half of almost continuous conflict has led some observers to assume that the twenty-first century will indeed be a 'Pacific Century'. This belief has been occasioned by the end of the Soviet–American Cold War in Asia, but also by the operative assumption that the economic dynamism and complimentarities of Asia–Pacific nations build interdependencies that will anchor bilateral and multilateral relationships, restrain commercial competition from stimulating strategic conflict, and maintain the balance of regional power and security.

The end of the Cold War in Asia has been largely beneficial to the region. Many regional civil wars and insurgencies have dissipated, ended, or been quelled (East Timor notwithstanding). Many animosities that were fixtures of the post-war era have been relaxed in recent years: China–Russia, Japan–Russia, China–South Korea, China–Vietnam, China–India, Cambodia–Vietnam, North Korea-Japan, Russia-South Korea, Vietnam–ASEAN, Myanmar-ASEAN, and (prior to 1995) China-Taiwan. These intra-regional *détentes* have made many positive contributions to regional security in recent years.[1] The normalisation of ties and relaxation of tensions between China and many of its neighbours have been particularly important. Australia's improvement of defence links with ASEAN is also notable.

Despite these factors that are conducive to peace and stability, a variety of unstable situations exist in Asia that could prove disruptive. Territorial disputes throughout the region, the continued stand-off on the Korean peninsula, and the China–Taiwan problem all have potential to erupt into armed conflict. More broadly, regional fears of a resurgent Japan, a strong and assertive China, an unpredictable North

Korea, and growing Indian power are all keeping regional strategists working overtime.

Doubts about the future of regional security are fuelled by the uncertain roles that Russia and the United States will play. Neither commands the respect or power of five years ago. Russia has virtually disappeared as an actor on the Asian security scene, while the US military presence in the region is being questioned by both Asian and American politicians alike. Washington's aggressive trade policy toward Asia during the Clinton administration[2] and the multiple disputes with China have added to the decreased respect for the United States in the region.

Further compounding the fluidity is the absence of any regional collective security regime to deter and contain conflicts. Regional security dialogues are underway bilaterally and multilaterally at the governmental and non-governmental levels, while confidence building measures have been implemented between some regional nations, but an integrated security framework is lacking. Various political and cultural factors exist which mitigate against the emergence of a cooperative or collective security framework.

Thus, despite the optimism brought about by recent diplomatic initiatives and confidence building measures, the assumption of a pacific Asia is by no means a foregone conclusion. The Cold War between the United States and former Soviet Union may be over, but remnants of that era are still present in Asia (notably a divided Korea and China). Tensions between Washington and Beijing continue to bear an ideological hue characteristic of Cold War rivalry, and some wonder whether the growing animosity between the US and China bears the seeds of a new Cold War.[3] The Cold War rivalries across the 38th Parallel in Korea and across the Taiwan Strait still have the potential to erupt into hot wars. As in other parts of the world, regional and civil conflicts long suppressed by the Cold War bipolar structure now have potential to re-emerge. These lingering historical rivalries and national divisions join new asymmetries that are taking shape and have the potential to disturb the peace and cause a fundamental realignment in the regional balance of power. Mutual perceptions are also shifting – particularly of China. Thus bilateral relationships and security in the region remain in great flux, while there exists no regional security mechanism to control crises and contain conflict. The Association for Southeast Asian Nations (ASEAN) Regional Forum remains an embryonic organisation with no power of enforcement. It offers little more than a forum for polite discourse between its members and 'dialogue partners' once a year.

Potential Flashpoints

While the Asia–Pacific is presently devoid of hot war or active inter-state conflict, instability exists in several places that could trigger the outbreak of hostilities. Short-term potentialities must be distinguished from medium-term possibilities. In the near term, there exist three potential conflict zones: the Korean peninsula, the Taiwan Strait, and the Indo–Pakistani border.

The continuing division of the two Koreas, the nature and uncertain future of the North Korean regime, and North Korean nuclear ambitions continue to make the Korean peninsula the most dangerous situation in the region. The more isolated and destitute the North Korean regime becomes, the greater risk it poses. North Korea is presently on the verge of a national famine, the economy is at a standstill and experiencing negative growth, the political succession to Kim Il-sung is far from settled, the regime is isolated internationally and deeply in debt, while Pyongyang no longer enjoys the unquestioned patronage of Moscow and Beijing. The agricultural situation is particularly pressing, with nearly a million homeless and hungry. Many analysts fear that, under such conditions, North Korea may strike at South Korea. South Korean and US forces (37,000) are preparing for just such an eventuality at present, while US intelligence estimates that the North Korean regime will not last out the decade and could well collapse in one or two years.[4] This highly fluid and volatile situation thus remains the primary flashpoint in Asia.

Tensions across the Taiwan Strait are rising and come a close second. The unresolved division of Taiwan and China, and the island's growing aspirations for independence, makes the Taiwan issue loom larger as a source of instability in the region than at any time since the Sino–US rapprochement of 1971–72. Since 1995, when Taiwan President Lee Teng-hui paid a private visit to the United States, tensions have escalated dramatically, with China carrying out large-scale military exercises and ballistic missile tests near the island. Beijing's stance toward Taipei has toughened as result of a variety of factors, but can be expected to continue. The use of force by China cannot be ruled out, and is an increasingly distinct possibility.

Continuing rivalry between India and Pakistan is the third potential flashpoint in Asia. While dormant for over twenty years, tensions have been rising of late over the Kashmir issue, while India's deployment of the Prithi medium-range missile and both nations' clandestine programmes to develop nuclear weapons are further destabilising factors.

While not necessarily pressing flashpoints, the territorial maritime disputes in the Sea of Okhotsk, Sea of Japan, the East China Sea, and the South China Sea also have potential to bring Asian nations into conflict with one another. China also shares disputed borders with India and Vietnam – which caused wars in 1962 and 1979 respectively – although bilateral boundary commissions have been established in each case to discuss the disputes. Progress has been made in each case and all parties have begun the process of disengaging military forces from the contested borders. The demarcation of the Sino–Russian frontier and reduction of tensions between Beijing and Moscow must be counted as a major enhancement to regional stability and security, as is the pacification of the Cambodian conflict.

Militarising Asia

While the predominant post-Cold War trend in Asia has been towards peace and prosperity, potential near-term flashpoints still exist. Because of these continuing conflicts, latent regional rivalries, and increasing wealth throughout the region, Asia remains a heavily militarised region. It has not enjoyed the same 'peace dividends' from the end of the Cold War enjoyed by other regions. There are more than 10m service personnel under arms in Asia.[5] After the United States and Russia, Asia retains six of the world's eight largest standing armies (China 2.9m; India 1.14m; North Korea 1.12m; Vietnam 572,000; South Korea 633,000; Pakistan 587,000).

Asian military establishments are increasingly armed with sophisticated, state-of-the-art weaponry.[6] The introduction of F–16, MiG–31, and Su–27 fighter-interceptors and a range of modern naval vessels into the region has led some analysts to conclude that a regional arms race has commenced,[7] although the majority view among specialists is that Asian military establishments are undertaking necessary force modernisation programs that are not part of an action-reaction arms spiral. Regional defence spending is also dramatically rising as most countries in the region seek to modernise their forces. Unlike other regions of the world where the end of the Cold War has meant the building down of military establishments, the trend has been the opposite in Asia.

Historically, individual military modernisation programmes tend to fuel fears and misperceptions among neighbours which, like the outbreak of the First World War, can easily ignite an arms race and trigger hostilities. Lack of transparency in military spending and modernisation programmes, and non-institutionalised confidence building and security measures (CBSMs), fuel such fears and misperceptions in Asia. Such contemporary fears are often anchored in ancient animosities. Historical regional rivalries that could re-emerge in Asia include China/Japan, China/Vietnam, China/India, China/Indonesia, Indonesia/Vietnam, Thailand/Vietnam, Japan/Korea, and Russia/Japan. All have historical precedents. It is interesting to note in this regard that Asia's potential conflicts are primarily of an *inter*-state nature, whereas elsewhere on the globe the post-Cold War world has been predominantly characterised by *intrastate* civil conflicts in Europe, Africa, Central and Southwest Asia.

Interactions Among the Powers

The post-war order in Asia was cast by the Korean War, out of which grew the Asian Cold War. A bipolar balance emerged initially with Washington and Tokyo confronting Beijing and Moscow. This basic configuration held for more than two decades, although following China's rupture with the Soviet Union in 1960 a more complex quadrangle of power took shape between the Soviet Union, China, Japan, and China.

With President Nixon's visit to Beijing and the normalisation of diplomatic relations between China and Japan in 1972, a new era in Asian international relations opened. For the first time in the 20th century the United States, Japan, and China enjoyed productive and amicable relations with each other, and all shared a strategic orientation to contain Soviet power in Asia. This was to last a decade. In 1982–83 leaders in Beijing and Moscow initiated a cautious rapprochement, while China distanced itself from its strategic alignment with Washington. Meanwhile, Beijing and Tokyo proceeded to build a close commercial and political relationship, while increasing strains in the US–Japan relationship emerged. Considerable fluidity remained in these inter-relationships throughout the remainder of the 1980s. The Tiananmen massacre of 1989 and implosion of the Soviet Union in 1991 only served to increase the fluidity.

With the collapse of the Soviet Union and end of the Cold War the regional 'strategic quadrangle' has been essentially reduced to a triangle, as Russia is not at present a principal strategic actor in the Asia–Pacific region.[8] There are calls from nationalistic quarters in Russia to 'reclaim the empire', including territories *beyond* the former Soviet Union in Asia, but this latent imperial thrust is unlikely to materialise or meet with success. Russia's armed forces are in disarray, and the once feared Pacific Fleet lies literally rusting in the Vladivostok harbour. Its ground forces in the Far Eastern Military District have been cut by more than half, and those that remain are at a very poor state of readiness. The defence pacts and alliances that Moscow had with India, Vietnam, North Korea, and Mongolia are defunct. Commercially, Russia is a virtual non-player in the booming Asia–Pacific trade. Russia's total trade turnover with the Asia–Pacific region was a paltry $6 bn in 1995. It has little to trade with the Asian nations except natural resources and weapons.

Since 1991 dynamics between each of the four regional powers have intensified and become more complex. Despite its declining role as a regional power, Moscow has developed an extensive relationship with Beijing. The blossoming of the Sino–Russian relationship is particularly noteworthy, and it has certainly contributed to China's national security and strategic leverage. High-level exchanges, including between Presidents Boris Yeltsin and Jiang Zemin, occur annually. Ministerial-level officials shuttle between the two countries regularly. More than 50 bilateral accords have been signed since 1991. Two-way trade, negligible just a few years ago, totalled $7.6 bn in 1993. In an ironic twist of history, China has become a creditor to Russia, extending several large loans and commodity credits. Moscow's debt to Beijing stood at $1.07 bn in 1993.

A significant indicator of the warming relationship between the two formerly bitter adversaries is in the military sphere. Various confidence building measures have been implemented, including the considerable reduction of forces across their 4,550 mile-long shared frontier. With the minor exception of the navigation channel in the

Amur River, agreements have been reached to demarcate the entire border. A non-aggression treaty is said to be under negotiation, and Presidents Yeltsin and Jiang agreed in September 1994 to no longer target nuclear weapons against each other. Military delegations are now exchanged on a monthly basis. Russian engineers have returned to upgrade defence factories constructed during the 1950s and to help upgrade several categories of Chinese weapons systems (including the long-plagued submarine-launched ballistic missile program). Russia has also sold sophisticated arms to China in recent years – including twenty-six Sukhoi–27 high altitude interceptors, ten Ilyushin–76 transports, four S–300 anti-aircraft batteries with 80 surface-to-air missiles, 12 Mi–17 attack helicopters, and two *Kilo* class attack submarines. Visiting Chinese military delegations have examined and expressed interest in a wide variety of other systems – including an aircraft carrier, T–72 main battle tanks, MiG–29 and MiG–31 interceptors, advanced avionics, and more Su–27 fighters and *Kilo* submarines – but to date these sales have not materialised. They are unlikely to do so, at least in any large numbers, because the People's Liberation Army lacks the foreign exchange for large-scale purchases and China is very reluctant to become dependent on foreign suppliers. The PRC learned a harsh lesson in this regard in 1960, when Soviet advisors, supplies, and joint projects were abruptly terminated. Chinese strategy today exhibits a preference for co-production arrangements on Chinese soil.

Sino–Japanese relations have been strengthened following a brief interlude after 1989, when Tokyo had to acquiesce to Western sanctions against Beijing. Political disputes over Taiwan, mutual fears about the growing strength of each other's military, and lingering distrust stemming from the war years plague the Sino–Japanese relationship and are beginning to rise to the surface. Frictions between Tokyo and Beijing are noticeably on the increase, as are the constituencies in each country that advocate a 'get tough' policy with the other. While there are numerous stabilising elements in the bilateral relationship, one senses that perceptions are shifting and a long-term strategic rivalry is brewing.[9]

In the medium term, stability and security in Asia will likely revolve around relations among the larger regional powers and the United States on the one hand, and among the stronger Asian nations on the other (Japan, China, India, Indonesia, Vietnam, Thailand, Republic of Korea, Pakistan). The dislocations to the established balance of power caused by the emergence of China as an economic and military power will be a central challenge to the region and the world in the years to come. The growing assertiveness of Japan in regional and international affairs is also changing the strategic landscape, while the rapidly growing economies and power projection capabilities of India and Indonesia are also being felt.

Equally important are the declining roles played by Russia and the United States in Asia. Since the collapse of the Soviet Union, Russia has become a marginal player in regional affairs, and it is unclear if Moscow will be in a position to exert any real influence for the foreseeable future (even if it does succeed in reasserting a relative sphere of influence in the 'near abroad'). Russia's growing relationship with China could, however, shape a new balance of power in East Asia and serve to polarise relations with the United States and Japan.

The role of the United States is also in doubt. Throughout Asia one encounters the *perception* that Washington is pulling out of the region. Whether or not this is true (American officials hotly deny it and tangible evidence contradicts it),[10] Asians increasingly see the US to be pulling back. For its part, the United States remains committed to maintaining 100,000 ground forces in East Asia (backed by the Seventh Fleet and forces deployed in Alaska and the continental United States) and is exploring new arrangements for military cooperation in South Asia.[11] Subjective perceptions are often more important than objective realities in international relations, therefore the widespread belief that the United States is not committed to sustaining a formidable presence in Asia has already contributed to the fluidity and post-Cold War uncertainty in the region.

Despite the rise of China and Japan, and the relative decline of Russia and America in East Asia, the inter-relationships between these four powers are likely to determine whether the Pacific Century will be pacific.[12] The flashpoints noted above would not only bring into conflict the principal antagonists, but could also trigger involvement by these major powers. Presently cooperative and competitive elements are evident in each bilateral relationship, but the potential for strategic rivalry exists in each case.

Japan's New Assertiveness

The Cold War ensured that Washington and Tokyo contained their economic competition and commercial conflicts in the interests of a larger strategic partnership. This was sustained by broadly shared values and democratic political systems. The two argued about market access, trade, and defence 'burden sharing,' but their political commonalties and allied partnership contained the disputes. This no longer appears to be the case – with the intensification of trade frictions resulting from the Clinton administration's enforcement of 'Super 301' trade legislation, and strains over US forces deployed on Okinawa and the Japanese home islands. A change in Japan's reaction to the United States is evident in recent years. The 'just say no' school is in the ascent. This is indicative of broader changes in Japan's self-image and definitions of international interests, as well as the coming to power of a post-war generation which is far less encumbered with the burdens of the past.

Tokyo's new posture towards Washington is reflective of Japan's growing self-confidence in a variety of international arenas and desire to be more than a one-dimensional power. This has caused some concern in the Asia–Pacific, notably from China.[13] In Japan there are also rising voices for a greater assertiveness vis-à-vis China, as many intellectuals and politicians are openly expressing concern about the prospects of a strong and powerful China.[14]

The main manifestation of Japan's new consciousness and confidence is the emerging consensus over a more activist foreign policy, maintaining a strong defence, and increasing Japan's international stature. This consensus was forged under former Prime Minister Hosokawa, was maintained under the socialist-led coalition that came to power in 1994 and strengthened under the Hoshimoto government. To some extent, the new confidence represents a rising nationalism and declining pacifism among politicians and intellectuals in Japan, although it should not be mistaken for a new militarism or *revanchisme*. The rationale has simply been to bring Japan's global political and, to a lesser extent, military clout in line with its economic power – to become a 'normal' power. This has resulted in Japan's decision to contribute troops to international peacekeeping forces (PKO) and to play a role in brokering conflicts (such as Bosnia); to seek a seat as a permanent member of the UN Security Council; to increase military spending and provide the Japanese Self Defence Forces (JSDF) with state-of-the-art equipment (possibly including a high altitude anti-ballistic missile system).

Japanese diplomacy has also become more assertive in Asia. Tokyo has sought to take the lead in pushing for a regional security mechanism in East Asia. While the United States has generally welcomed (and indeed has encouraged) Japan's new international activism, China has not. Like many other Asians, Beijing remains highly sceptical of any increase in Japan's international or regional political or military roles. This partly stems from the legacy of the war and Beijing's long-standing fears of revived Japanese militarism, but it is also related to China's own aspirations to become the dominant power in the region.[15]

Coping with China

The principal challenge facing Washington and Tokyo in the coming years will not be each other, but China. The challenges posed to both by China's economic dynamism, modernising military, and authoritarian political system may serve to breathe new life into the bilateral relationship and alliance. At present, both the US and Japan are working to engage with China and bring the PRC peacefully into the regional and international order. But both are uneasy about nationalistic trends in China, Beijing's muscular posture towards Taiwan and the South China Sea, and the modernisation of the People's Liberation Army. Neither wishes to move to a policy of containment, but both realise that this is an option that may require further contemplation in the future.

Washington and Tokyo have overlapping but also divergent interests in, and policies toward, China. The essential difference lies in the political domain. Japan's highest priority is that China remain socially and politically stable, whereas the United States favours – and even seeks to foster – political change in China. The greatest fear of the Japanese government and people is that China will convulse in civil conflict, resulting in the splintering of the nation and bringing a massive refugee exodus to Japan's shores. This has been demonstrated in numerous public opinion polls. Unlike Washington, human rights concerns rank relatively low on Tokyo's agenda with Beijing. This was evident during former Prime Minister Hosokawa's visit to Beijing in March 1994. Hosokawa pleased his hosts by publicly stating that human rights were relative to each nation, and that governments should not impose their definitions upon one another. Instead he concentrated on economic, security, and military issues.

Of considerable concern to Tokyo is China's rapidly rising military budget, force modernisation programme, continued nuclear testing, new doctrine of rapid deployment and peripheral defence, and lack of transparency in most aspects of its armed forces. While the rest of the world is cutting military expenditure and establishments, the Chinese People's Liberation Army (PLA) has received eight consecutive years of double-digit budget increases (since 1988); is engaged in buying a range of sophisticated weaponry from Russia; has aspirations to build a blue water navy and modern air force; is upgrading its nuclear weapons arsenal; and is slowly developing a force projection capability. This is all of great concern to Japan and China's neighbours, particularly because Beijing has shown a willingness to use force in the past and has a number of contested territorial claims in the region.

China's military modernisation programme is also of increasing concern to the United States, but Washington's China agenda remains dominated by human rights, trade, and political concerns. The US seeks to improve human rights in China, but the American stance is also shaped by the lingering ideological/political struggle of the Cold War. The Chinese Communist regime is seen by many American politicians and officials as a pariah state, that should join the former Communist parties of the former Soviet bloc in the annals of history. Nonetheless, President Clinton has opted for the policy of 'constructive engagement' with China fashioned by President Bush. By extending 'Most Favoured Nation' trading privileges to China, the Clinton administration recognised that China is critical to key US commercial interests, while at the same time trying to balance deep American concerns over China's human rights record. President Clinton's delinkage of trade and human rights has not, however, improved human rights in China; to the contrary, they have sharply deteriorated.

For China's part, Beijing continues to cling to a myopic view of state sovereignty that mandates an exclusive position on 'interference in internal affairs'. Such a position in today's interdependent world is not viable. Beijing's foreign policy is also premised on its struggle against 'power politics' and 'hegemony'.

Thus America seeks to change China domestically while China

desires to change American behaviour internationally. The struggle between the two has been intense for at least a decade, albeit subliminally, and is not likely to end. The struggle does not command the attention of 'high politics', yet it is very fundamental. It is deeply rooted in divergent world views, political systems, and national interests. Various American and Chinese politicians have sought to divert this fundamental divide in the interests of broader national concerns, yet the contradiction remains.

Japan's ties with China are, by contrast, more solid. The two governments watch each other's military capabilities warily and each is mindful of the legacy of the Second World War, but their commercial and cultural linkages are particularly thick. Trade and Japanese investment in China have shot up in recent years. Since the 1960s Japan has been China's largest trading partner, and continues to be so today. Japan does more trade with China than any other country except the United States. Bilateral trade increased from $19.7 bn to nearly $35 bn between 1989–93. Japanese investment in China more than quintupled during the same period, from $438m to approximately $2.5 bn. The dramatic increase in Japanese investment is particularly noteworthy, since Japanese businessmen have always been more willing to trade with than to invest in China. The burgeoning of Sino–Japanese commercial interaction is indicative of their economic complimentarities.

American trade and investment with China has similarly increased in recent years, although the US runs a much higher trade deficit with China than does Japan. The US trade deficit with China during 1995 reached $50 bn – second only to Washington's trade deficit with Tokyo. This has resulted in a toughened trade policy towards both countries by the Clinton administration, which in turn is spurring both Beijing and Tokyo to resist American pressure.

The challenge that China poses to US–Japanese relations will be considerable in the years to come. Before 1989 Washington and Tokyo shared the same views and policies toward China, but after Tiananmen they have diverged somewhat. The major divergence is over how to handle the human rights issue and, relatedly, how to press for political change in China. The Japanese side prefers gradual change and quiet diplomacy while Washington seeks rapid progress and tends toward public diplomacy. On other issues – particularly military and economic – the two sides continue to hold an essential identity of interests. But there is little doubt that co-ordinating and managing the two nation's respective policies toward China will be one of the principal challenges facing US–Japan relations in the future. Security concerns may well become more important than commerce in the future, as China modernises its military. Among Asian nations Tokyo has been the most forthright in pressing Beijing for military transparency, but the United States and the member nations of ASEAN became more vocal during 1994–95.

Of course, the greatest concern about Chinese military modernisation is on Taiwan. Since 1995 military tensions across the Taiwan Strait have heated up as the government in Taiwan has sought to enhance its international standing and the voices for independence in Taiwan have increased. The main catalyst was a private visit by Republic of China on Taiwan President Lee Teng-hui to the United States in June 1995. Beijing responded with large-scale military exercises and ballistic missile 'tests' off the coast of Taiwan. Should the mainland be tempted to use force against Taiwan (as it has long maintained it will if there is any movement towards independence), Taiwan's forces appear sufficient to inflict heavy losses if not repel the attack.[16] Taiwan's anti-submarine warfare (ASW) capability appears sufficient to cope with a submarine blockade, and its new Perry destroyers and Knox frigates armed with Harpoon anti-ship missiles (recently leased from the US) could probably break a surface blockade. Nonetheless, a naval blockade (be it submarine and/or surface) would undoubtedly undermine confidence on the island and among commercial shippers – driving up insurance rates, driving down the stock market and making Taiwan pay a dear price economically. An M–9 or M–11 ballistic missile strike against Taiwan would be even more devastating. In general, since 1995 the Taiwan issue has again become an explosive situation with real potential to erupt in conflict.

Cooperative Security in Asia?

Asians are aware of the potential for military conflict in their region. They are also paying increased attention to unconventional security threats in the Asia–Pacific: piracy and smuggling; refugees; environmental degradation (especially acid rain) and depletion of strategic resources; drug trafficking; nuclear proliferation; and terrorism. To address the conventional and unconventional threats to security in the Asia–Pacific, numerous 'dialogues' have been initiated over the last few years. These have taken place at both the governmental and non-governmental levels, although the vast majority fall in the latter category.[17] The Asia–Pacific security conference circuit is a busy one.

Official regional security dialogues take place bilaterally and multilaterally. The most important multilateral channels are the ASEAN Post-Ministerial Conference (PMC), the ASEAN Ministerial Meetings (AMM), the ASEAN Regional Forum (ARF), and the Asia–Pacific Economic Cooperation (APEC) organisation. Each of these annual gatherings brings together representatives of different nations at different levels. The APEC summit is attended by heads of state, and although economics is the *raison d'être* of the organisation, security and political matters are discussed bilaterally. Security issues are also on the agenda of the annual ASEAN summit and the important series of post-summit meetings. The PMC, AMM, and ARF each bring together foreign ministers, but from different countries. For example, neither Russia or China are 'dialogue partners' of the PMC, although they do attend AMM meetings as guests.

Potentially the most important multilateral forum is the ASEAN Regional Forum. Established in 1993, the ARF is specifically tasked with discussing regional security issues. It is held every year in conjunction with the AMM and ASEAN–PMC meetings. Since its inception ARF meetings have not accomplished much of substance (they only last for one day and are consumed by pleasantries and procedural matters). It is difficult to even agree an agenda of what constitutes regional security 'problems' that should be addressed multilaterally. China is proving a stubborn player because it refuses to discuss either the Taiwan or South China Sea problems or its own military since Beijing claims these are 'internal affairs.'[18] China also refuses to allow Taiwan to participate in the forum or any other unofficial 'Track 2' security discussions.

Security dialogues also take place bilaterally between governments in the region. For example, Chinese Foreign Ministry and PLA officers meet annually with their counterparts in Japan, South Korea, and Russia. The United States has the most wide-ranging series of bilateral security exchanges in the region, concomitant with its multiple alliances and security pacts.

Regional security dialogues have proven an important channel of communication, even though little of significance has resulted to date.

They are especially important for articulating perceptions, voicing concerns, seeking clarification, improving transparency, and building confidence. Such dialogue can act as a tripwire for ascertaining misperceptions that could lead to broader conflict.

Three issues will likely be of key importance in such dialogues in the years to come. First, there is a need to improve military transparency concerning issues of defence budgets and military expenditures; force structures and order-of-battle; defence doctrines; arsenals; and deployments. This particularly applies to China, whose military establishment is extremely opaque. Second, there is a need to discuss national arms procurement policies, force modernisation programmes, and foreign weapons purchases. Regional militaries are legitimately being modernised, but an arms race in Asia could be brewing. If a classic action-reaction spiral is to be avoided these procurements must be discussed multilaterally and restraint must be exhibited by external suppliers. Both of the first two objectives would benefit from the publication of national defence White Papers. Third, territorial disputes must be opened to multilateral discussion and resolution. The map of Asia and the Pacific is littered with disputed lands and waters, many of which hold significant potential for armed conflict.

Having initiated regional security dialogues at the governmental and non-governmental levels, the future task will be to improve the substantive interaction. But to be successful, all nations in the region must be represented at the table (including Taiwan, North Korea, and Myanmar) and all regional security issues must be open for discussion.

Ultimately the goal should be to create an Asian version of the Organisation on Security and Cooperation in Europe (OSCE), or even an institutionalised regional collective security regime. Since the collapse of the system set up at the Washington Conference of 1922, Asia has never had a region-wide collective security regime. Several have been proposed and tried, but none have taken root. Those imposed by external powers – such as the US-sponsored Southeast Asia Treaty Organisation (SEATO) – have been limited in their scope or duration. Only the Five Power Defence Arrangement – which binds together Malaysia, Singapore, Great Britain, Australia, and New Zealand – has demonstrated endurance. The bilateral security treaties the United States maintains with Japan, Republic of Korea, the

Philippines, Thailand, and Australia have survived the Cold War, and do much to stabilise Asian security. As noted above, the US appears committed to maintaining 100,000 forward-positioned troops in East Asia for the foreseeable future, backed by the Seventh Fleet and further deployments in Guam, Hawaii, and California. But if they were to be drawn down or out of Japan and South Korea, US extended deterrence would lack credibility. If a regional security regime is to evolve in Asia it will have to do so indigenously, but it must also take account of US national security interests and commitments in the region.

A Pacific Century?

The Asia–Pacific region embarks on the Pacific century at peace. Will it last? If history is any guide, the chances are poor. This is a regrettable prognosis, but there exist at least six reasons for the prediction.

Firstly, rapidly growing economies produce inter-state competition and trade frictions. Although there do exist substantial complimentarities among regional economies that will build trade interdependencies, there is also considerable scope for contention. Dumping of inferior goods on regional export markets has already become a problem. Illegal movement of capital and shady investment chains are also increasingly frequent. So too is smuggling and piracy.

Rapid growth also stimulates social dislocations domestically, that have the potential to spill over borders. In recent years East Asia has had to cope with refugees from Vietnam, Cambodia, and East Timor. As the situation in North Korea deteriorates, a refugee exodus becomes increasingly likely in Northeast Asia. The region might also brace itself for an exodus the likes of which the world has never seen – from China. By the Chinese government's own admission, China today has 105 million transients moving about the country. This 'floating population' (other estimates run as high as 150 million!) could easily begin to migrate beyond China's shores if agricultural output continues to have shortfalls and employment cannot be found in coastal cities. Taiwan officials already report a greatly increased flow across the Strait. Should China convulse in civil conflict after the death of Deng Xiaoping, as some predict, Asia would be confronted with a major refugee crisis.

Third, growing economies contribute to increased military power. The rapidly developing capacities of regional militaries is on the verge of triggering an expensive and explosive regional arms race. Asian governments have demonstrated a propensity to use force to solve political problems; with modern armies the temptations will increase.

Fourth, rapidly growing economies and military establishments will inevitably shift the regional balance of power. The main catalyst for a re-configured balance, in the view of many, will be China's growing power. China is an aggrieved power which seeks restore its position as the dominant regional power. The PRC's growing strength will likely stimulate an informal alignment of offshore nations to contain continental Chinese power.

Fifth, historical rivalries and animosities may re-emerge during the Pacific century. As in other parts of the world, the dismantling of the Cold War superstructure has exposed latent rivalries and long-smouldering scores that need to be settled. In Asia, both China and Korea harbour great resentment towards Japan resulting from invasion and occupation, colonisation, and war atrocities. India and Vietnam are still smarting from the damage inflicted by China in 1962 and 1979. The civil wars that resulted in a divided Korea and China/Taiwan have yet to be resolved. And India–Pakistan rivalry will probably be eternal.

Finally, territorial conflicts and the need for strategic resources could be a catalyst to conflict. Some of these disputes result from artificially drawn colonial boundaries, but others derive from national aspirations and thirst for resources and monetary gain. The Pacific Rim seabed is particularly rich in oil and natural gas – which is not a coincidental factor in the territorial disputes in the East and South China Seas.

Thus, while the Asia–Pacific region is in an unprecedentedly peaceful state, it is by no means certain that this state is sustainable. This is a dynamic region, but such fluidity concomitantly causes instabilities. For the Pacific century to be pacific regional security mechanisms must be substantially strengthened and the United States must maintain its military commitments to the region. Even if these conditions do obtain, Asia is likely to experience as much conflict in the next as in the previous century.

Notes

This chapter is an adapted, expanded and updated version of my 'Pacific Security in the Pacific Century?' *Current History* (December 1994). It is reprinted with permission from *Current History*.

1 See the essays in Leslie Palmier (ed.) *Asia in Détente?* (MacMillan, London, 1992).

2 See Barry Bosworth, 'Growing Pains: Trade Frictions Corrode the US–Asian Relationship' *The Brookings Review* (Winter 1996) pp. 4–9.

3 See David Shambaugh, 'The United States and China: A New Cold War?' *Current History* (September 1995) pp. 241–7.

4 See 'U.S. Review Korea War Plan', *South China Morning Post International Weekly*, 13 January 1996, p. 8.

5 International Institute for Strategic Studies, *The Military Balance 1995–96* (Oxford University Press, Oxford, 1995).

6 For an excellent analysis see Paul Dibb, 'The Future Military Capabilities of Asia's Great Powers' *Janes Intelligence Weekly* vii/5 (1995), pp. 229–33.

7 See Andrew Mack and Desmond Ball, 'The Military Build-up in the Asia–Pacific' *Pacific Review* v/3 pp. 197–208; Gerald Segal, 'Managing New Arms Races in the Asia/Pacific' *The Washington Quarterly* (Summer 1992) pp. 83–101; and 'Asia's Arms Race', *The Economist*, 20 February 1993, pp. 21–3.

8 For an excellent discussion of Russia's role in Asia today see Charles E. Ziegler, 'Russia in the Asia–Pacific: A Major Power or Minor Participant?' *Asian Survey* xxxix/6 (June 1994) pp. 529–43.

9 See Gerald Segal, 'Confrontation Between China and Japan?' *World Policy Journal* xx/2 (Summer 1993).

10 See Joseph S. Nye, 'East Asian Security: The Case for Deep Engagement', *Foreign Affairs* (July/August 1995) pp. 90–102.

11 See US Department of Defense Office of International Security Affairs, *United States Security Strategy in the East Asia–Pacific Region* (The Pentagon, Washington, 1995).

12 See Michael Mandelbaum (ed.) *The Strategic Quadrangle: Russia, China, Japan, and the United States in East Asia* (Council on Foreign Relations Press, New York, 1995).

13 See Valérie Shimizu-Niquet, 'Japan's New Strategy: A New Menace' *The Pacific Review* vii/2 (1994) pp. 163–70.

14 See, for example, Masashi Nishihara, 'Japan Has Cause to Worry About Chinese Ambition', *International Herald Tribune*, 12 July 1994, p. 4. Nishihara is a leading defence intellectual at the Institute for Defence Studies in Tokyo. He is one of the few to have expressed the growing Japanese concern about China in print, although such anxieties are readily apparent in discussions with, and among, the Japanese defence establishment and – to a slightly lesser extent – the Foreign Ministry, Diet officials, and journalists.

15 See David Shambaugh, 'China and Japan: Complex Interdependence or Rivals for Pre-eminence?' in Christopher Howe (ed.) *China and Japan: History, Trends, and Prospects* (Oxford University Press, Oxford, 1996).

16 For an extended analysis see David Shambaugh, 'Taiwan's National Security' *The China Quarterly* (December 1996), forthcoming.

17 For a summary of the NGO forums see Appendix 1 in Paul Evans, 'Building Security: The Council for Security Cooperation in the Asia–Pacific (CSCAP)' *The Pacific Review* vii/2 (1994) pp. 133–6. For consideration of the issues see Sheldon Simon (ed.) *East Asian Security in the Post-Cold War Era* (M. E. Sharpe, Armonk, NY, 1993); and Desmond Ball et al, *Security Cooperation in the Asia–Pacific Region* (CSIS and Pacific Forum, Washington and Honolulu, 1993).

18 See Banning Garrett and Bonnie Glaser, 'Multilateral Security in the Asia–Pacific Region and its Impact on Chinese Interests: Views from Beijing' *Contemporary Southeast Asia* xvi/1 (1994) pp. 14–34; and Lee Lai To, 'ASEAN-PRC Political and Security Cooperation', *Asian Survey* xxxiii/11 (1993) pp. 1095–104.

6 Thinking Globally from a Regional Perspective: Chinese, Indonesian and Malaysian Reflections on the Post-Cold War Era

Rosemary Foot

Academic studies of the post-Cold War era until recently have demonstrated a relative neglect of the Asian and African dimension.[1] The majority of the empirically-based studies, especially those emanating from the trans-Atlantic international relations academic community, have tended to concentrate on the major states in the global system, on US–European relations within the context of NATO, on European Union policy developments, and on the future of the Central and Eastern European relationship with those two bodies.

In theoretical terms, and arising out of the substantive focus on US–European developments, such literature has shown signs of stabilising around two competing paradigms: the 'back to the future' school which laments the passing of the form of stability it associates with bipolarity, and which fears the resurrection of old rivalries that had been suppressed by common concentration on the external Soviet threat; and the neo-liberal institutionalist argument which contends that the institutionalised cooperation of an earlier era continues to shape policy choices in the current period, contributing to the maintenance of cooperative behaviour patterns.[2] Only recently have these two positions begun to influence debate about other areas of the world.[3]

This chapter is intended to contribute to this shift in focus away from US–European relations and towards East Asian perceptions of the strategic and political environment in the post-Cold War era. It examines some of the perspectives that are held in the region about the nature of the current order, highlighting especially the views of government officials, but also the analyses of influential individuals in some of the leading research institutes in the three countries selected. In addition to the modest goal of providing some information on Chinese, Indonesian and Malaysian thinking, it also provides one means of assessing the extent to which these perceptions about the global order might help to underpin or undercut a cooperative future for the region.

These three states have been chosen for comparison for a number of reasons: in terms of self-assessment, leaders in each country have frequently depicted themselves as champions or representatives of developing country positions; with regard to concepts of security, and as former colonies or semi-colonies, each state has been concerned about the West's challenge to sovereign jurisdiction; and each has articulated a concept of national security in this and past periods that gives primacy to national resilience and unity. Because each has been concerned about internal subversion, there has been a close connection between internal and external security and, since national resilience has been deemed important, a socio-economic dimension to security is also prominent. Although these states are divided along other important political, cultural and economic dimensions, the perceived capacity to represent wider developing country opinion and the similarities in their concepts of security ensure in the former case the ready articulation of positions regarding global developments, and in the latter at least provide the opportunity for a common perspective to emerge. In this respect, therefore, there is the possibility of tempering the argument with regard to East Asia that predominates: that it is an area made up of states seriously divided along a number of crucial dimensions, including political systems, religious affiliation, ethnicity, culture, and language, that render its ability to deepen areas of cooperation problematic.

In order to determine positions, government statements and some of the published material from the major research institutes have been examined. To a greater or lesser extent, within the three countries, and for political reasons, there is a closeness of view between government and academic analysis.[4] Such similarity is further reinforced by the fact that the research institutes in each country are strongly policy-oriented, thus making it difficult to allow time for theoretical or conceptual reflection.[5] Moreover, since both leaders and policy-oriented researchers are reacting to contemporary developments, their analyses are strongly affected by such immediate and pressing events. For example, the 1990–91 Gulf War, developments in the former Yugoslavia and Somalia, the advent of a new American administration in January 1993, the debate over the Uruguay Round, domestic political unrest and/or repression together with its generation of external concern and comment – all have had their impact on perceptions in official and non-official arenas. A further consequence of this, therefore, is that perceptions are evolving – an obvious drawback to the approach adopted in this chapter. Nevertheless, it is suggested that there is sufficient stability in positions, based on certain similarities in articulated conceptions of security, to make the objective of determining and comparing perspectives a viable one.

The Post Cold War Global Structure

Governmental and academic opinion in all three states has reached the unsurprising conclusion that the international system is en route to a multipolar order which it will reach at some future time impossible to determine. In a clear rejection of Waltzian notions of bipolar stability[6], multipolarity tends to be depicted as being more conducive to world peace, but only in its ideal form – that is to say, in circumstances where no single power dominates but where differences among the various poles narrow allowing each pole to act to balance and constrain another.[7]

In the meantime, however, the transition from bipolarity is seen to have greatly complicated the strategic picture. Commentators in all three states have depicted the current era as one of great turbulence, unpredictability and instability, and as noted earlier there are few guesses as to when these tendencies will abate.[8] Currently, all basically agree that the world is in a 'unipolar moment', with important, mainly negative, consequences for the Third World, of which they see themselves to be a part.

Both Indonesia and Malaysia emphasise that one thing that bipolarity afforded (and implicitly that Third World states currently miss) was the opportunity to play off one superpower against another. Their primary concern is that such a loss of leverage is likely to have serious economic consequences: with a shortage of global capital, the former Soviet Union, Central and Eastern Europe and to a lesser degree the Middle East are expected to absorb the West's resources, leaving countries such as their own on the sidelines. The Prime

Minister of Malaysia, Datuk Seri Mahathir Mohamad, also has put the marginalisation argument in more overtly political terms, most starkly at the Non-Aligned Summit (NAM) in September 1992. Pointing to the inauspicious circumstances for the weaker states in the post-Cold War era, he described their current options as being 'to submit or resist. Both involve a loss of leverage, and weak nations with no leverage can only become weaker. And the strong will truly inherit the world.' He went on: 'Without the option to defect to the other side, we can expect less wooing but more threats.'[9] Similarly, Noordin Sopiee, then the influential Director of the Institute of Strategic and International Studies in Kuala Lumpur, has written of the accelerated 'peripheralisation of most Third World countries,' of the 'erosion of superpower generosity' and loss of great power tolerance of behaviour deemed detrimental to their interests, especially when compared with their relative indulgence during the period of the 'heroic contest' between East and West.[10]

Chinese leaders too have frequently reflected on the extent to which their country has lost political leverage as a result of the ending of the 'strategic triangle'. Most emphatically, Beijing has noted the increased threat that a unipolar moment poses in political and cultural terms to itself and to other parts of the Third World. The fear is that the West (or the United States in particular) will be bolder in attempting to impose its values, intervening in domestic affairs where necessary to ensure this imposition. As Foreign Minister Qian Qichen put it at the UN General Assembly in October 1993: 'The new international environment has landed many developing countries in an even more dire plight. Increasing foreign intervention has heightened the various factors of instability therein and compounded their difficulties.'[11] The Malaysians appear to agree, Noordin Sopiee, writing in terms close to Mahathir's own views, that there has been a 'rise of a doctrine of interventionism' in the West which will be 'generally threatening to the interests of the weaker nations since double standards will abound and it will be the strong who will determine its very selective application.'[12] To some degree, the debate over Asian values, which relates to issues of human rights, democratisation and development (and in which Malaysia has played a particularly prominent role), has been fuelled by these concerns over an interventionist West attempting to impose 'conditionality', and its view of the relationship between these complex issues.[13]

All three countries pay lip service to the need for greater South–South cooperation but in Malaysia's expression of this its pessimism is evident: as Mahathir put it, such states must 'pool what little strength we have'. Worse still, in his view, the countries in the South in their striving to develop have found that 'their records on human rights, democracy, and so on are [being] scrutinised in order to obstruct their progress.'[14] The Chinese have advocated a number of reforms of the global economic system, calling for the developed world to open its markets, provide development aid, transfer technology and reduce the debt burden.[15] In Indonesia's case, it promotes more forcefully than South–South cooperation a 'Brandtian' vision of North–South, arguing that the way to deal with the North is not to confront it but to cooperate with it: 'whether one likes it or not, the West or the North has continued to be the primary source of capital and technology which the non-aligned nations badly need for development.'[16] According to one author, Indonesia has a strong and influential group of liberal economists with some access to policy makers. Their ideas on economic liberalisation obviously help to underpin this perception of the value of foreign capital.[17]

The US Role as Sole Superpower and Regional Security Partner

Inevitably, there has been a focus on US behaviour, both as sole superpower and as actual or potential security guarantor in East Asia, in official and non-official writings and statements in all three countries. Indonesian elites seemingly have had a somewhat more benign public attitude than Chinese or Malaysian commentators about the US role in the post-Cold War era. After the Gulf War, leading commentators in Djakarta at the Centre for Strategic and International Studies (CSIS), and the Centre for Information and Development Studies (CIDES), such as Dewi Fortuna Anwar and A. Hasnan Habib, both drew the lesson that regional hegemons would not be allowed to get away with bullying smaller nations[18] (although the latter author pointed to the requirement that an American direct and vital interest had to be involved). China's paramount leader, Deng Xiaoping, on the other hand, allegedly characterised the action, as an example of 'big hegemonists beating up on small hegemonists,' or as a Hong Kong newspaper reflecting Beijing opinion described it, it was a 'war for the interests of the USA, a war contending for hegemony over petroleum, a war between world hegemony and regional hegemony.'[19]

Despite US criticism of Indonesian actions in East Timor and of its labour legislation, there is still a clear desire in Djakarta to see Washington remain globally active to include involvement in the East Asian region. All ASEAN states to a greater or lesser degree want to see the United States remain an involved Pacific as well as Atlantic power, the broad argument being that too swift a US disengagement from their region will create a power vacuum that would probably be filled by either China, Japan, or India. Malaysia in particular, however, has tried hard to move beyond the power vacuum argument and to put emphasis on the need to reassure rather than to deter traditional or potential enemies. As Mahathir has put it: 'There are now tremendous opportunities to go by a different path, to cooperate with those with whom one disagrees, with whom one has yet to come to an agreement ... This is the path of cooperative security, of trying to get along, of trying to understand one's adversary and the security concerns of others, of trying to accommodate and to embrace.'[20] The Indonesian government has also demonstrated its interest in regional security cooperation, sponsoring a series of meetings designed to deal with the management of tensions in the South China sea, and actively working to establish the multilateral security organisation, the ASEAN Regional Forum (ARF), of which the United States is a member.[21]

China, on the other hand, is more ambivalent about the US role. It recognises that the ASEAN countries want the United States to remain in the region, and has acknowledged that its presence can be valuable in sustaining regional stability and in containing Japan; but it also views Washington as a brake on the emergence of multipolarity, a world structure which it would like to see in place. Moreover, certain key figures in Beijing, especially within the military, believe that the United States has targeted China as a potential enemy and is exacerbating China's relations with other states in the region through the depiction of the PRC as a future threat to others.[22] This encourages China to seek to allay these fears by participating in the various multilateral security forums that have emerged at official and non-official levels in East Asia. Yet, it is fearful that the United States will try to set the agenda at such gatherings, and use them as a 'platform for China-bashing.'[23] Thus, while it has become more active within the ARF – the most significant multilateral security organisation yet to emerge – it also fears that the ARF might be used by Washington to construct its own preferred security structure for the area.[24]

A More Activist and Restructured UN

Attitudes towards the United States and fears regarding Third World marginalisation inevitably influence reactions to the more active United Nations that has emerged in the post-Cold War era. The UN-authorised action in Iraq was followed in 1992 by a five-fold increase in the numbers of troops deployed in peace-keeping operations, but more significantly also by an increase in the types of activities such forces engage in, including the monitoring of elections, peace-enforcement, and humanitarian intervention.[25]

Again, the three governments' reactions to these developments have been somewhat different. As noted earlier, Chinese statements emphasise that the West, and especially the US, is using the United Nations in this new era to promote its interests. During the Gulf War, for example, one commentator, noting that the UN had been strengthened as a result of its actions in the Gulf, also argued that one outcome had been that the 'United States and some Western countries have taken advantage of the drastic changes in the international situation and given enormous publicity to their values and priorities within the UN. They have attempted to force their views and policies upon others in order to achieve their own interests.'[26] Beijing fears the implications of the constant reference to chapter VII rather than chapter VI provisions within the UN charter as a means of dispute settlement. It constantly reminds those willing to listen that the UN is a gathering of sovereign states and is in danger of riding roughshod over the statist principles enshrined in its charter, especially the basic principles of 'respect for the sovereignty and non-interference in the internal affairs of member states.'[27] China has ruled out the integration of its armed forces into a UN task force, and has ignored the basic tenor of Boutros-Ghali's *Agenda for Peace*, which advocated the expansion of UN activities. Chinese commentators reported only his references to the sovereignty of states as an 'untouchable principle' and his statement that under article 2, paragraph 7 of the charter, the UN would 'never intervene in the domestic affairs of a member state either in the guise of preventive diplomacy or for a humanitarian aim.'[28] In summing up the achievements of the UN over its past 50 years, Foreign Minister Qian commended it for its 'major contributions to the peace and prosperity of mankind.' But he also advised this 'irreplaceable' organisation, where peacekeeping was concerned, to learn the lessons of the more recent past, to move forward only on the basis of those aspects of the Charter that gave due weight to domestic jurisdiction, that emphasised the settlement of disputes through mediation, and that sought the prior consent of the parties concerned.[29]

Although Indonesian and Malaysian perspectives on this question are less fully articulated, and though they certainly would not disagree with Chinese views about Western dominance of the institution, both nevertheless seem to favour a more active UN provided it is made more representative and democratic. Malaysia, for example, and with Bosnia in mind, has attacked UN activity primarily on the basis of its selectiveness, which leads it to 'apply principles when it suits the interests and convenience of certain prominent members.' In 1994, Malaysia's deputy prime minister, Anwar Ibrahim, reiterated his government's view that 'many of us will not be willing to accept that these powers should continue to be Charter-privileged to intervene wherever and only when their own interpretations of peace and security warrants intervention.' Mahathir's blunt warning to those who sought a seat on the UN Security Council was that they would have to 'be interested in everything' in every part of the world.[30]

The Indonesian foreign minister, Ali Alatas, has also put the case for activism and reform, but somewhat more circumspectly. He spoke in October 1993 of a 'renewed confidence in multilateralism as a viable approach to the resolution of the crucial issues of our time' and the head of Indonesia's UN delegation suggested that the body 'should become fully effective as the central instrument for a new and revitalised international order.' Alatas also called in 1994 for the promotion of the organisation's 'transparency, legitimacy, accountability and efficiency.'[31] In contrast to the Chinese foreign minister's view of recent peacekeeping operations (PKOs), the Indonesian foreign minister, while admitting that not all such operations had been successful, stated that such efforts nevertheless had 'consistently promoted progress in negotiations between the parties in conflict'. He went on to note, apparently with approval, the expansion of PKO protective functions to include 'humanitarian aid, refugees and displaced persons, as well as assistance to countries holding elections.' President Soeharto at the 50th commemorative meeting of the UN called for a further enhancement of the organisation's capabilities 'through more effective global and regional mechanisms for peacemaking, peacekeeping and post conflict peace-building as well as preventive diplomacy'.[32]

Obviously, their respective positions in the United Nations, with China the only one of the three that is a permanent member of the Security Council, shape their attitudes towards any restructuring of the UN.[33] The Malaysian government, with no chance of a permanent seat on the Security Council, has launched the most far-reaching attack on the current structure of the organisation, calling it undemocratic and unrepresentative of the body at large. Claiming to be strongly committed to enhancing the UN capacities in preventive diplomacy, peace-keeping and peace-making, it has argued that the body as currently constituted would be unable to carry out the work load envisaged for it in Boutros-Ghali's *Agenda for Peace.* Moreover, Mahathir has gone further than this and launched a direct attack on the Security Council and on the veto: 'I don't see why the last great war should influence us forever'; and on another occasion claiming that some of the veto-power holders had now become 'second-raters'. He has also argued: 'They talk about democracy and the need for us (the Third World) to practice democracy but, on the other hand, when it comes to international democracy, there is no one country one vote, it is a question of how strong you are.' In his address to the United Nations in October 1993 and again in September 1995 he called specifically for the overthrow of the veto. Although in 1993 he acknowledged that some additional weight for the Permanent members might be acceptable, he argued that 'for each of them, alone, to be more powerful than the whole membership of the UN' was not, 'not before, not now and not for the future ... the veto must go.' Although other of Malaysia's officials tend to be less specific about the veto, stating for example that it was a 'creation of power politics of the past', and therefore had to be 'part of the total reform of the Council,' or that it should be reviewed with 'a view to its total elimination', there is little doubt that it is Kuala Lumpur that has mounted the most serious attack of the three on this particular feature of the Security Council.[34] Moreover, it is Malaysia that has sought the most significant changes with regard to the matter of representation, to include an increase in the numbers of non-permanent members of the Security Council, and the giving of permanent seats to regions, 'possibly [to be] determined by a regional mechanism.'[35] Mahathir's government thus represents an outspoken proponent of structural change.

The Indonesian position has been similar in some respects to that of Malaysia, but has also reflected its own agenda and desire to become one of the permanent members of the Security Council, although not necessarily with full veto power. President Soeharto, and his foreign minister, Ali Alatas, are on record in support of increasing the numbers of developing states sitting as permanent members of the Security Council, to be chosen from the most populous countries in Asia (India and Indonesia), Africa, and Latin America. As Ali Alatas put it in October 1994 and in almost identical vein in 1995: 'while the principle of geographic representation is important, it should not be the only criterion to determine eligibility for new permanent members. We believe that other objective criteria are equally important such as political, economic and demographic realities and a country's capability and record of contributing to the promotion of peace, security and economic development, both regionally and globally, as well as the commitment of states to assume the responsibilities inherent to such a status.' Soeharto has also argued that, while it would prove impossible to remove veto rights from the permanent 5, the use of the veto should be regulated: the five permanent members of the Security Council 'can use their vetoes, but there must be rights to counter the veto power. This means that a veto can be countered by two vetoes. Two vetoes can be countered by four vetoes and so on.' In 1995, the foreign minister put reform of this aspect of the UN less specifically, calling for a review of the veto 'with a view to mitigating its arbitrary use and to ensuring a more democratic decision-making process.' Like Malaysia, Indonesia has also called for a more equitable distribution of power within the UN among the Security Council, the General Assembly, and UN Secretary General.[36]

Unlike these two states, and because it is on the Security Council, China has been in a more exposed position in this era of an activist UN, and will be directly affected by any change in the UN structure. Beijing has stated that it supports a 'further enhancement and strengthening of the UN's constructive role in preventive diplomacy, in peace-making and peace-keeping' but, as noted earlier, Beijing's Foreign Minister has also gone on to suggest that, as the scope and frequency of UN operations increases, 'we deem it important and relevant to stress such basic principles of the Charter as respect for sovereignty and non-interference in the internal affairs of member states.'[37] China has argued for a strengthening of the 'function and role' of the General Assembly. It has also called for the Security Council to become more democratic in the sense of being more representative geographically. As its various spokespersons have put it, expansion should take into account the 'principle of equitable geographic distribution' and should 'pay attention to the fact that the overwhelming majority of the UN membership was developing countries.' But Beijing has also suggested indirectly its reluctance to see any tampering with veto power: 'no reform measures should adversely affect and weaken the role and existing viable mechanism of the council.'[38] The twin evils, from the Chinese perspective, of a revitalised UN coupled with a weakening of the veto, reinforced by Beijing's wariness about multilateral decision-making, make this an extremely uncomfortable era for China, and the UN debate a difficult issue for the PRC to finesse. It represents a considerable dilemma for a country that wants to champion Third World opinion, but also to maintain its privileged position as a (potentially) veto-wielding member of the UN.[39]

State-Centrism v Globalisation

China's position with respect to UN reform is a further reflection of its predominantly realist, state-centric view of the world. Chinese researchers and even more so its leaders generally put great emphasis on the fact that the international community is made up of sovereign states and that sovereignty remains a fundamental principle of international law. This is not to argue, however, that there have been no changes at all in China's formulations on such questions. On economic issues, for example, these ideas have been tempered to an extent. In October 1995 at the UN's 50th anniversary commemorative meeting, President Jiang Zemin argued: 'No country can afford to stand aloof from the international community and isolate itself from the global market. The internationalisation of economic life requires that all countries conduct extensive exchanges and cooperation in the economic, technological, financial, trade and other fields.'[40] There has also been some softening in China's realist approach to security, as shown by its willingness to explore cooperative security ideas; nevertheless, state-centrism still remains predominant in official formulations.[41]

Malaysian commentators, given the country's long-standing commitment to regional organisation, do not put as much emphasis as China has tended to on the state as the sole focus of activity and authority. Government statements in the early 1990s have paid increasing attention to the benefits of regional cooperation, especially those that they perceive to have derived from the establishment of ASEAN. Such statements also suggest a determination to build on that success. Additionally, there was much discussion (in light of the establishment of NAFTA and the coming into being of the Single European Act in 1992) of the necessity in the economic realm to promote 'open regionalism'.[42]

Indonesia, however, has gone further than this. Various scholars at CSIS and CIDES, particularly Jusuf Wanandi[43], but also A. Hasnan Habib, Dewi Fortuna Anwar and J. Soedjati Djiwandono, have all emphasised in their recent writings the fact of global interdependence, the globalisation of economic activities, and the greater awareness within the global community of concepts associated with freedom: the rule of law, political pluralism, and the like. For Anwar, growing interdependence has meant that world politics can no longer be seen as a zero-sum game but should be viewed as positive sum, where, with regional and international cooperation, everyone can benefit. Wanandi in a discussion in 1993 on human rights has argued that international relations based on sovereign states is undergoing fundamental change since an essential part of global activity involves relations among individuals and groups of people. States, he has noted, were being challenged by international organisations, interest groups, by the globalisation of the economy, advancement in information technology, and developments in transportation. Habib, writing in 1994, has claimed that the cold war era has given way to the 'promise of global cooperation in the maintenance of international peace and security ... pushed by the unique combination of global trends' of the last quarter century: 'economic globalisation and interdependence, economic and political integration of nations even regions, common concern about global environmental degradation and depletion of natural resources, the spread of plural democracy, the declining importance of military power and the ascend [sic] of trade and economic issues in international relations.'[44]

At a time when there is much to indicate that Djakarta remains an authoritarian state still focused on the problems of national unity and resilience, it is perhaps foolish even to hint through these quotations that a genuine and fundamental change in thinking is afoot in Indonesia. However, at a minimum we can say that, while an alteration in values may not have occurred at the highest policy making levels, such views of the world are being reflected in official government statements. As part of Soeharto's pitch at the NAM summit for moderation in the approach of the movement towards North–South relations, he dwelt on the effects of economic globalisation, and of the rapid progress of science and technology and its impact on the changing patterns of production, trade and finance. In January 1993, Foreign Minister Alatas argued in an interview that, while major power tension and competition would remain a feature of international life, old style colonial patterns of relations could be ruled out: 'increasing interdependence and integration, the technological advances that make this earth smaller and smaller, becoming one community, whether we like it or not, the globalisation of factors of production – all make for an increasing awareness of interdependence.'[45] Where Chinese leaders seem to prefer to regard interdependence as a route to obtaining greater national power,[46] Alatas's statements suggest that such a choice is no longer possible.

Some Implications

Despite the 'econophoria' that one associates with the East Asian region and with these three states in particular,[47] this examination of their perspectives on global change since the end of the cold war, incomplete as it is, conveys an underlying sense of vulnerability and unease borne out of that transition. Each has characterised the new era as one that is unstable and unpredictable. As is the case for other Third World states, the world still appears to be a hostile and insecure place. Such states are also concerned about being ignored by the West in economic terms, but pressured by it politically, demonstrating that the North–South argument of the cold war years has survived, even intensified, in the new era. And, as with those earlier years, such states see themselves as being faced with the options of resistance or adaptation. Despite their impressive economic successes of recent years, when they contemplate global developments, long shadows of doubt are cast across their apparent optimism. There is a clear sense that, although their relative power has increased since the 1980s – especially in economic terms – their ability to shape the global agenda has not increased commensurately.

There is, then, a basic level of agreement among these three countries about the nature of the post-Cold War era and their place within it – a perception that is reflected elsewhere within the developing world, and which perhaps demonstrates the psychological basis and the continuing pertinence of this particular categorisation of states. Nevertheless, the three states do divide in different ways on different, specific issues, and from these specific findings it is apparent that the unease is at its greatest in Beijing and at its lowest in Djakarta.

Indonesia and Malaysia seem to be looking to the UN as the one credible multilateral organisation to fulfil the 'promise' of the Gulf War (if one can put such an optimistic spin on it): that regional hegemons, wherever they may arise, will not be allowed to get away with threatening the weak. But to reduce its tendency towards selectivity, these two states want to make the United Nations a more democratic institution, mainly by making the UN Security Council more representative and accountable. Within the region, they wish to see the United States remain engaged – in Malaysia's case, temporarily, in Indonesia's, remaining by right as a Pacific power – and at the same time they are working to promote multilateral security cooperation in the area. To this end, they want to strengthen and remain in control of security frameworks such as the ASEAN Regional Forum. These states' greater attunement to ideas connected with 'globalisation' or at least 'regionalisation' reinforces these particular policy directions.

For Beijing, the picture is more complex than this and it is under a number of conflicting pressures. This reflects problems with its own self-identification: is it a great power, a Third World state, or something in between? With respect to the UN, it is faced with responding to some of the ideas about the restructuring of the Security Council, or having to play a more active role on behalf of developing country interests than it does at present, lest it disappoint this constituency yet again. One difficulty with being responsive to such Third World opinion is that Djakarta and Kuala Lumpur suggest they want not only a more democratic UN but a more active one, too. It will take a long time to convince China of the benefits of this given its preoccupations with matters of state sovereignty, and its concerns about humanitarian intervention especially given the possibility of domestic unrest in Tibet and Xinjiang, or elsewhere on the mainland.

With respect to the East Asian security structure that is emerging out of the ending of the cold war, China remains cautious about the benefits of multilateralism even as it recognises that it is better to be a participant in such a process than to be left outside of it. Beijing's attitude towards the US regional role seems equally ambivalent. Its own bilateral relationship with Washington has been extremely volatile in the period since 1989,[48] and there is a danger that the specific tensions between these two states will reduce Beijing's tolerance of Indonesia's and Malaysia's desire to retain a US presence in the region. On the other hand, it acknowledges the US role in sustaining regional stability, an important value given China's wish to continue with its concentration on domestic economic advancement. Overall, therefore, China emerges as a more conservative and cautious state than its Asian partners, more uncertain about the benefits of organisational reform and development, and about how to deal with the United States as a Pacific power.

There are also nuanced differences among these three states in their attitudes towards the structural changes that have occurred in the global system since 1989. China and Malaysia seem more fearful of and defiant in response to the consequences of unipolarity, the latter recommending a binding together of the weak in order to mount some resistance, the former advocating sanctuary in the five principles of peaceful coexistence. Indonesian perspectives, on the other hand, in their reiteration of the phrase 'whether we like it or not' and reference to the processes of globalisation, suggest that the confrontationist, state-based, approach is neither sensible nor in accordance with the realities of the current international order.

Clearly, then, assuming a desire for cooperative relationships among the three within both global and regional organisations, there are divisions of approach and interest that will need to be recognised and reconciled. This finding, when added to the realisation that such states are divided in many other significant ways – in cultural, political, religious and linguistic terms – underlines the value of the various dialogues at the regional level that have been initiated, both official and unofficial, as venues for the airing of perspectives and the building of confidence and understanding. When these three countries reflect on the global changes that have occurred in the post-Cold War era, they demonstrate a sense of disquiet and feelings of injustice with respect to their own positions. It will be an extraordinarily difficult project to remove the basis for those perceptions at the global level.[49] Regional developments, however, hold out the promise that such concerns and frustrations can be addressed and even alleviated.

Notes

* This chapter was first published in *Contemporary Southeast Asia* xviii/ 1 (1996) and is reproduced here with the kind permission of the publisher, Institute of Southeast Asian Studies, Singapore.

1 For a sampling of some recent publications on the Asia–Pacific see both Denny Roy, 'Assessing the Asia–Pacific "Power Vacuum"', *Survival*, xxxvii/3 (1995) and notes 1 and 2 in his article, together with the useful compilation of essays in Robert S. Ross (ed.) *East Asia in Transition: Toward a New Regional Order* (M. E. Sharpe, Armonk, N.Y., 1995).

2 John J. Mearsheimer, 'Back to the Future: Instability in Europe After the Cold War', *International Security* xv/1 (1990) and Correspondence, 'Back to the Future, Part II: International Relations Theory and Post-Cold War Europe', *International Security* xv/2 (1990). Further detail on the latter position is provided in Robert Keohane, Joseph Nye, and Stanley Hoffmann, (eds) *After the Cold War: International Institutions and State Strategies in Europe, 1989–1991,* (Harvard University Press, Cambridge, Mass., 1993). See too the continuation of the debate in *International Security* xx/1 (1995).

3 A prominent example is Barry Buzan and Gerald Segal, 'Rethinking East Asian Security' *Survival* xxxvi/2 (1994).

4 Note, however, the recent important argument advanced by Andrew MacIntyre. MacIntyre argues that in Indonesia, 'In both the economic and security policy domains we can identify active, innovative, and reasonably independent networks of intellectuals and policy research specialists linked in with particular policy factions or camps in the state elite.' See his 'Ideas and Experts: Indonesian Approaches to Economic and Security Cooperation in the Asia–Pacific Region', *The Pacific Review* viii/1 (1995) p. 160.

5 A point noted by Herman Joseph S. Kraft in 'Security Studies in ASEAN: Trends in the Post Cold War Era', in Paul M. Evans, (ed.) *Studying Asia Pacific Security: The Future of Research Training and Dialogue Activities* (University of Toronto/York University Joint Centre for Asia Pacific Studies, Canada, 1994) p. 11.

6 Kenneth N. Waltz expounds on the benefits of bipolarity in, for example, his *Theory of International Politics* (McGraw Hill, New York, 1979) especially pp. 170–6.

7 For example, see Wang Jisi, 'International Relations Theory and the Study of Chinese Foreign Policy: A Chinese Perspective', in Thomas Robinson and David Shambaugh, (eds) *Chinese Foreign Policy: Theory and Practice* (Oxford University Press, Oxford, 1994) p.491; J. Soedjati Djiwandono, 'The Security of Southeast Asia in a Changing Strategic Environment: A View from Indonesia' *Indonesian Quarterly* xix/3 (1991) p.252.

8 See for example Alatas and Mahathir's statements at the UN General Assembly, 48th session, 13th plenary session, 1 Oct. 1993; David Armstrong, 'Chinese Perspectives on the New World Order' *Journal of East Asian Affairs*

Summer/Fall 1994, no. 2, p.461; and Qian Qichen's statement at the UN in *Beijing Review* xxxvi/41 (1993).

9 *Foreign Broadcast Information Service,* reports, East Asia, (FBIS-EAS) FBIS-EAS-92-173-S, 4 September 1992, p.2. Or as Hedley Bull was to put it, one impact of the Cold War had been to constrain Western intervention in the Third World, in part because the growing Soviet capability 'facilitated Third World resistance to Western intervention' and there 'emerged a balance among the interveners which has worked to the advantage of the intervened against.' In Hedley Bull (ed.) *Intervention in World Politics,* (Clarendon Press, Oxford, 1984) pp. 135–6.

10 Noordin Sopiee, 'The New World Order: Implication for the Asia–Pacific', in Rohana Mahmood and Rustam A. Sani (eds) *Confidence Building and Conflict Reduction in the Pacific* (ISIS, Kuala Lumpur, Malaysia, 1993).

11 *Beijing Review,* xxxiv, 11–17 Oct. 1993.

12 Sopiee Noordin, 'The New World Order', p. 10.

13 For some insight into this debate see Daniel Bell, et. al. *Towards Illiberal Democracy in Pacific Asia* (Macmillan, London, in association with St. Antony's College, Oxford, 1995); Bilahari Kausikan, 'Asia's Different Standard', *Foreign Policy* lxxxii (Fall 1993).

14 UN General Assembly, 50th Session, 12th Plenary Session, 29 September 1995.

15 See Qian Qichen's statement to the UN General Assembly 49th session, 28 September 1994, quoted in *Beijing Review* xxxvii/41 (1994).

16 J. Soedjati Djiwandono, 'The Tenth Summit Meeting of the Non-Aligned Movement', *The Indonesian Quarterly* xx/4, (1992) p.368. This article reflects the tenor of President Soeharto's address to the NAM.

17 MacIntyre, 'Ideas and Experts', especially pp. 162–3.

18 Dewi Fortuna Anwar, 'Indonesia in a Changing Regional and International Environment' *The Indonesian Quarterly* xx/4 (1992), p.386; A. Hasnan Habib, 'Asia Pacific Developments in the 1990s' *The Indonesian Quarterly* xix/3 (1991) p. 258.

19 *Wen Wei Po,* 30 January 1991. For discussion of Chinese policies during the Gulf War see J. Mohan Malik, 'Peking's Response to the Gulf Crisis' *Issues and Studies* (September 1991); Hwei-ling Huo, 'Patterns of Behaviour in China's Foreign Policy: The Gulf Crisis and Beyond', *Asian Survey* xxxii/3 (1992); Yitzhak Shichor, 'China and the Gulf Crisis', *Problems of Communism*, November–December 1991.

20 Speech by the Prime Minister of Malaysia at the 27th International General Meeting of the Pacific Basin Economic Council, Kuala Lumpur, 23 May 1994. Malaysia's Defence Minister, while alluding to the concern about a power vacuum in the region that 'may be filled by countries like China or Japan', has also suggested that the armed forces of regional states should 'intensify cooperation and dialogue with each other as another confidence booster'. See FBIS–EAS–93–110, 10 June 1993, p. 1.

21 Michael Leifer, 'Chinese Economic Reform and Security Policy: The

South China Sea Connection' *Survival* xxxvii/2 (1995) p.52; MacIntyre, 'Ideas and Experts', pp. 168–9. Harry Harding discusses these regional developments in more detail in 'Cooperative Security in the Asia–Pacific Region' in Janne E. Nolan, (ed.) *Global Engagement: Cooperation and Security in the 21st Century,* (The Brookings Institution, Washington DC., 1994).

22 David Shambaugh, 'Growing Strong: China's Challenge to Asian Security', *Survival* xxxvi/2 (1994) p.51. China's aggressive behaviour towards Taiwan, especially after President Lee Teng-hui's visit to his *alma mater,* Cornell University, in June 1995 does not help its case in undermining this depiction of its intentions. China, of course, would regard the Taiwan issue as an entirely internal affair.

23 Banning Garrett and Bonnie Glaser, 'Multilateral Security in the Asia–Pacific Region and its Impact on Chinese Interests: Views from Beijing', *Contemporary Southeast Asia* xvi/1 (1994) p. 25. See also Paul Evans, 'Building Security: the Council for Security Cooperation in the Asia Pacific (CSCAP)' *Pacific Review* vii/2 (1994).

24 Shambaugh, 'Growing Strong', p. 50. See also David Shambaugh's chapter in this volume where he discusses some of the multilateral and bilateral security dialogues that have been established in the East Asian region, together with Harding, 'Cooperative Security in the Asia–Pacific Region'.

25 Adam Roberts, 'The United Nations and International Security', *Survival* xxxv/2 (1994) p.3; and Adam Roberts, 'The Crisis in UN Peacekeeping', *Survival* xxxvi/3 (1994).

26 *Beijing Review* xxxiv/3 (1991).

27 *Beijing Review* xxxvi/41 (1993). Chapter VII refers to Security Council action, including the use of force, to maintain or restore international peace and security; Chapter VI focuses on the pacific settlement of disputes.

28 FBIS-Chi-92-200, 15 October 1992. See also Qian Qichen's address on 23 September in FBIS-Chi-92-191, 1 October 1992.

29 UN General Assembly, 50th session, 8th Plenary Meeting, 27 September 1995.

30 FBIS-EAS-93-190, 4 October 1993, p.32. See also the Malaysian representative's address to the General Assembly, 48th session, 41st meeting, 28 October 1993, and Anwar Ibrahim's speech to the 49th session of the General Assembly, 5 October 1994.

31 UN General Assembly, 48th session, 13th meeting, 1 October 1993 and 52nd meeting, 28 October 1993; 49th session, 4 October 1994.

32 UN General Assembly, 50th session, 14th Plenary meeting, 2 October 1995, and 38th Plenary meeting, 23 October 1995.

33 Presumably, the fact that China alone has nuclear weapons and missiles would probably also lead to a different position between it and the other two governments on, for example, the Missile Technology Control Regime and the Comprehensive Test Ban Treaty.

34 FBIS-EAS-92-116, 16 June 1992; UN General Assembly, 48th session, 13th meeting, 1 October 1993; Anwar Ibrahim to 49th session of

UN General Assembly, 5 October 1994; UN General Assembly, 50th session, 12th Plenary meeting, 29 September 1995, and 37th Plenary meeting, 23 October 1995.

35 See UN General Assembly statements referred to in note 34.

36 FBIS-EAS-92-190, 30 Sept. 1992; Alatas's statement at the UN General Assembly 48th Session, 13th meeting, 1 October 1993, at the 49th Session, 4 October 1994, and at the 50th session, 14th Plenary meeting, 2 October 1995.

37 Qian Qichen as quoted in *Beijing Review,* xxxvi/41 (1993) p.9. See also his statement in 1994 to the UN General Assembly, in *Beijing Review* xxxvii/41 (1994).

38 FBIS-Chi-93-126, 2 July 1993 and FBIS-Chi-93-225, 24 November 1993; Qian Qichen's address to the 49th session of the UN General Assembly, 28 September 1994. During Boutros-Ghali's visit to Beijing in 1994, *Beijing Review* xxxvii/39 (1994) quoted him as stressing that 'the enlarged Security Council will play exactly the same role'.

39 For a recent analysis that refers to China's UN behaviour see Sally Morphet, 'The influence of states and groups of states on and in the Security Council and General Assembly, 1980–1994', *Review of International Studies* xxi/4 (1995).

40 Speech given 24 October 1995 and quoted in *Beijing Review* xxxviii/45 (1995) p. 21. Note, however, the use of the term 'internationalisation' rather than 'globalisation', the former of which retains the focus on the state as the primary actor in this process.

41 Rosemary Foot, 'Chinese-Indian Relations and the Process of Building Confidence: Implications for the Asia–Pacific', *Pacific Review* ix/1 (1996); Banning N. Garrett and Bonnie S. Glaser, 'Chinese Perspectives on Nuclear Arms Control', *International Security* xx/3 (1995–96); Susan Shirk, 'Chinese Views on Asia–Pacific Regional Security Cooperation' in *NBR Analysis,* v/5 (1994); Armstrong, 'Chinese Perspectives', p. 471. See also Wang, 'International Relations Theory', pp. 497–8.

42 For example, see Mahathir's speech to the Asia Society Conference on 'Asia and the Changing World Order', Tokyo, *The Star,* 14 May 1993.

43 For a helpful portrait of Wanandi see MacIntyre, 'Ideas and Experts', pp. 169–70.

44 Dewi Fortuna Anwar, 'Indonesia in a Changing Regional and International Environment' *The Indonesian Quarterly* xx/4, (1992) p.386; Jusuf Wanandi, 'Human Rights and Democracy in the ASEAN Nations: the Next 25 Years' *The Indonesian Quarterly* xxi/1 (1993) pp. 14–15; A. Hasnan Habib, 'The Post-Cold War Political-Security Landscape of the Asia Pacific Region', *The Indonesian Quarterly* xxii/1 (1994) p. 51.

45 FBIS-EAS-92-171-S, 2 September 1992; FBIS-EAS-93-009, 14 January 1993.

46 Or as Thomas Robinson has recently put it, to maximise the benefits of interdependence in resource terms, while avoiding the political, economic,

and military costs: see 'Interdependence in China's Foreign Relations', in Samuel S. Kim, (ed.) *China and the World: Chinese Foreign Relations in the Post-Cold War Era,* (Westview, Boulder, 1994) pp. 190–2.

47 The term is used in Barry Buzan and Gerald Segal 'Rethinking East Asian Security', *Survival* xxxvi/2 (1994) p. 11.

48 For a discussion of the difficulties in the bilateral relationship in the mid-1990s see David Shambaugh, 'The United States and China: A New Cold War?' *Current History* lxxxx/593 (1995).

49 For an argument outlining the need to extend democracy to the international realm, see David Held, 'Democracy: From City-States to a Cosmopolitan Order', in David Held, (ed.) *Prospects for Democracy; North, South, East, West* (Polity Press, Cambridge, 1993).

PART TWO

Democratisation and the Fate of Leftist Movements

7 ❧ International versus Domestic Pressures for Democratisation in Africa

Michael Bratton

> It was *man* who ended the Cold War in case you didn't notice. It wasn't weaponry, or technology, or armies, or campaigns. It was just *man*. Not even Western man either, as it happened, but our sworn enemy in the East, who went into the streets, faced the bullets and the batons and said: 'We've had enough'. [George Smiley in John Le Carré, *The Secret Pilgrim*.]
>
> The Clinton Administration can 'talk the talk' on African democracy as well as anyone. Will it also 'walk the walk' as African regimes back away from their democratic commitments, and as African autocrats gain leverage when conflicts erupt in countries in their region?[Richard Joseph, *Africa Demos*, 3, 3 September 1994, p. 15.]

Introduction

It has become a cliché to assert that world politics were transformed by the end of the Cold War. The collapse of the Soviet Union was accompanied by a fundamental reordering of political relationships at both the international and domestic levels. Internationally, the bipolar structure of global political conflict was superseded by a hegemonic coalition of Western powers led by the United States. With reference to domestic politics, authoritarian leaders came under pressure for political reform and many surrendered some or all of their powers to more liberal, even democratic, regimes. This chapter explores putative connections between these general changes at different levels of world politics. Has the end of superpower rivalry contributed directly to the global trend of democratisation? If the end of the Cold War has encouraged democratisation, by what mechanisms has it done so? What other factors – particularly those deriving from domestic political processes – help to explain why authoritarian regimes have collapsed so frequently in recent years?

These questions are addressed here in the context of sub-Saharan Africa between 1990 and 1994. During this period, a wave of democratisation crested in Africa. Almost all African regimes – 40 out of 47 in the sub-Saharan subcontinent – underwent a measure of political reform.[1] To be sure, by December 1994 only 16 African countries had achieved a transition to a democratic regime, defined minimally.[2] By this standard, a democratic transition requires only (a) a single election (b) that is open to all parties or candidates, (c) which is freely and fairly conducted, (d) in which the losers accept the results. Obviously, elections are not the be-all and end-all of democracy, but they do constitute an irreducible minimum for holding leaders accountable. The majority of African countries did not meet even these minimal conditions, instead experiencing transitions that were flawed (with the incumbent stealing an election) or blocked (by an intransigent dictator, a military backlash, or by civil conflict). Because of the generally problematic and incomplete nature of African regime transitions, the term democratisation is used with caution throughout the discussion.

What were the origins of these transformations? One argument is that the world-wide trend of democratisation derives from the diffusion of Western liberal values.[3] This argument locates the source of political change in Africa outside the continent and emphasises the influence of ideas exported by the victors of the Cold War. Another related argument for 'the predominance of the international context' has been made for Eastern Europe where 'the USSR's changed policy of allowing ... countries to liberalise in their own way [was] the most decisive single cause of the shift to democratisation.'[4] According to this interpretation, Gorbachev's decision to withhold military protection from discredited communist governments was a signal to opposition forces in Eastern Europe that pro-democracy movements could prevail.[5]

The case for an externally inspired process of political change might seem particularly persuasive for Africa. The rash of political openings in African countries from 1990 onwards occurred almost simultaneously, implying a common response to a single external stimulus, such as the fall of the Berlin Wall in November 1989. Moreover, African countries are among the most economically dependent in the world, with their governments relying heavily on foreign aid to underwrite public investment. Thus political developments in sub-Saharan Africa seem particularly susceptible to political pressures imposed by the international donors and creditors. In this vein, Barry Munslow contends that 'the move for democratisation is being driven primarily from outside the African continent',[6] echoing an earlier commentary that 'the principal cause of Africa's wind of change is the World Bank and the donor countries ... [who] are explicitly demanding political change as a condition for further loans to Africa.'[7]

One can challenge whether external events and pressures are so formative. After all, the 'third wave' of democratisation noted by Huntington,[8] of which the African cases represent the trailing edge, began in the mid-1970s long before an end to the Cold War and the ascendance of liberalism were anywhere in sight. Moreover, even if one accepts that recent political transitions in Africa are a response to a common external stimulus, one still has to account for the divergent political paths taken by different African countries.[9] Indeed, the consensus in the theoretical literature on regime transitions is that 'the immediate prospects for political democracy are largely to be explained in terms of national forces and calculations.'[10]

In other words, a country's political development derives from the evolution of domestic political forces in its particular state and society. Even the most dependent regimes have their own distinctive institutional structures and political histories which propel regime change from within. Thus, the rise of pro-democracy movements in Africa can be explained in terms of internal trends such as the failure of one-party and military regimes to deliver economic benefits and the rising frustrations of newly educated groups at declining living standards within African civil societies. Because the independence generation of leaders was incapable of halting economic decline and unwilling to surrender political power, ordinary Africans decided that they had to be removed. In this vein, Jean-François Bayart has commented that, 'external dynamics played an essentially secondary role in the collapse of authoritarian regimes ... Demands for democracy in Africa are not exceptional and, just as with the logic of authoritarianism, they are grounded in their own historicity.'[11]

The thesis of this chapter is that recent efforts to install democracy in African countries can best be explained by the convergence and interaction of international and domestic factors.[12] On one hand, one cannot account for the extent or timing of the second wind of change in African politics without reference to the withdrawal of superpowers from involvement in African regional conflicts or the realignment of their foreign policies away from Cold War strategic considerations. The main effect of the end of superpower rivalry in Africa has been to reduce and reallocate sources of external economic and political support for authoritarian regimes. No longer is it possible for African dictators to play one superpower off against another solely on the basis of professed affinity to Marxism–Leninism or anti-communism.

But the impact of changing international conditions is mediated through domestic state–society relations. Withdrawal of international political validation and economic wherewithal from an extant regime shifts the balance of power between state and civil society. The end of the Cold War has created new constraints for political incumbents and fresh opportunities for opposition social movements. Whether democratisation subsequently unfolds, however, depends on whether domestic political actors are able to adapt to, and make the most of, the resources that changed circumstances put at their disposal. As Keohane and colleagues suggest, 'when the structure of politics – that is, the resources available to actors and therefore their capacity to exercise influence – is transformed, state strategies and the characteristics of institutions can be expected to change as well.'[13] With reference to civil society, Spalding has suggested that we should probe 'the conditions under which protest movements might succeed', especially 'the openness of the political opportunity structure and the organisational resources available.'[14]

Thus, transformations in the international political environment alone are insufficient to account for actual regime changes on the ground. At best, the end of Cold War helped to precipitate political openings and weaken authoritarian regimes in Africa at the end of the 1980s. The end of superpower rivalry provided the occasion – but not the basic cause – for long-dormant political energies to bubble to the surface after a prolonged period of repression. A complete analysis of political transitions in Africa requires an account of the wills, actions and capacities of state elites and social movements at the country level. The behaviour of these domestic actors is more fundamental than a changing international context in determining the onset, dynamics, and outcomes of political transitions.

This argument is developed in three steps. First, the chapter reviews changes in the foreign policies of the major powers towards Africa with particular reference to the promotion of democracy as a policy goal, noting instances in which political conditionalities attached to foreign aid appear to have moved the democratisation process forward in selected African countries. The chapter then changes tack in an effort to demonstrate the relatively limited effect of these international pressures. Evidence is presented that the foreign policies of external actors – especially the former colonial powers – display at least as much continuity as change, in some cases favouring political stability over the full flowering of African democracy movements. Finally, the paper seeks to show that international pressures are best understood in terms of their interactions with domestic political factors such as the presence and timing of mass protest and the relative resourcefulness of state and social actors.

International Pressures for Democratisation

Africans experienced the end of the Cold War principally through shifts in the foreign policies of the major world powers.[15] By the late 1980s, foreign policy makers in Washington and Moscow abandoned the notion of African states as geostrategic outposts in a global struggle between communism and capitalism. Indeed, the Soviet Union faded from the scene as a contender for a sphere of influence within Africa. In response, the Western powers found it possible to emphasise more idealistic foreign policy goals – including preferred democratic values – in appraising existing and prospective African involvements. As will be shown, the emerging approaches of the major world powers were not always consistent, and different Western countries pursued divergent policies. But, as the major foreign policy legacy of the cessation of superpower rivalry, the declining salience of geostrategic competition had profound implications for Africa.

While the Soviet Union gained considerable access to independent Africa, it achieved little success in reaching its objectives of building socialism and blocking Western encroachment.[16] In the 1960s, the Soviets discovered that weak African governments made unreliable Cold War allies, as indicated by the military ouster of socialist-leaning leaders such as Ahmed Ben Bella in Algeria, Kwame Nkrumah in Ghana, and Modibo Keita in Mali. Even so, the Brezhnev administration became deeply involved in intractable regional conflicts,

for example helping to consolidate MPLA rule in Angola and assisting Mengistu Haile Meriam of Ethiopia to suppress
Because the Soviet clients in Africa were some of the most impoverished countries in the world, they failed not only to pay for arms shipments, but also to demonstrate the viability of socialism as a model of development. As such, debates began within the Soviet foreign policy establishment about the high costs of, and meagre returns from, African ties. Scepticism about the prospects for socialist transformation in Africa was reflected in Moscow's advice to countries like Benin, Congo and Mozambique to seek development assistance from the West.[17] After a quarter century of growing economic and especially military commitments to struggling client states in Africa, conditions were ripe for a change of Soviet policy.

Thus, Soviet disengagement from Africa began well before the break-up of the Soviet Union in December 1991.[18] Especially after 1985, under the reformist influence of Mikhail Gorbachev's 'new thinking', Soviet foreign policy came to stress the re-establishment of good relations with the West. The revival of détente required mediation and settlement of nettlesome and expensive regional conflicts in Africa.[19] Landmark events followed in quick succession which together signified a Soviet withdrawal from the continent. On December 22, 1988 – the date which probably marks the end of the Cold War in Africa – the Soviets and Americans brokered a tripartite agreement between Angola, Cuba and South Africa to permit the independence of Namibia in return for the extraction of Cuban troops from Angola. The Soviets subsequently advised Mengistu that Ethiopia would receive no further arms shipments. Indeed, by March 1990, Moscow revealed a pragmatic new policy of contact with richer African countries like South Africa. The subsequent dissolution of the Soviet Union in December 1991 and the preoccupation of the Soviet successor states with their own internal travails, ensured that 'Moscow's venture into the African interior [would] not be resumed.'[20] In the 1960s and 1970s, the United States sought to counter what were perceived as strategic gains by the enemy, especially in the Horn of Africa. By the early 1980s, the Reagan Doctrine called for aid to guerrillas fighting against Soviet-backed governments, notably for UNITA in Angola. The lion's share of US assistance went to egregiously dictatorial regimes: the six largest African recipients of official development assistance were all rated 'not free' by Freedom House.[21] But by mid-decade, responding to signals that the Soviets were gradually pulling back and acknowledging that neither superpower would benefit from further competition, the US also adjusted its Africa policy. US military assistance to Africa was reduced significantly after 1985, including to client governments in Kenya, Somalia and Sudan. In 1986, the US Congress grasped control of a key aspect of Africa policy by passing the Comprehensive Anti-Apartheid Act which imposed economic sanctions on South Africa over an attempted presidential veto. Thereafter, the United States openly urged the South African government and African National Congress to seek a negotiated escape from apartheid, a task that was facilitated by withdrawal of Soviet military assistance to the ANC's armed wing.

The end of the Cold War marked two departures in US foreign policy in Africa. First, having concluded that the Soviets were no longer poised to take advantage of political turmoil overseas, the United States itself began to disengage. In particular, Washington 'lost the urge to intervene in African conflicts.'[22] For example, the Bush administration passively observed the armed overthrow of heads of state in Liberia, Chad and Somalia, all former allies. Even when military intervention was ordered, as by Bush in Somalia in 1992 and by Clinton in Rwanda in 1994, the US president justified the measure as a non-combatant action to deliver humanitarian relief. Such detached neutrality from internal conflicts would have been unthinkable at the height of the superpower rivalry. At the same time, the US reduced its permanent presence through triage: it decided to concentrate aid on approximately 17 countries undertaking simultaneous political and market reforms,[23] closed nine aid missions,[24] and put the remaining countries on an intermediate 'watch' list. US aid personnel were redirected from Africa to new priority assignments in Eastern Europe and the former Soviet Union.[25]

Second, the end of the Cold War provided an opportunity for Americans to indulge a moralistic streak in their national temperament by embarking on a crusade to promote democracy. Echoing a theme that has informed American diplomacy since Woodrow Wilson's time,[26] US Secretary of State James Baker declared in February 1990 that 'our first and pre-eminent challenge is consolidating democracy.'[27] Later that same year the US Agency for International Development announced its Democracy Initiative;[28] henceforth, eligibility for American economic assistance would require recipient governments to demonstrate adherence to human rights and progress toward democracy. The goal of US development assistance was 'sustainable development', defined to include the 'strategic objective' of democratisation: projects would be designed to establish 'democratic institutions, a vibrant civic society, and a relationship between state and society that encourages pluralism, inclusion, and peaceful conflict resolution.'[29] By 1994, the USAID Administrator[30] had created a Center for Democracy and appointed advisors to spawn programmes to strengthen democratic institutions in Ethiopia, Kenya, Mozambique, South Africa, Uganda and Zambia.[31]

These two strands of the new US Africa policy may well have been connected. Because both superpowers always accorded Africa a low priority in foreign policy, the US may simply have been awaiting a pretext to withdraw from its commitments on the continent. If so, the claim that in future the US will only support democratic regimes provided a morally comfortable rationale for a basically self-interested policy to abandon the continent and leave Africans to their own devices.

Africa retains a much higher priority in the foreign policies of the former colonial powers. France has maintained particularly intimate relations with erstwhile colonies in Africa as a means of projecting France's prestige in the world.[32] During the Cold War, France's practices in its '*chasse gardée*' went unchallenged by the outside world. Washington perceived West and Central Africa as a diplomatic backwater and was content to allow Paris to retain its supremacy, thus keeping the region out of Soviet hands.[33] For half a century, the special relationship between France and Africa was cemented by the CFA franc zone, which guaranteed a fixed value and free convertibility for the currencies of 14 African member states, and which granted Paris extensive influence over African economic affairs. Where political stability unravelled – as in Chad, Djibouti and the Central African Republic – French legionnaires were dispatched to restore order.

France's Africa policy in the early 1990s was marked by a reduction in the personal oversight of the French president[34] and the increasing influence of technocratic considerations.[35] These changes arose less from the end of the Cold War than from leadership turnover in Paris and the growing costs of maintaining a quasi-empire. Reformers in the Ministries of Foreign Affairs, Development Cooperation, and Defence warned against open-ended policies of bailing out discredited

African leaders, inaugurating a policy of *les ouvertures* which was endorsed publicly by President François Mitterrand at the June Franco–African summit at La Baule. 'From now on,' he declared, 'France will link its aid to the efforts of those heading toward more freedom.'[36] The current French approach was cautious and moderate, proffering support to established African heads of state, while at the same time urging the delegation of authority to competent technocrats and a gradual opening of the political process to opponents. 'The idea', according to one commentary 'is to usher in multi-party politics and inspire cleaner government without provoking revolution.'[37]

The policies of other Western powers moved in tandem. British Foreign Secretary Douglas Hurd declared that 'poverty does not justify torture, tyranny, or economic incompetence'[38] and that overseas development assistance would favour countries tending towards pluralism. The European Union agreed to insert human rights clauses in cooperation agreements and, by April 1991, Japan followed suit. As early as 1989 the World Bank had acknowledged that the performance of its economic development projects required improved political accountability and sounder public management.[39] And Western-based private, non-governmental organisations helped to build sources of power in African societies that could serve as counterweights to the state.

In sum, the end of the Cold War provided an opportunity for Western leaders and institutions to distance themselves from dictatorial governments and exercise preferences for democratisation. A consensus evolved among donor agencies on a new agenda of increased attention to political reforms as a core dimension of international development.[40]

How are such international preferences implemented? Because the metropolitan powers relate to African governments principally as donors of concessional assistance, foreign aid has become the main mechanism for disseminating the gospel of democracy and good governance. Western donors now openly grant and withhold military and economic assistance as means to support, persuade – and often to pressure – African governments to introduce political reforms.

The biggest policy change, with the most profound results, was the withdrawal of superpower military assistance to former client states and movements. Drastic declines in Soviet and American military assistance to Africa clearly contributed to the overthrow of several entrenched African leaders. Soviet military cutbacks – along with failing domestic political control resulting in Soviet weapons making their way into opposition hands – contributed to the collapse of the Ethiopian army, the fall of Addis Ababa to guerrillas, and Mengistu's flight from the country in 1991. During the same period, Siad Barré's grip on Somalia was significantly weakened by a progressive reduction of US military assistance, which in turn contributed to his being driven out by rival faction leaders. The departure of some 60,000 Soviet and Eastern European 'technical-economic cooperants' from Africa undermined state capacity, particularly with regard to internal security, in a range of left-leaning African countries from Ghana to Zimbabwe.[41]

At the same time, Paris signalled that so-called mutual defence treaties with African states would no longer be activated to dispatch French paratroopers to protect autocrats against political opponents. Significantly, the French government informed Felix Houphouet-Boigny, its key African ally, that he could no longer count on French military reinforcements to contain domestic unrest, a factor that apparently entered into his decision to hold snap elections in November 1990. In Chad in November 1990, France denied incumbent president Hissan Habré's request for a military rescue mission to repel the insurgent forces of Idriss Deby; France initially provided an air defence force to his successor government but, by mid-1992, began to move away again when Deby arrested opponents and failed to honour promises of political reform. And when military strongman Kolingba of the Central African Republic tried for a second time in August 1993 to annul elections which he had lost, the French threatened to cut off his military lifeline unless he surrendered power.

Donors also introduced political conditionality on aid allocations, whereby recipient countries had to demonstrate progress on human rights, governance, and democracy.[42] The US government was most publicly vociferous in stating political conditions (followed by the Germans and the Scandinavians) with the former colonial powers and the international financial institutions opting for more muted approaches. US ambassadors Smith Hempstone in Kenya and Frances Cook in Cameroon publicly condemned governments for restricting basic freedoms and avoiding genuine elections. The US House of Representatives amended aid bills to require respect for human rights abuses and the conduct of free and fair elections. This resulted in substantial new aid infusions to fledgling democracies like Zambia and Benin and radical reductions to countries like Liberia and Nigeria where democratisation was precluded or stalled.

In order to encourage political change, the Western donors promoted multiparty elections. Major international entities – notably the United Nations, the Commonwealth, the United States and the Scandinavian governments – joined in consortia to deliver electoral assistance.[43] Support was provided to induce electoral law reform, to train and equip electoral offices, and to sponsor delegations of election observers. The French limited their involvement to electoral administration in selected francophone countries, for example providing computers to the Ministry of the Interior for voter registration in Niger and military air transport to ferry ballot boxes in CAR. In the poorest and most strife-torn locations – like Angola, Ethiopia, Mozambique and the Sahelian states – international actors carried such a large portion of the financial burden that elections could not have been mounted without external support. One cost of donor-driven elections in Africa was that the level of political commitment from the incumbent regime of the host country was limited or unknown.[44]

Where carrots failed to induce democratisation, donors occasionally resorted to sticks. Temporary suspensions on aid disbursements[45] were actually used quite sparingly in Africa, the two prominent examples being Kenya in November 1991 and Malawi in May 1992. A consortium of Western donors, acting through the World Bank-chaired Consultative Group, suspended quick-disbursing programme aid to these countries in order to urge governments to reduce repression and legitimate their rule.[46] Shortly thereafter, Daniel Arap Moi agreed to hold competitive elections (December 1991) and Hastings Banda announced a referendum on multiparty democracy (October 1992). In these instances, an international ultimatum clearly contributed to hastening political opening.

In West Africa, the French government was less overt in the use of political conditionality but quietly ended the long-standing practice of balancing annual budgets of several non-democratic client states. For example, the French backed up their demands for political opening in Benin by withholding funds for government salaries.[47] Denied Soviet support since the mid-1980s, Benin's treasury was bankrupt by the end of the decade, forcing President Matthieu Kérékou to tour

Europe in 1986 and eject Libyan diplomats from Cotonou in 1988 efforts to win Western backing. When these stop-gap measures were exhausted, he renounced Marxism–Leninism as Benin's state ideology in December 1989 and agreed to convene a national conference to revise Benin's constitution in February 1990. Only then did the French government release funds to pay salaries to civil servants.

Where human rights abuses were particularly egregious, Western aid agencies pulled out entirely, at least for a while. Take the example of Zaire. By 1991, following a massacre of university students and military riots, Zaire's 'big three' donors (Belgium, France, and the United States) withdrew ambassadors and aid representatives and sharply cut support. At Congressional initiative, the US eliminated all military and economic assistance to the government and announced that henceforth humanitarian assistance would be funnelled only through non-governmental organisations. In 1990, the IMF and World Bank decided to reduce their presence to a minimal core programme and in 1993, dropped Zaire completely. Similarly, in Sudan, Western donors eliminated all multilateral loans and government-to-government aid when the Islamic regime of Mohammed al-Bashir stepped up its military campaign to prosecute the civil war against non-Muslims in the South. In 1993, the US blacklisted Sudan as a terrorist nation on evidence that it was allowing Iranian-based guerrilla groups to organise on its soil.

For the moment, let us summarise the effects of international pressures for political reform in Africa in the 1990s. The withdrawal of superpower military assistance undermined the viability of authoritarian regimes that depended on outside military aid and contributed to the demise of some of their strongmen. The announcements by Western financiers that economic assistance would flow mainly to political reformers weakened other national leaders of indebted or aid-dependent countries, shaking their confidence and ability to govern. But, the Western powers rarely went so far as to cut off current financial flows to African regimes. And, as we shall see below, even where they did so, the results were mixed.

Countervailing Interests: Effects on Democratisation

Just how committed is the international community to genuine democratisation in Africa? This section of the chapter argues that, because the Western powers pursue numerous and sometimes conflicting goals in Africa, they are regularly led to maintain support for some less-than-democratic regimes. Indeed, the West is primarily interested in an orderly and stable world in the aftermath of the Cold War and will pursue democratisation only to the extent that it contributes to this larger strategic objective.[48] Nelson and Eglinton have noted that 'human rights ... are often subordinated to other foreign policy concerns'[49] and that 'donors are reluctant to invoke or sustain sanctions against large and important nations.'[50] These arguments are confirmed with recent evidence from Africa where Western security and economic interests have sometimes contributed more to political continuity than to regime change.

Most African countries have completed some sort of political transition. With the denouement of democratic struggles in key countries – especially the annulled election in Nigeria in June 1993 and the peaceful transfer of power in South Africa in April 1994 – the current wave of political transitions in Africa is essentially over. Moreover, just as opposition movements within Africa were inspired by the success of pro-democracy compatriots in neighbouring countries, so African strongmen have learned from one another. The most skilful leaders have discovered ways to control the process of competitive elections so that they can win a grudging stamp of approval from Western donors but still hang on to political power. With few remaining prospects for further dramatic democratic changes in Africa, Westerners and Africans alike are turning attention from regime transition to regime consolidation. Rather than pressing for new political openings, democratic reformers now aim to sustain and institutionalise fragile gains and to maintain political order. Because the next steps in democratic institution-building appear uncertain and arduous, the reach of reformers is now tempered with realism.

The occurrence of violent ethnic conflicts and the collapse of states in places such as Liberia, Rwanda and Somalia have helped to push considerations of political stability to the fore. Some African conflicts – Angola, Mozambique, Somalia – are legacies of Cold War antagonisms where the West bears direct responsibility for finding solutions. Wherever the West risks being drawn into regional conflicts in Africa, the US and French governments especially have become preoccupied with preventative measures. The Clinton administration has always listed conflict management as a major goal of Africa policy[51] and much the same can be said for the policies of France and Britain.[52]

In practice, Western policies toward Africa since the Cold War have been highly improvisational, reactive, and influenced by media coverage of crisis events. Since the mass refugee exodus from Rwanda in mid-1994, foreign policy officials have elevated conflict prevention above all other goals.[53] The political crises in Somalia and Rwanda created complex military entanglements and expensive humanitarian crises that were not immediately resolvable by efforts at 'nation-building' (Somalia) or democratisation (Rwanda).[54] Elsewhere, Western efforts to use elections as a means of ending civil wars failed patently in Liberia and Angola. Hence the Western powers began to downgrade democratisation in favour of alternate approaches, for example seeking to forestall the spread of civil conflicts and the collapse of states, especially within large and populous countries like Zaire and Nigeria. A concern for political stability necessarily pulls the Western powers into closer engagement with existing regimes and extend credibility to incumbent political leaders.

Other national security objectives potentially contradict the Western goal of democratisation in Africa:[55] these include the control of immigration, the prevention of terrorism, and the containment of militant Islam.[56] The case of Algeria provides clear evidence of the willingness of the Western powers to subordinate democratisation to the goal of stabilising incumbent regimes against this range of perceived threats. In December 1991, the Algerian military cancelled elections and seized power after the Islamic Salvation Front won a first round of multiparty elections and were poised to take control of the national government in a second round. Led by France, the West has since underwritten the military-backed government of Lamine Zeroual by pledging aid, securing debt rescheduling, and mobilising bank loans.[57] The principal motivation for the European Community's redirected Mediterranean policy is apparently to prevent conditions 'which could provoke new waves of immigration and even the emergence of another maverick regime to join Libya in the Southern Mediterranean.'[58] Western perceptions of an 'Islamic threat' are more pertinent to North Africa than to sub-Saharan Africa, though the Western diplomatic isolation of Sudan is evidence that such considerations are affecting policies further south. It seems likely, for instance, that the EPRDF government in Ethiopia garners more US support than its democratic credentials alone would allow because of Meles Zenawi's posture as an orderly buffer against Sudan's aspirations to promote Islamic revolution in the region. Thus the Western powers are being tempted once again to define international relations in terms of a global ideological struggle in which client states are valued more because they are stable than because they are democratic.

In addition to these security and strategic considerations, the former colonial powers continue to possess economic and commercial interests in Africa. The French business community retains significant trade and investment ties with former colonies (especially Cote d'Ivoire and Cameroon), as do the British (for example in Kenya, Zimbabwe, and South Africa). Even the United States – which is commonly held to have no significant economic interests in Africa[59] – wishes to retain access to oil supplies from Nigeria and neighbouring states.[60] The low sulphur, 'sweet' grades of crude oil found on Africa's west-central coasts are particularly attractive to industrial countries that have enacted environmental restrictions on automobile emissions. Thus, 'securing oil and gas concessions in Africa is a dominant policy imperative at a time when in almost all other respects Western interest in the continent is static or declining.'[61]

These types of commercial considerations have motivated France to continue cultivating friendly relations with the long-standing single party regimes of Biya in Cameroon and Bongo in Gabon and have inhibited the United States from enacting oil sanctions against the military dictatorship of Sani Abacha in Nigeria. Notably, all the largest African oil producers – Angola, Nigeria, Gabon, Congo and Cameroon – face long-standing political crises culminating in recent failed or flawed attempts at democratic transition. In part this reflects the general problem of democratisation in rentier states where overwhelming resources are concentrated in the hands of centralised regimes that can be used to buy off both internal and external pressures. While it may be true that oil supplies are accessible to the West regardless of the nature of the incumbent regime, oil supplies would certainly be threatened if such states were allowed to collapse.

Thus, economic interests give rise to security concerns. Because the Western industrial countries lack energy security, they remain interested in friendly relations with nations in the Horn of Africa that are proximate to Persian Gulf oil fields and oil shipping lanes. In order to protect these assets, the US and its allies wish to retain access rights to ports, airfields and other military facilities. The reliance of Western governments on strategic installations in north-east Africa during the Persian Gulf War of 1991 may have had a moderating influence on Western demands for political liberalisation in Kenya and Ethiopia. Moreover, other Western national security concerns are becoming relevant for Africa such as the interdiction of narcotics, for instance via South Africa, Nigeria and Zambia. The official reason for the US decision to suspend aid to Nigeria in July 1993 was the government's failure to control drug rings, rather than its poor performance at democratisation. The US also withheld new aid commitments to the newly elected government in Zambia for several months in early 1993 until President Chiluba dismissed cabinet ministers suspected of drug trafficking. Thereafter, the US signalled that security considerations remained important in its Zambia policy, by withholding praise from Chiluba as a model democratic reformer.[62]

France especially among the Western powers has opted for the *status quo*. Even at La Baule, Mitterrand announced that France would not insist on formal political conditions for aid, instead encouraging each African country to find its 'own route to democracy'. Since that time, the French government has endorsed flawed election victories by incumbent political leaders in Cameroon, Togo, and Gabon, even though each had campaigned violently. And, notwithstanding military aid cutbacks, French troops continued to underpin unpopular regimes, for example by training soldiers of the Juvenal Habyarimana government in Rwanda – possibly even the notorious Hutu militias (*khmer noir*) – until shortly before their genocidal killing spree of 1994.

For its part, the United States has not broken completely with its Cold War alignments, continuing to associate pragmatically with President Mobutu Sese Seko of Zaire.[63] Installed and protected with support from the CIA, Mobutu has been one of the more durable aspects of US policy in Africa, especially as a conduit to anti-communist rebels in the Angolan civil war. His announcement of political reforms in April 1990 convinced no-one that he was a born-again democrat, but his dire warnings – '*après moi, le déluge*^' – seem to have resonated among donors. While the Clinton Administration announced support for the transition programme of the national conference of popular forces in Zaire, it allows that Mobutu has a temporary role to play as a force for stability by exercising a modicum of control over the armed forces. Despite Mobutu's presence as the single greatest obstacle to democratisation in Zaire, the Western powers have been unwilling and unable to force him to leave.[64]

The British commitment to democratisation has been modest and selective at best. British aid has been directed at the technical aspects of improved governance rather than the more overtly democratic prerequisites of civil and political rights. A landmark speech by Minister of Overseas Development Lynda Chalker in June 1991 was criticised by African political activists for failing to insist that African governments embrace multiparty political competition.[65] And like France, Britain has maintained close ties with important former colonial countries, such as Ghana and Uganda that have demonstrated commitment to orthodox economic adjustment reforms. The gradual political transitions initiated by military leaders in these countries – a tightly managed return to civilian rule in Ghana and 'no party' elections in Uganda – fall well short of a transition to democracy.

Throughout the 1990s, the World Bank and International Monetary Fund have also voiced political pragmatism. Despite rhetorical commitment to good governance, these agencies in practice have continued to extend credits to any government that adopts an approved economic stabilisation or adjustment programme and makes adequate progress toward meeting programme targets. During the early 1990s, countries like Chad, Guinea, Mauritania, Sierra Leone and Togo were rewarded financially for having adjustment programmes in place, despite scant progress on democratisation.[66] In some cases, compliance with economic adjustment conditions is used by skilled leaders to purchase protection against donor demands for political reform.[67]

Moreover, Western donors are already relaxing political conditions for less-than-democratic regimes in economically or strategically important African countries. Aid cuts have been restored even though political conditions have not been fully met. For example, in Kenya in April 1993, the World Bank and IMF agreed to resume its suspended aid programme, notwithstanding negative assessments by observer delegations about the conduct of the December 1992 elections.[68] Similarly, following the disputed October 1992 election in Cameroon, the French government bailed out the Biya government on debt arrears and increased aid contributions to the point that Cameroon became one of France's largest African aid recipients in Africa. Even in Zaire, Western donors began to coalesce around the technocratic government of the Mobutu-appointed prime minister, Kengo wa Dondo in 1994; France promised aid and Belgium assisted in reopening negotiations with the IMF. This major softening of Western policy toward Zaire – which extended Mobutu's lease on political life – was apparently motivated by strategic considerations: the new regime provided international access to manage the Rwanda refugee crisis.[69]

By way of concluding this section, let us note briefly several other factors that blunt the impact of democracy promotion by outsiders in Africa. The first is resource constraints. With the exception of Japan, all Western donors anticipate major cuts in development assistance to Africa for the remainder of the decade.[70] While the US protected USAID's Development Fund for Africa from nominal depletion in the 1990s, it is now outspent in Africa by Japan, Germany and Italy.[71] Thus individual donors possess limited leverage to attain democratisation objectives; increasingly they rely on indirect influence through donor consortia and multilateral channels, approaches which tend to dilute political conditionality. Moreover, given declining aid levels, donors have fewer opportunities to reward fragile new democracies with new resource flows than to punish authoritarian regimes with cutbacks. As a result, Africa's leaders have recognised that there could be little payoff for engaging in risky political reforms.

Second, bureaucratic obstacles within the foreign policy establishments of Western countries have forestalled a full commitment to democratisation. Generally speaking, the agencies responsible for diplomatic representation (State Department, Foreign Office, Quai d'Orsay) have promoted democracy against scepticism from the agency responsible for foreign assistance. Diplomats have asserted their prerogative to take the lead on political affairs, whereas aid officials are often professionally and personally unsympathetic to assistance programmes aimed at political objectives. Moreover, both embassies and aid agencies lack knowledge and experience in designing and managing projects to strengthen democratic institutions. And donors have sometimes found democracy programmes blocked by their own public laws and regulations.[72]

Finally, despite apparent policy consensus, Western countries increasingly disagree with one another about whether, where and how to promote democracy in Africa. Put bluntly, the Europeans regard the pro-democracy proclamations of the Americans as hopelessly naive, and the Americans suspect that European support for old-guard African leaders is cynically motivated by commercial self-interest. Moreover, the French government jealously guards its special relationship with francophone states, perceiving rivalry in the pro-democracy initiatives of Americans or Northern Europeans. Take relations with Cameroon, for example, around the time of the October 1992 election: whereas France refused to send election observers and sided with incumbent president Paul Biya after his questionable victory, the US and Germany issued statements critical of election irregularities, downgraded diplomatic representation, and cut back on aid.[73] US and French policies also split over Algeria; by 1994, the Clinton administration regarded an Islamic take-over in Algiers as virtually inevitable and opened contacts with moderate groups in society in an effort to avoid the opprobrium earned by the US after the Islamic victory in Iran. And the French policy of backing the Habyarimana government in Rwanda appears to have been motivated at least in part by an unwillingness to concede territory to a guerrilla movement (the Rwanda Patriotic Front) based out of a country (Uganda) that was perceived in Paris to be backed by 'Anglo-Saxon' interests.

Thus the end of the Cold War revealed long-standing rivalries in Africa among the Western allies, especially the former colonisers, that had been papered over by the Soviet threat. These differences are accentuated by real clashes of economic interest, for example among French, British and American energy companies that seek to exploit oil and natural gas reserves in the West African coastal zone.[74] Precisely because security concerns and economic imperatives intrude on foreign policy, the Western commitment to democratisation in Africa has been half-hearted. The policies of the former colonial powers have only been consistent in a concern for political stability. Even where policy has changed, resource and bureaucratic constraints limit real impact. These considerations have constrained Western support for democratic reformers in Africa and provided incumbent leaders with breathing space. Those leaders who survived the political transitions of the early 1990s can now anticipate reincorporation into Western circuits.

Interactions with Domestic Political Pressure

Because international pressure is ambiguous, attention must be paid to domestic considerations in explaining political change in Africa. What is the political impact of the popular groundswell against autocratic rule in so many African countries? How does the strength of incumbent regimes affect opposition prospects? Beyond assessing the independent influence of domestic political initiatives, one would wish to know how they interact with donor demands. Have donor aid flows influenced the relative strengths of incumbent and opposition forces? And have international pressures ever actually changed the outcomes of regime transitions?

The argument in this section is that international donor pressures have generally played a subordinate role in political change in Africa. The process of political reform there has been driven principally from within; it takes the form of an internal struggle between incumbent political leaders and opposition social movements. Domestic political dynamics take primacy both for reasons of proximate causality – transitions occur even when international pressures are absent – and for reasons of timing – international pressures are usually introduced during the late stages of already well-advanced transition processes. Moreover, considerations of political leverage apply. In poor countries, the resources that donors bring to bear may be sufficient to change the existing balance of power between contending forces in state and society; in richer countries, however, domestic political actors may be sufficiently resourceful to resist donor requirements. These propositions are explored against recent African evidence below.

Political transitions in African countries commonly began with spontaneous popular protests.[75] Of the 40 countries in sub-Saharan Africa that undertook political reforms in the first five years of the 1990s, a majority of 28 involved protests. In some countries (such as Madagascar, Mali and Zambia) protesters filled the streets of the capital city with mass marches and rallies; in other countries (such as Cameroon, Gabon and Nigeria) they chose the weapon of the general strike, which paralysed commerce and administration and created deserted *villes mortes* (ghost towns).

Do popular political protests lead to democratic transitions in Africa? What about the effects on democratisation of donor political conditions? Do domestic and international pressures combine to jointly bring about democratic outcomes? To address these questions, a simple empirical analysis is presented in Table 1. The reader is reminded that a minimalist definition is used to denote a democratic transition based on a single free election whose outcome participants accept. A flawed transition refers to a situation in which an election is held but either election observers deem it unfair (Cameroon, Ghana, Kenya) or the

Table 1: Democratic Transitions in Africa:Interaction of International and Domestic Pressures (November 1989–December 1994)

Pressure		Transition Outcome				Examples
International[1]	Domestic[2]	Blocked	Flawed	Democratic*	Incomplete	
Yes	Yes	4	5	6	0	Benin, CAR, Madagascar, Malawi, Namibia, S. Africa
Yes	No	6	0	2	2	Mozambique, Seychelles
No	Yes	0	6	5	2	Congo, Guinea–Bissau, Mali, Niger, Zambia
No	No	1	0	3	0	CapeVerde, Lesotho, São Tomé and Principé
Totals		11	11	16	4	

losers refuse to accept the results (e.g. Chad, Comoros, Equatorial Guinea, Gabon, Guinea, and Mauritania), or both. A blocked transition refers to a situation in which political reform is either precluded by civil conflict (e.g. Liberia Sudan, Djibouti) or the political elite uses repression to shut down the process of political change (e.g. Nigeria, Togo, Zaire).

The findings are as follows. Democratic transitions in Africa are associated with the presence of domestic pressures for political reform. Of the 16 cases of transition to democratic regimes in the sub-Saharan region between November 1989 and September 1994, 11 (i.e. 69 per cent) occurred in the presence of popular protest. This does not mean to say that mass political action always led to democratic outcomes; indeed, popular protest in the African cases was even more strongly associated (11 out of 11 cases) with political transitions that involved flawed elections. Nevertheless, mass action by Africans always resulted in at least a measure of political change away from the authoritarian status quo. And when domestic political protest was the sole initiative for reform, the transition was never blocked. In other words, even if domestic demands for political reform were diverted down a path of flawed transition, they still resulted in the liberalisation of autocratic regimes.

International pressures, conceived as the presence of explicit political conditions for development assistance, occurred in more than half the cases under review (25 out of 42). But political conditionality appears to have a much less positive effect on democratisation than did political protest. Of the 16 cases of democratic transition in the sample, only 8 (i.e. 50 per cent) occurred in the presence of international pressure. Strikingly, six of these eight cases were instances in which international pressure occurred in combination with domestic pressure. To put it differently, donor political conditionality appears to have been the sole effective agency of democratisation in only two cases: Mozambique and the Seychelles. Indeed, the efforts of donors to induce political reform were often counterproductive, accounting for 10 out of 11 (91 per cent) of the blocked transitions in the sample.

Thus international pressure for democratisation is a double-edged sword. Because the power relationship between donors and the leaders of resource-poor African states is asymmetrical, donors can enforce acceptance of political conditions. But the level of commitment of leaders to democratisation will be dubious under these circumstances.

Moreover, perhaps because political conditionality infringes on national sovereignty, it can apparently lead resistant or resourceful African leaders to dig in their heels, resist reform, and even intensify repression.

In sum, democratisation is by no means guaranteed in Africa; as of 1994 political transitions were more likely to be blocked, flawed or incomplete. But in the few cases where fragile democracies emerged, they did so more commonly in the presence of domestic than international pressure. While a combination of internal and external factors was regularly effective, the most compelling condition for democratic transition was a mobilised domestic constituency for political change. One cannot go so far as to claim that popular protest was a necessary condition for democratisation, given that at least three small African countries (Cape Verde, Lesotho, São Tomé and Principé) transited to democracy at the top-down initiative of political elites. But, again, the initiative came from a set of domestic political actors rather than explicitly from abroad.

This last anomaly cannot be explained fully without reference to international considerations. Why did incumbent leaders in some African countries announce political reform measures in the absence of mass demands? For example, political openings were initiated by political elites acting alone in countries such as Angola, Burundi, Cape Verde, Ethiopia, Lesotho, Mozambique, Rwanda, Somalia and São Tomé. This group includes several military regimes – in which one would expect any transition to be tightly managed from above – but also several former Portuguese colonies and Marxist regimes. Leaders of regimes that always lacked a foreign patron (the lusophones) or suddenly lost one (the Soviet client states) may well have instigated reforms as urgent bids to attract Western aid flows. Even in the absence of explicit conditionality, they may have anticipated that their actions would win international approval.

Let us now turn to the timing of domestic demands. African politics displays a long history of mass protest.[76] Lacking opportunities for participation in genuine elections and political representation under one-party and military regimes, urban Africans have consistently employed strikes and demonstrations as means of political expression. As Africa's economic crisis deepened during the 1980s, disaffected corporate groups in society accelerated the pace of popular demonstrations. Typically, outbursts began when students or consumers expressed distress at austerity measures imposed by indebted governments. In some cases, governments were forced to reverse economic policy decisions: for example, in Liberia in 1984 and Zambia in 1986, official price increases for staple foodstuffs were rescinded. In other cases, governments recognised the political implications of economic protest and sought to assuage and contain dissent by guardedly opening the political system. For example, the governments of Mali in 1978 and Congo in 1979 permitted political opponents to re-enter the country from political exile. In 1985, governments in the francophone West African bloc of Cameroon, Gabon, and Togo decided to allow multiple candidates to stand for elections within the single ruling party. And, in Sudan, military governments conceded brief interludes of civilian multiparty rule in 1964 and 1986 when they could no longer resist organised street action by occupational and religious interest groups. Thus, a home-grown cycle of popular protest and political reform was underway within Africa well before the introduction of international pressures for democratisation after the end of the Cold War.

The belated timing of international pressure can be confirmed even with reference to the two African cases identified earlier where political conditionality apparently had decisive consequences. In Kenya, the suspension of donor assistance in November 1991 followed in the wake of a series of domestic demands for democracy: a campaign of public criticism of the Moi regime by church leaders and lawyers especially after 1986, a series of mass protest protests in Nairobi and regional towns in July 1990, and calls for multiparty politics by prospective candidates for the presidency. In Malawi, the suspension of aid in May 1992 responded to, rather than stimulated, the March 1992 publication by the country's Catholic bishops of a pastoral letter condemning political abuses and the first worker demonstrations in a generation. At very least, one can infer multi-causality, that is, that domestic and international pressures interacted to co-produce political movement in Kenya and Malawi. But, in both cases, domestic initiatives came first.

But what explains the timing of the politicisation of economic protests? Why did protests turn political when they did? After all, demonstrators only began to demand the ouster of corrupt leaders and the introduction of multiparty competition in the late 1980s and early 1990s, that is, at the same time that donors were announcing political conditions. Yet these two sets of events are related indirectly, if at all; other international developments were probably more important than donor demands. In condemning single-party rule, opposition activists – especially labour leaders such as Frederick Chiluba in Zambia and churchmen like Timothy Njoya in Kenya – made explicit reference to the example of democratisation in Eastern Europe.[77] For most Africans, however, the sources of inspiration were international events closer to home: the dissolution of single-party rule in Algeria in 1988, the release of Nelson Mandela in South Africa in February 1990, and the independence of Namibia under a liberal constitution in March 1990. Thus, if international donor pressure had any effect on the politicisation of protest, it probably did so only in conjunction with these other, broader international influences.

Further evidence of the internal dynamics of political change in Africa can be found in the persistence of popular protest in the aftermath of flawed or blocked political transitions. If domestic opposition forces perceived that the transition process had been aborted, street demonstrations did not ease up and sometimes even intensified. In Madagascar and Nigeria, for example, popular opposition became more coherent and relentless after promising transitions were interrupted by recalcitrant leaders. Thus, confrontation between state and society escalated according to an intrinsic logic that made little reference to the alignment of external forces. Indeed, the determination of domestic protesters to persist against unpopular regimes stood in marked contrast to the equivocation of external donors, first condemning, and later endorsing, dubious transitions.

Let us conclude our discussion of the role of international pressures on democratisation in Africa with reference to the role of political resources, and the political leverage they provide. Political transitions involve multiple players; each donor is one participant among many. Even if donors coordinate their actions – which, as was shown earlier, occurs increasingly but is never guaranteed – they must still compete for influence with political forces in domestic society. Incumbent political elites and opposition social movements – which themselves may be internally divided – each have their own political agendas for political transition. The actual processes and outcomes of transitions depend critically on the autonomy, cohesion, and resourcefulness of these various organised forces.

Donors are resourceful players since they can manipulate flows of development assistance to political actors in government and opposition camps. Incumbent elites commonly have at their disposal the resources of the state and opposition movements can call upon resources from civil society. The influence of international actors depends on their relative standing vis-à-vis domestic groups, particularly in respect to the resources – human, material, coercive, organisational, and ideological – that each can bring to bear in efforts to direct the transition process. In some cases, donors will have adequate leverage to alter the behaviour of domestic political actors, but in other cases they will not.

The capabilities of domestic political actors vary considerably across African countries, depending mainly on the physical resource endowment of the country and the extent to which incumbent political elites monopolise these resources. Consider first the capabilities of incumbent political elites. At one extreme were African strongmen in resource-rich countries who controlled revenue flows from export products. Their ideologies (usually some variant of African socialism) and their single party apparatuses (a product of the spread of Leninist ideas during the Cold War)[78] had long lost popular appeal and were used instead to intimidate citizens. Yet, even *in extremis*, such leaders were able to maintain themselves in power by buying the loyalty of key elements within the armed forces and deploying military coercion to repress opposition. At the other end of the spectrum were national leaders who presided over bankrupt treasuries, whose parties had collapsed, and who could not even regularly pay civil servants or soldiers. Such leaders were highly vulnerable to political pressures from within and without their countries.

Whether African leaders were forced to embark on a path of political liberalisation depended principally on the relative strengths of the opposition movements they faced at home. Such movements usually held an ideological advantage, being able to protest against corruption and human rights abuses, and sometimes even invoke multiparty democracy. But because the private economy was underdeveloped, the material base for resourceful opposition social movements in Africa was virtually non-existent. General strike strategies often ultimately collapsed when participants could no longer bear the material burden of withholding their labour. Organisationally, opposition movements had difficulty transcending the early protest phase of political transition and creating well-funded and cohesive political parties that could attain state power peacefully by winning elections. Only where churches, professional associations, and labour movements were strong could opposition movements overcome common flaws of fragmentation, personalisation, and ineffectiveness. But in regimes where the incumbent elites were themselves weak, even a weak opposition movement could make some impact on political change.

Seen from this perspective, democratic transitions in Africa occurred where relatively resourceful opposition social movements confronted severely weakened states. In Zambia, for example, an unusually well-organised, country-wide coalition of business, labour and white-collar groups faced the most deeply indebted government on the continent. Donors stood on the sidelines, issuing occasional diplomatic warnings to the incumbents and rhetorical encouragement to the opposition, but never issuing explicit political conditions for political liberalisation. The result was a democratic transition.

By contrast, political transitions were blocked where a relatively resourceful incumbent was able to withstand pressures from both domestic and international quarters. Mobutu Sese Seko of Zaire outmanoeuvred both international and domestic opponents with false promises of reform, and by buying off opposition elements with material inducements made possible by his direct personal access to the country's foreign exchange revenues. The withdrawal of Western aid from Zaire seriously undermined government capacity but was insufficiently consequential to force a genuine distribution of political power. In Sudan, the al-Bashir government was able to resist the continent-wide trend of political opening by drawing upon flows of aid from Iranian and Arab sources to substitute for Western aid embargoes. And Western aid sanctions on the military government of General Sani Abacha were ineffective in restoring democracy in a context where aid constituted a tiny proportion of public revenues. Instead, the strongman's position was underpinned by control over oil revenues, even through a protected oil workers strike in mid-1994.

Thus, the outcomes of international political pressure varied in relation to the aid dependence of the recipient country and the relative resourcefulness of domestic political protagonists. The effectiveness of donor pressure was mediated through these domestic political factors. Strong incumbents resisted the entreaties of donors and deployed material and coercive resources (notably the military) to hold on to power. Donor pressure was more effective in situations where incumbent political elites were so economically weak and fiscally strapped (to the point of being unable to pay the military) that they had few options but to submit to outside demands.

Given that domestic power relations are pre-eminent, donors could conceivably promote democratisation by seeking to strengthen independent power centres in civil and political society. Indeed, the realignment of post-Cold War foreign policies has involved shifting Western aid away from the state and towards the non-governmental sector.[79] In some African countries, the United States embassy has provided diplomatic support and political asylum for opposition activists; and Scandinavian donors have set the pace for other donors in providing modest grants to nurture civic associations and a free press. But, for the most part, donor flows of material and technical assistance to non-state political actors have followed the general pattern of external intervention noted in this chapter: too little, too late. Responding to governments' sensitivities about national sovereignty, donors have generally preferred to work with neutral development associations rather than with civic organisations that have explicitly political orientations. Any concrete support to civic associations has usually come during the end game of the transition, for example in the form of assistance to monitor a founding election. Donors are still embroiled in internal policy debates about whether, and to what extent, they should extend assistance to African political parties. As such, autonomous political organisations in African countries have remained largely beyond the reach of Western contact and influence. In short, the potential for concerted action by international and domestic coalitions of democracy advocates was barely explored in the period of political openings in Africa in the early 1990s.

Conclusion

The end of the Second World War encouraged a global wave of democratic transitions as the European powers reassessed their commitments abroad and granted independence to colonies in Africa.[80] So too the end of the Cold War encouraged democratisation in Africa as overextended superpowers pulled back from the continent, reformulated their foreign policies, and reduced and redistributed aid resources.

The principal mechanism of international pressure for the latest round of democratisation in Africa was political conditionality on development aid. While the donors have arrived at a broad consensus on this new approach, in practice they applied political conditions selectively. Western powers have insisted most firmly on political reform in resource-poor African countries in which they have few economic and strategic other interests; in richer and larger African states, donor demands for political reform have been much more muted and leavened with pragmatic considerations of political stability.

Moreover, the implementation of international political conditions has been compromised by countervailing interests and has had mixed impact. It has assisted regime change in Malawi and South Africa, prompted superficial reform under entrenched leaders in Kenya and Cameroon, and – at least to date – failed to dislodge military dictators in Zaire and Nigeria. Generally speaking, international aid conditionality is generally ineffective against rich African countries where incumbent political leaders have captured domestic economic resource flows. These are often the very same countries where external political pressures are weakest because of cross-cutting Western interests.

This paper has argued that the effects of a changing international environment are mediated through domestic politics. A unicausal explanation of change and continuity in African regimes based on international pressures alone is likely to be partial at best. Rather, the impetus for political transition originates importantly – indeed, predominantly – from within. As Haggard and Webb[81] note for economic reform, there is scant evidence that 'external actors tipped the political scales in favour of reform when the domestic institutional and coalitional environment was unfavourable'. The same lesson applies to democratisation, only more so. If donors have limited influence when they provide considerable resources in the form of structural adjustment loans, they are likely to have even less influence when the principal instrument of conditionality is withholding aid. Outsiders are only likely to be effective, and then only at the margins, where they can act in support of a strong domestic constituency that is committed to, and capable of, installing democracy. These conditions do not pertain in many parts of Africa.

Indeed, the wave of democratisation that swelled in Africa in the early 1990s has now peaked. This is so because of a conjunction of international and domestic trends. From an international perspective, Western donors are increasingly granting higher priority to conflict management than to democratisation. Domestically, pro-democracy movements are largely exhausted, either through victory as in South Africa, or because they are worn down by adamant dictators, as in Nigeria and Zaire. Even where transitions have occurred to fragile or flawed forms of democracy, opposition movements have yet to learn how to function as a united, organised and loyal force within a democratic process. The current challenge, for outsiders and insiders alike, is how to consolidate slim democratic gains before they gradually dissipate or are reversed.

Notes

1 Research for this chapter was conducted under the auspices of a project on 'Explaining Political Transitions in Africa' funded by National Science Foundation Grant No. SBR 9309215. Thanks are due to Joel Barkan, Linda Beck, Christopher Clapham, David Gordon, Peter Lewis, Nicolas van de Walle and the editor of this volume for comments on a first draft and to Kimberly Ludwig for research assistance. The figures on regime transitions refer to events up to December 1994 and are drawn from the database of the research project. Data are published in Michael Bratton and Nicolas van de Walle, *Political Regimes and Regime Transitions in Africa: A Comparative Handbook*, MSU Working Papers on Political Reform in Africa, No. 14 (Center for the Advanced Study of International Development, Michigan State University, East Lancing, Michigan, January 1996).

2 A minimalist definition of democracy focuses on elections as 'an institutional arrangement for arriving at political decisions in which individuals acquire the power to decide by means of a competitive struggle for the people's vote': Joseph A. Schumpeter, *Capitalism, Socialism, and Democracy* (Harper, New York, 2nd ed., 1947) p. 269; see also Samuel Huntington, *The Third Wave: Democratization in the Late Twentieth Century* (University of Oklahoma Press, Norman, Oklahoma, 1991) p. 6.

3 Francis Fukuyama, *The End of History and the Last Man* (Free Press, New York, 1992); Joshua Muravchik, *Exporting Democracy: Fulfilling America's Destiny* (American Enterprise Institute, Washington, 1991); Henry Kissinger, *Diplomacy* (Simon and Schuster, New York, 1994).

4 Geoffrey Pridham, Eric Herring, and George Sandfors (eds), *Building Democracy? The International Dimensions of Democratization in Eastern Europe* (Leicester University Press, Leicester, 1994). See also Geoffrey Pridham, *The International Context of Regime Transition in Southern Europe* (Leicester University Press, Leicester, 1991).

5 The causal direction of this relationship could be inverted, that is, with democratisation as the engine of change. In the former Soviet Union

and Eastern Europe the end of the Cold War looks as much like an effect as a cause of political opening and electoral transition. As Diamond and Plattner write, 'most dramatically of all, the democratic revolutions of 1989–91 precipitated the collapse of communism in Eastern Europe and the former Soviet Union and thus brought an end to the Cold War that had been the central feature of international relations for almost half a century': 'An Introduction to the Forum for Democratic Studies' (National Endowment for Democracy, Washington, August 1994).

6 Barry Munslow, 'Democratization in Africa', *Parliamentary Affairs*, xlvi/3 (1993) p. 483; see also Claude Ake, 'Democratization of Disempowerment in Africa', paper presented at the Transnational Institute, Cologne, Germany, November. 1991, and Claude Ake, 'Rethinking African Democracy', *Journal of Democracy* ii/1 (1993) pp. 32–44.

7 *Africa Confidential* xxxi/15 (1990) p. 3.

8 Huntington, *Third Wave*.

9 As Fishman notes, 'to emphasise the distinctiveness of specific cases in no sense implies that the comparative enterprise has been abandoned. It simply avoids the false assertion that there is one comprehensive causal constellation accounting for significantly different outcomes and processes'. See Robert M. Fishman, 'Rethinking State and Regime: Southern Europe's Transition to Democracy', *World Politics* xlii/3 (1990) p. 440.

10 Guillermo O'Donnell, Philippe Schmitter and Laurence Whitehead, *Transitions from Authoritarian Rule: Comparative Perspectives* (Johns Hopkins University Press, Baltimore, 1986) Vol. 1, p. 4; see also Huntington, *Third Wave*, p. 112.

11 Jean-Francois Bayart, *The State in Africa: The Politics of the Belly* (Longman, London, 1993) pp.x–xi.

12 Others have recently drawn attention to the 'complex dynamic process of interaction between global and national politics': Gabriel Almond, 'The National-International Connection', *British Journal of Political Science* xix/2 (1989) p. 257.

13 Robert Keohane, Joseph Nye and Stanley Hoffmann (eds), *After the Cold War: International Institutions and State Strategies in Europe, 1989–1991* (MIT Press, Cambridge, Mass., 1993) p. 2.

14 Nancy L. Spalding, 'Resource Mobilization in Africa: the Role of Local Organizations in the Tanganyika Independence Movement', *Journal of Developing Areas* xxvii (October 1993) pp. 92 and 94.

15 This paper intentionally defines the end of the Cold War in narrow foreign policy terms, the better to manage the subject matter. The notion of 'international pressure' used here is limited to diplomatic and economic measures used by Western donor countries to induce democratic political reforms. It is therefore far less comprehensive than Pridham's notion of 'the international dimension', which includes long-term 'developments' such as the spread of market forces and communications technologies or the demonstration effects of successful pro-democracy movements in other

countries: see Pridham, Herring and Sandfors, (eds), *Building Democracy?* pp. 1–3.

16 Eric Herring, 'The Collapse of the Soviet Union: The Implications for World Politics', in John Baylis and N. J. Rengger (eds), *Dilemmas of World Politics: International Issues in a Changing World* (Clarendon Press, Oxford, 1992) pp. 375–7; see also Jerry Hough, *The Struggle for the Third World* (Brookings Institution, Washington, 1986). On these grounds, Herring (p. 355) questions whether the Soviet Union was a superpower at all: while it could project its power to various world regions, it achieved little success. He attributes these shortcomings to the one-dimensional nature of Soviet power which was based upon military might at the expense of a proven model of economic development.

17 See Winrich Kuhne, 'What Does the Case of Mozambique Tell Us About Soviet Ambivalence Toward Africa?' *CSIS Africa Notes*, No. 46 (Center for Strategic and International Studies, Washington, 1985) and Jeffrey Herbst, 'The Fall of Afro–Marxism', *Journal of Democracy*, i/3 (1990) pp. 92–101.

18 See Elizabeth Valkenier, *The USSR and the Third World: An Economic Bind* (Praeger, New York, 1983) and Margot Light, 'Moscow's Retreat from Africa', *Journal of Communist Studies*, viii/2 (1992) pp. 21–40.

19 John Harbeson and Donald Rothchild (eds), *Africa in World Politics* (Westview, Boulder, 2nd, edn. 1994) p. 8 and Donald Rothchild, 'Responding to Africa's Post-Cold War Conflicts: The Need for Strategy' in Edmond Keller and Donald Rothchild (eds), *Africa in the New International Order: Rethinking State Sovereognty and Regional Security* (Lynn Riennes, Boulder, Col., 1996).

20 Light, 'Moscow's Retreat', p. 34.

21 Larry Diamond, 'Promoting Democracy in Africa: US and International Policies in Transition' in Harbeson and Rothchild (eds), *Africa in World Politics* , p. 10.

22 Michael Clough, *Free At Last? US Policy Toward Africa and the End of the Cold War* (Council on Foreign Relations, New York, 1992) p. 12.

23 President Clinton's appointee as USAID Administrator, Brian Atwood, testified to the the US Senate on 29 April 1993: 'We cannot be everywhere. In particular, we can no longer afford to be in countries where corruption, authoritarianism and incompetence makes development doubtful': US Agency for International Development, *Frontlines*, (USAID, Washington, June 1993) pp. 3–4.

24 This action trimmed US aid missions in Africa from 30 to 21 in 1994, with further reductions to come. Fifteen intelligence posts were also closed.

25 To avoid military intervention, the US voted funds to supranational organisations (like the OAU and ECOWAS) and regional African powers (notably South Africa) to deploy military forces on behalf of United Nations peace-keeping efforts in African trouble spots.

26 Joel Barkan, 'Can Established Democracies Nurture Democracy Abroad? Lessons from Africa' (paper presented at a Nobel Symposium on

Democracy's Victory and Crisis, Uppsala University, Uppsala, Sweden, 27–30 August 1994) notes that 'promoting democracy as a [US] foreign policy objective is not new', with current policies being 'replications or partial replications of earlier efforts in selected countries' (e.g. Germany and Japan after World War II, in Vietnam and Latin America in the 1960s). See also Thomas Carothers, *In the Name of Democracy* (University of California Press, Berkeley, 1991).

27 Quoted in Clough, *Free At Last?* p. 57.

28 US Agency for International Development, *The Democracy Initiative* (USAID, Washington, December 1990).

29 US Agency for International Development. *USAID Strategy Papers* (USAID, Washington, draft paper, 5 October 1993) p. 36.

30 Atwood (see note 23) was formerly President of the National Democratic Institute, a non-governmental entity that provided technical assistance worldwide on election administration and monitoring, as well as training for legislators and political party personnel.

31 During 1994, USAID conducted assessments for additional democracy support programmes in Guinea, Mali, Madagascar, Niger, Namibia and Tanzania. For a concise summary of these programmes see Barkan, 'Established Democracies', pp. 10–12.

32 John Chipman, *French Power in Africa* (Basil Blackwell, London, 1989).

33 Howard French, 'Cote d'Ivoire: Closing a Chapter', *Africa Report* xxxix/2 (1994) pp. 19–22.

34 Since Charles de Gaulle, the French president has exercised authority over Africa policy and has communicated directly with African heads of state through personal networks. Traditionally, the Ministry of Foreign Affairs and other executive branch departments were bypassed in the foreign policy decision-making process. Because of the lobbying strength in Paris of French business interests in Africa and because French political parties receive campaign funds from African leaders, Africa policy became quite salient within French domestic politics; (see Stephen Smith, and Antoine Glaser, *Ces Messieurs Afrique: Le Paris-Village du Continent Noir* (Calmann Levy, Paris, 1992).

35 As graphically illustrated by France's acceptance in January 1994 of the devaluation of the CFA franc, a policy reform long recommended by the multilateral financial institutions and by the French Treasury. Smith and Glaser, *Ces Messieurs Afrique:* Serge Michailof, *La France et l'Afrique: Vade-mecum pour un nouveau voyage* (Karthala, Paris, 1993).

36 *Marchés Tropicaux*, 12 June 1990, p. 87.

37 *Africa Confidential,* xxxi/14 (1990) p. 7.

38 *Financial Times,* 1 October 1990.

39 World Bank, *Sub-Saharan Africa: From Crisis to Sustainable Growth* (World Bank, Washington, 1989): World Bank, *Managing Development: The Governance Dimension* (World Bank, Washington, 1991): World Bank, *Governance: The World Bank's Experience* (World Bank, Washington, 1994).

40 The 'Washington consensus', which embraces a commitment to economic liberalisation confronts recipients with narrowed options for pursuing development: John Williamson, 'Democracy and the "Washington Consensus"' *World Development* xxi/8 (1993) pp. 1329–36: Atul Kohli, 'Democracy Amid Economic Orthodoxy: Trends in Developing Countries' *Third World Quarterly* xiv/4 (1993) pp.671–89.

41 Herbst, 'The Fall of Afro–Marxism'; Light, 'Moscow's Retreat'.

42 Joan M. Nelson and Stephanie J. Eglinton, *Global Goals, Contentious Means: Issues of Multiple Aid Conditionality* (Overseas Development Council, Policy Essay No. 10, Washington, 1993): Joan M. Nelson with Stephanie J. Eglinton, *Encouraging Democracy: What Role for Conditioned Aid?* (Overseas Development Council, Policy Essay No. 4, Washington, 1993); see also R. Stephen Brent, 'Aiding Africa', *Foreign Policy*, lxxx (Fall 1990) pp. 121–40.

43 Jennifer McCoy, Larry Garber and Robert Pastor, 'Pollwatching and Peacemaking' *Journal of Democracy*, ii/1 (1991) pp. 102–14: Larry Garber and Clark Gibson, *Review of United Nations Electoral Assistance* (United Nations Development Program, New York, 18 August 1993); Michelle Wozniak Schimpp and Lisa Peterson, 'USAID and Elections Support: a Synthesis of Case Study Experiences' (Center for Development Information and Evaluation, USAID, Washington, May 1993).

44 For other criticisms of electoral assistance see Marina Ottaway, 'Should Elections be the Criterion of Democratization in Africa?' *CSIS Africa Notes*, no.145 (Center for Strategic and International Studies, Washington, 1993) and Gisela Geisler, 'Fair? What has Fairness Got to Do with It? Vagaries of Election Observations and Democratic Standards', *Journal of Modern African Studies* xxxi/4 (1993) pp. 613–37.

45 The targeted funds are usually, quick-disbursing, non-project assistance, that is, cash disbursements to cover deficits on the trade or public budget accounts.

46 In the case of Kenya, the donors also wished to signal displeasure at growing corruption and the government's dilatory implementation of agreed-upon structural adjustment reforms: Joel Barkan, 'Kenya: Lessons from a Flawed Election', *Journal of Democracy*, iv/3 (1993) pp. 85–99; Garber and Gibson, *United Nations Electoral Assistance.*

47 Chris Allen, '"Goodbye to All That": the Short and Sad Story of Socialism in Benin', *Journal of Communist Studies*, viii/2 (1992) pp.63–81; John Heilbrunn, 'The Social Origins of National Conferences in Benin and Togo', *Journal of Modern African Studies*, xxxi/2 (1993) pp. 277–99; Richard Westebbe, 'Structural Adjustment, Rent Seeking, and Liberalization in Benin', in Jennifer Widner (ed.), *Economic Change and Political Liberalization in Sub-Saharan Africa* (Johns Hopkins University Press, Baltimore, 1994) pp. 80–100.

48 Peter Savigear, 'The United States: Superpower in Decline?', in Baylis and Rengger (eds), *Dilemmas of World Politics,* argues that, despite gyrations in US foreign policy (due to a string of one-term presidencies and growing

divisions between the executive and legislative branches) the quest for a stable world order provides a thread of continuity in US policy over the past half century.

49 The argument in this section is organised partly around, and expands upon, themes identified in the groundbreaking studies of political conditionality by Joan Nelson and Stephanie Eglinton *Encouraging Democracy,* and *Global Goals.*

50 Ibid. They cite the West's muted responses to the suppression of unarmed pro-democracy protesters to China over Tiananmen Square in 1989 and to Indonesia in East Timor in 1991.

51 US Congress, Statement by Assistant Secretary of State for African Affairs, George E. Moose, before the House Foreign Affairs Subcommittee on Africa, 22 April 1993: see also Carol J. Lancaster, *The United States and Africa: Into the Twenty-First Century,* (Overseas Development Council, Policy Essay No. 7, Washington, 1993).

52 Philippe Leymarie, 'La France et le maintien de l'ordre en Afrique', *Le Monde diplomatique,* 28 June 1994. See also the statement of British Foreign Secretary Douglas Hurd at the United Nations, 28 September 1994.

53 See Center for Strategic and International Studies, 'The White House Conference on Africa', *CSIS Africa Notes* no. 162 (CSIS, Washington, July 1994) pp. 4–5.

54 Ironically, Rwanda was one of the first countries in which USAID launched a 'democratic governance' project, following an assessment in 1992 that commented favourably on the prospects for democracy there.

55 Peter J. Schraeder, '"It's the Third World, Stupid!" Why the Third World Should be a Priority of the Clinton Administration', *Third World Quarterly,* xiv/2 (1993) pp. 215–37: Peter J. Schraeder, *United States Foreign Policy Toward Africa: Incrementalism, Crisis and Change* (Cambridge University Press, Cambridge, 1994).

56 For debates on whether the West really faces an 'Islamic threat' see James Piscatori, 'Islam and World Politics' in Baylis and Rengger (eds), *Dilemmas of World Politics:* Samuel P. Huntington, 'The Clash of Civilizations', *Foreign Affairs* (Summer 1993): Leon T. Hadar, 'What Green Peril?' and Judith Miller, 'The Challenge of Radical Islam', both in *Agenda 1994: Critical Issues in Foreign Policy* (Council on Foreign Relations, New York, 1994). Islam gained unprecedented visibility in US policy with the arrest and conviction of religious fundamentalists from Egypt for the bombing of the World Trade Center in New York. US Secretary of State Warren Christopher condemned attacks on Jewish targets in Buenos Aires and London in July 1994 by asserting that 'Hezbollah's patron, Iran, must be *contained*'. (Testimony to the House Foreign Affairs committee, quoted in the *New York Times,* 29 July 1994, emphasis added). The choice of terminology, so redolent of America's grand design against communism during the Cold War, can hardly have been accidental.

57 Two French international civil servants, IMF managing director

Michel Camdessus and EC president Jacques Delors, along with the outspoken French Foreign Minister Alain Juppe, took a leading role in marshalling Paris Club support to refinance more than $5 billion in June 1994.

58 *Africa Confidential*, xxxv/12 (1994) p. 4.

59 Michael Clough, *Free At Last? US Policy towards Africa and the End of the Cold War* (Council on Foreign Relations, New York, 1992); Carol J. Lancaster, *The United States and Africa: Into the Twenty-First Century* (Overseas Development Council, Policy Essay No.7, Washington, 1993).

60 Walter Kansteiner, 'U.S. Interests in Africa Revisited', *CSIS Africa Notes*, No.157 (Center for Strategic and International Studies) Washington, February 1994.

61 *Africa Confidential*, xxxv/1 (1994).

62 See Brian Atwood, 'The White House Conference on Africa', *CSIS Africa Notes*, No.162, (Center for Strategic and International Studies, Washington, July 1994).

63 Michael Schatzberg, *Mobutu or Chaos? The United States and Zaire, 1960–1990* (Foreign Policy Research Institute, Philadelphia, 1991); Sean Kelly, *America's Tyrant: the CIA and Mobutu of Zaire* (American University Press, Washington, 1993) p. 250.

64 Notably, the US has never intervened directly in post-Cold War Africa to facilitate the exit of an unpopular leader as it did, however belatedly, for Ferdinand Marcos of the Philippines. Sean Kelly claims that the US did hatch an evacuation plan to extricate Samuel Doe from Liberia but that 'he apparently took too long to make up his mind and was tortured and killed': Kelly, *America's Tyrant*, p.256. In contrast to their policies on Haiti, the Western countries or the United Nations have never committed themselves to military invasion as a means to remove a military regime and restore democracy in an African country.

65 Linda Chalker, *Good Government and the Aid Programme* (Royal Institute for International Affairs, London, 1991).

66 World Bank, *Adjustment in Africa: Reforms, Results, and the Road Ahead* (World Bank, Washington, 1994).

67 On the day after he capitulated to a key World Bank demand to liberalise maize marketing in 1994, President Moi of Kenya began to arrest opposition MPs.

68 For critical observer reports see National Electoral Monitoring Unit, *The Multi-Party General Elections in Kenya, December 1992* (NEMU, Nairobi, January 1993): International Republican Institute (IRI), *Kenya: The December 22, 1992 Elections* (IRI, New York, 1993). In April 1993, $85m was released for an export development programme even though the Kenya government had also failed to meet reform targets in the monetary and banking sectors. *Africa Confidential* comments that 'given continuing criticism of IMF and World Bank policies in Africa, neither organisation can now afford the defection of a key state such as Kenya': *Africa Confidential*, xxxiv/20 (1993)

p. 5.

69 In a September 1994 interview with the author, a top former policy maker for Africa from the Bush administration characterised the Western policy switch toward Zaire this way: 'France led the way: it needed Mobutu to mount Operation Turquoise in Rwanda; the Belgian government was too weak to stand up to its own business lobby; and the Americans agreed to go along'.

70 *Africa Confidential*, xxiv/20 (1993) p. 1.

71 Michael Bratton, 'Academic Analysis and U.S. Economic Assistance Policy on Africa', *Issue: a Journal of Opinion*, xix/1 (1990) p. 25.

72 For example, when the US sought to reward economic and political reforms by the Ethiopian government of Meles Zenawi with a modest $60m aid programme, it was blocked by legislation forbidding assistance to countries with debt arrears and by the defeat of the 1992 foreign aid bill which included a waiver for Ethiopia. See Nelson and Eglinton, *Encouraging Democracy*, p. 21. In Rwanda, the World Bank was restricted from releasing $250m to the Twagiramungu (RPF) government, despite its desperate basic needs, until the Rwandans cleared $3.75m worth of arrears on earlier loans (*New York Times*, 17 September 1994).

73 The Western donor bloc also fractured over political conditionality on Kenya, with Britain being the last to join, and first to abandon, the November 1991 aid freeze. Thereafter, Britain and France tended to give Moi the benefit of the doubt for nominal compliance to political reform goals, whereas the US, German and Scandinavian governments introduced new conditions, such as an end to ethnic massacres.

74 See 'The French Keep Africa under Economic Wing', *New York Times*, 11 September 1994, and 'Africa: Finding Oil in Troubled Waters', *Africa Confidential*, xxxv/11 (1994) pp. 3–4.

75 Michael Bratton and Nicolas van de Walle, 'Popular Protest and Political Reform in Africa', *Comparative Politics* xxiv/4 (1992) pp.419–42: Michael Bratton and Nicolas van de Walle, 'Neopatrimonial Regimes and Political Transitions in Africa', *World Politics* xliv/4 (1994) pp. 453–89.

76 For example, see Peter Anyang' Nyong'o, *Popular Struggles for Democracy in Africa* (Zed Press, London, 1987).

77 Even so, French, 'Cote d'Ivoire' p.22, claims a different causal sequence: 'Beginning with a wave of contestation in 1988, West Africa preceded, rather than followed, Eastern Europe in shaking up its old dictatorships and seeking a democratic way of life.'

78 While only a handful of Afro–Marxist leaders attempted to recreate the extensive apparatus of a communist party during the Cold War, single-party constitutions gained wide currency among African leaders of all ideological stripes as means of controlling political opposition. These same regimes often received technical and financial assistance from communist regimes in Eastern Europe to create state capacity, especially for internal security. However weak, the single-party in Africa did at least offer ambitous

political leaders an instrument with which to penetrate the state apparatus in order to extract rents for personal consumption. This institutional legacy will not disappear overnight. The intertwining of party and state and the habits of monopolistic rule, ingrained in the sentiments of elites and masses alike, will survive political transitions. In this sense, the Cold War legacy of one-party rule will constitute a long-lasting constraint on the transition to, and consolidation of, democratic rule in Africa.

79 Lester Salomon, 'The Rise of the Non-Profit Sector', *Foreign Affairs*, lxxiii/4 (1994) pp. 109–22; Barkan, 'Established Democracies'.

80 Huntington, *Third Wave*, p. 40.

81 Stephen Haggard and Steven B. Webb (eds), *Voting for Reform: Democracy, Political Liberalization and Adjustment* (Oxford University Press, Oxford, 1994) p. 5.

8 ❧ Authoritarianism Liberalised: Syria and the Arab East after the Cold War

Eberhard Kienle

Authoritarianism, or at least strong authoritarian features, have been identified as the hallmarks of most of the political systems which have coexisted or succeeded each other since the Second World War in the geographical area known to us as the Middle East. With the exception of the rather special case of Israel, only Syria immediately after independence, Lebanon prior to its second civil war, and Turkey between (or after) its various military coups managed to appear as more democratic than authoritarian, to the extent that this Manichaean dichotomy makes sense. Even the parliamentary trappings of the Egyptian and Iraqi monarchies were never solid enough to dispel the impression of a dictatorship of the palace and its cronies.

Though a trait common to most regimes in the area, authoritarian features vary significantly from case to case, depending on time and place. Unelected and entirely unaccountable monarchies in most of the Arab Peninsula, 'democratic centralism' in the heyday of Arab socialism and nationalism, and military regimes without any 'democratic' or party façade differ from each other in important respects but nonetheless share authoritarian features as a sort of minimal common denominator. In all these political systems 'power is highly centralised, pluralism is suspect and ... the regime seeks to exercise a monopoly over all legitimate political activity.'[1] Authoritarian features remain pre-eminent where the art of domination is developed further towards totalitarian models as, for example, in late Ba'thi Iraq.[2] In the latter case indoctrination may have produced 'spontaneous' compliance, acclamatory 'participation' and thus a semblance of legitimacy, but as in the more 'classical' authoritarian regimes the survival of the rulers largely depends on power and coercion. Finally, authoritarian features are also the prerequisites of the forms of despotism or tyranny which some authors have identified in the region.[3] From the latter point of view, authoritarianism could be seen as no more than the modern bureaucratic and sanitised version of old-fashioned despotism, be it 'Oriental' or not.

While there is considerable agreement when it comes to identifying authoritarian forms of government, there is obviously non over the terminology to be used, and there is even less over the explanation of the phenomena described. Some authors prefer germane notions such as 'patrimonialism' or 'neo-patrimonialism' which nonetheless imply a considerable degree of authoritarianism.[4] Others emphasise the 'relative autonomy' enjoyed by a state which narrowly limits political participation.[5] Yet others, though highlighting important 'authoritarian' elements in the politics of Syria and Egypt, seek to qualify their importance analytically as well as terminologically.[6] As to the causes of the emergence and survival of this type of rule, the major divide separates what may be called universalists on the one hand from particularists on the other. Dominated by culturalists who largely and unconvincingly identify Islamic prescriptions, or whatever 'essence' of Islam as the prime cause,[7] the particularists also comprise authors who emphasise the role of certain social or societal features such as kinship or authority structures.[8] For their part, universalists tend to stress factors common to economically less developed countries inside and outside the Middle East such as processes of state-formation or the economic underpinnings of state and society, themselves largely shaped by centre-periphery relations.[9] The latter factors may also account for the absence or weaknesses of 'civil society.'[10]

One of the countries whose political system has consistently been described as authoritarian is Syria, and in order to pinpoint the specific character of the country's authoritarianism, populist, despotic and more or less totalitarian features have often been ascribed to its regime. In less abstract terms Syria, according to the literature, appears as a country ruled by an informally constituted power elite which is dominated by military officers; more often than not it is pointed out that in their great majority these officers are Alawites and thus 'members' of a religious minority. The power elite is said to rule the country from behind the scenes, through the Ba'th Party which under the constitution enjoys a privileged position, and through a state apparatus which imitates forms of democratic centralism known from the former Eastern Europe. The regime is not bound by its own laws and there is no political participation worth mentioning; on the contrary, people are mobilised by the regime to support its policies.[11]

Among the diachronic changes in the manifestations and intensity of authoritarian rule in the Middle East, those coinciding or correlating with policies of 'economic liberalisation' have attracted the greatest attention over the past few years;[12] 'transitions to democracy' along the lines of Southern Europe or Latin American cases are for obvious reasons rarely discussed in the literature.[13] The attempts to mobilise and strengthen the private sector, partly in response to the shortcomings of previous public sector-oriented development strategies, partly in response to the decrease in rent transfers from the major oil producing countries, in some cases coincided with processes of political restructuring which enhanced possibilities of political participation and also led to a greater respect for human rights on the part of governments. Egypt after the 1973 war and Sadat's October Paper of 1974[14] seemed to exemplify the nexus between economic and political liberation, though for a period in which there was no shortage of rent.

Since the mid-1980s Jordan and even Syria have embarked on new economic policies which have strengthened their private sectors far more than was the case under previous liberal or liberalising policies in the economic domain. Concurrently, or with some delay, the regimes in both countries also embarked on a process of political 'decompression'[15] on the levels of both human rights and political participation, which to an extent changed their authoritarian character.[16]

The cases of these, and numerous other countries, thus seem to confirm a close link between economic and political restructuring. However, this link should not be reduced to the liberal credo according to which economic liberalisation necessarily entails political liberalisation.[17] Rather, developments at the two levels seem to be linked in the sense that new economic policies, often but not always in response to resource crises, through their distributional effects strengthen or weaken different classes or other parts of society; in sometimes complex games of coalition-building, selective (dis)enfranchisement and a redefining of constituencies, economic winners and losers may gain or lose political rights, including that of participation.[18] In the best of cases even 'political pacts' might be concluded.[19]

On the other hand, political change in Syria, Jordan and other states coincided with, or followed chronologically, not only policies of economic liberalisation but also important global developments which are generally supposed to have favoured 'transitions to democracy'. With the advent of Mikhail Gorbachev as first secretary of the Communist Party of the Soviet Union (CPSU) in 1985, Moscow's foreign policy changed not only vis-à-vis the 'West' but also many of its allies in the so-called 'Eastern bloc' and in the 'South'. In particular, the USSR sought to distance itself from the more unsavoury and repressive actors in Asia and Africa which it had until then supported. As a consequence of its *rapprochement* with the United States and the growing economic decline at home, Moscow soon also began to redefine in financial terms relationships which had hitherto been defined as strategic; debtors were reminded of their duties and military hardware had to be paid for in cash. The net result for former allies and protégés was that Soviet support could not be taken for granted; indeed it rapidly declined and exposed existing regimes to internal and external pressures which they no longer had the resources to counter.

Finally, the failure of various Soviet policies to produce the expected results delegitimated them as models in the eyes of other regimes. Very few Third World regimes had chosen to organise their states politically and economically fully along Soviet lines; but many had adopted individual policies, often in key areas, which in one way or another resembled Soviet policies. Single-party systems, forms of 'democratic centralism', public sector-focused development planning and strategies of internal repression all had certain features in common with policies pursued by the Soviet government and its East European allies. Once such policies proved to be unsuccessful in the model case, their adequacy was also questioned by their imitators. In particular, 'socialist' public sector-oriented economic policies and the repression of internal dissent no longer seemed to guarantee either economic growth or political stability. Doubt thus reinforced the effects of declining resources.

The much-celebrated end of the Cold War and its major causes – the reformulation of Soviet foreign policy and the economic decline of the Soviet Union – therefore weakened numerous regimes in the

Third World on three levels: their own perception of the validity of policy choices, external moral support for those choices and external material support for their implementation. As the decline in external support could not be matched by a decreasing need for such support, the end of the Cold War increased the dependency of Third World regimes on the 'West' as the only surviving source of potential support. Certainly not unaware of their monopolistic or oligopolistic position, 'Western' actors roughly at the same time increasingly linked aid and support to political conditions generally epitomised by the notion of 'good governance'. From this perspective, the end of the Cold War together with its causes and consequences constitutes a second set of factors which may account for the political change observed in several Middle Eastern states over the last decade or so.[20]

Comparing Syria to a number of other Arab states, this chapter seeks to evaluate the relative importance that processes of economic liberalisation on the one hand, and factors related to the end of the Cold War on the other hand, have had for the reformulation of policies concerning human rights and political participation over the last decade. While in Syria domestic economic reform and global political change have so far correlated with a timid liberalisation of authoritarian rule, regime policies in Egypt since 1992 seem to have led to a considerable deliberalisation of what for years had been the most liberal polity in the Arab East (except for the rather special and contradictory case of Lebanon). The case of Egypt could confirm that factors often considered as favourable to political liberalisation, in particular economic liberalisation, can produce opposite outcomes, at least under certain conditions. Notwithstanding the analytical distinction between the two sets of factors central to this study they may, of course, reinforce each other as, for example, in the cases analysed by Michael Bratton elsewhere in this volume. To some extent it could also be argued that economic liberalisation, and therefore its political consequences, are linked to a decrease in rent and resource transfers, not only from the major oil producing states but also from those states which ultimately lost the Cold War.

Recent Political Change in Syria

After almost three decades of tight limitations on political participation and liberties, indeed their complete absence for the overwhelming majority of Syrians, the elections to the People's Assembly (Majlis al-Sha'b) or parliament in May 1990 injected a dose of liberalisation into the country's political system. Almost precisely five years after Gorbachev was elected secretary-general of the CPSU and less than a year after the fall, first of the Berlin wall and then of Ceauscescu, Syria's electoral law was modified to make the new assembly moderately more representative than its predecessor.

The total number of seats was raised from 195 to 250, and by contrast to earlier elections,[21] only about two thirds of the seats were reserved from the outset for the Ba'th Party and its junior partners in the Progressive National Front (PNF). The smaller parties obtained together 31 seats while 137 were filled by candidates of the Ba'th. The score of the Ba'th reflects its privileged position under the constitution of 1973, which clearly defines it as the ruling party, even though in practice state power is vested in the president and the military establishment. While the seats reserved for the Front were promptly filled with the respective candidates appearing on its list and therefore not subject to any actual vote, a serious campaign opposed the roughly 9,000 independent candidates who competed for the remaining 82 seats.[22] As independents these candidates could be members of PNF parties but not run under such a label. Organisations outside the PNF were not, and still are not, legalised and therefore, with a few exceptions, their members were unable to stand for election.[23] Moreover, candidates were thoroughly screened by various regime agencies before they could actually register as such. Finally, the counting process left sufficient room for vote rigging where this was deemed necessary; in some cases candidates who were first declared elected lost their seats after the sudden discovery of forgotten votes. Nonetheless, at least and at last non-regime candidates entered the Assembly.[24]

Not surprisingly, some debates of the fifth Assembly, elected in 1990, were far more lively and sometimes controversial than debates in the 1970s and 1980s. On several occasions during its four-year term the Assembly even used its right to pass a vote of no confidence in individual ministers leading to their resignation. However, various sorts of issues were never discussed in parliament, in particular internal security, defence and foreign policies. The major debates turned around questions of distribution, when either the annual budget or other economic policies had to be voted.[25]

Four years later, on 24 and 25 August 1994, a new Assembly was elected. Despite apparent hesitation on the part of the regime, the vote took place within the constitutional deadline of ninety days after the end of the preceding parliament. Again, roughly two-thirds of the seats were reserved for PNF candidates and one-third for independents; the latter third were contested by 7,366 candidates. Ultimately, 85 independents were declared elected. Since these included two Ba'this who ran as independents after they had failed to be nominated by their party, the PNF in practise obtained two more than the 165 seats initially allotted to it from he total of 250 seats.[26] Constituencies remained identical with the country's governorates. Depending on the number of voters, different numbers of seats continued to be allocated to different constituencies and thus to PNF and independent candidates within them. Among independent candidates of the same constituency, those who obtained most of the votes were declared elected, though within the limits set by the electoral law. The law still requires a 51 per cent majority of workers and peasants in the assembly, affecting independents and PNF deputies alike.[27] While the arrangements governing the 1994 elections failed to extend participation beyond the limits set in 1990, they nonetheless confirmed and consolidated the policy of restricted liberalisation; more would have been surprising at a moment when the regime had to make critical decisions concerning its negotiations with Israel.

There were also other areas in which political participation was extended to hitherto excluded individuals and groups. From autumn 1993 official Syrian delegations to the bi-annual meetings of the World Bank and the International Monetary Fund (IMF) in addition to government officials comprised prominent representatives of the expanding private sector such as the tycoon Sa'ib Nahhas.[28] In autumn 1993, and again in 1996, Damascus also saw a fully-fledged election campaign in which well-known business figures contested seats on the Damascus Chamber of Commerce. With election posters all over town, none of which portrayed President Asad, the vote resembled general elections elsewhere.[29]

At the same time and on a largely informal level, less visible relationships between the military establishment and other state officials on the one hand and private entrepreneurs, merchants or industrialists on the other in numerous cases changed in nature. In various cases private sector figures and their protectors in the state apparatus together invested in companies. Although the law prevents officers from open economic activity, many of them participated in such civilian-military joint ventures by hiding behind members of their own families. A certain number of business people or their offspring also entered family relations with officers and key representatives of the regime. These qualitatively new relationships enhanced their ability to represent their interests and to participate politically in informal ways.[30]

The changes at the level of political participation were accompanied by an equally modest liberalisation at the level of civil, political and more generally human rights. Foreign newspapers began to spend less time on the desks of censors in the Ministry of Information and the presence of secret police agents and special forces became less conspicuous in public places. In cafés and restaurants people began to talk more freely about subjects they would not have dared to address earlier. The occasional jamming of Jordanian television ceased and even openly displayed satellite dishes were tolerated.

Simultaneously, numerous political prisoners were freed, even though many others remained in jail and yet others were newly arrested or rearrested. In the major amnesties of December 1991, March 1992 and December 1992 as well as in the period since between 2,000 and 4,000 political prisoners seem to have been released, although an estimated 3–10,000 remain in detention. A semblance of the rule of law was set up for some of some of the remaining prisoners as they were formally charged and tried after years of detention.[31] In some cases relatively short sentences were handed down, but in others the procedure was clearly a way of legalising unlawful detention. In 1989 the Syrian authorities for the first time agreed to receive officially a delegation from Amnesty International. More recently, and contrary to their previous policy, the Syrian authorities have responded to individual inquiries and representations made by either Amnesty International or other organisations concerned with human rights such as the International Commission of Jurists or Middle East Watch; in various cases representatives of such organisations have been allowed to attend political trials as observers.[32]

In an article for the lawyers' journal *al-Muhamum* the president of the High Constitutional Court, who is directly accountable to President Asad, even stated that it was time to think about the abolition of the state of emergency which since 1962 has been the major legal instrument of repression. At the UN conference on human rights in Vienna in June 1993, Damascus first joined governments who criticised the draft declaration for its emphasis on individual as opposed to collective human rights and their universal nature; in the end, however, Syria was among the 171 states which adopted the declaration.[33] Finally, new legislation is being discussed and prepared to disentangle the trade unions from their present domination by the Ba'th Party. The new law is expected to be enacted by the parliament elected in 1994.[34] Collective bargaining and workers rights may therefore be reinforced legally, even though the overall process of economic liberalisation threatens to undermine them in practice.

Explaining Political Change in Syria

The timing of the political liberalisation coincinding with the 1990 parliamentary elections suggests a strong link with global processes associated with the end of the Cold War. The Berlin wall came down in October 1989 and President Ceauscescu of Romania was overthrown shortly afterwards in December. Ceauscescu's inglorious end, his death at the hands of a firing squad, was noted with particular interest – indeed concern – throughout the Arab world. Romania seemed very close in many ways. It had economic ties with many Arab states, and to an extent the Arab world seemed to share its semi-peripheral status on the fringes of Europe. But above all, its political system, on the face of it, had numerous features in common with the mobilisational authoritarianisms of Syria and Iraq. In Damascus Ceauscescu's violent death inspired the occasional graffiti about the life and opinions of 'Shamscescu', the word '*Sham*' being a synonym for 'Syria'.

The writing thus being on the wall, it seems plausible that the rapid disintegration of the Soviet order and the signs of crumbling in the Kremlin itself pushed the rulers of Syria first to stress, but then also to create, differences between their own regime and the *anciens régimes* of the Eastern hemisphere. The similarities which Syrians could perceive in this respect needed to be not only explained away rhetorically but also reduced politically in order to preclude the spread to Syria of *glasnost* or worse, with all the pernicious consequences which that might have for the regime.

The issue of change was sufficiently important for President Asad to address it himself in a major (and characteristically paternalistic) speech in February 1990:

> The right thing is not to do something because others do the same. We do something when we become convinced that it expresses our will and convictions and serves our people. Today, just as in the past, we do not do something influenced by others or pressured by specific circumstances. Had the pressures of circumstances and external events steered our work, we would have yielded to external pressures long before.

Referring to his own Corrective Movement which after 1970 recognised a highly limited degree of political diversity and activity outside the Ba'th Party, Asad insisted that 'since then, our decision has been for a multi-party system and political pluralism ....'[35]

Put differently, there was no need to follow the lead of others because others were ultimately following the lead of Syria and Soviet *perestroika* and *glasnost* were nothing but belated imitations of Syria's Corrective Movement.[36] Since change had already occurred in Syria, the country could now remain outside history as it unfolded elsewhere and time could be reduced to a variable dependent on place. Thus an almost ontological distinction, reminiscent of the premises of 'Orientalism' and 'Orientalism in reverse',[37] could be established between dynamics inside and outside Syria. In more concrete terms, political change in Syria was not and would not be influenced by political change in and around the Soviet Union and its wider global consequences.

Although Asad dismissed the importance of global developments for Syria, they nonetheless may have prompted him to introduce a measure of political reform. Considering the timing of reform, his remarks could have merely been a clumsy attempt to deny the obvious, especially as he made them at a dinner given in the honour of the outgoing parliament, three months before, in May 1990, a new assembly was elected according to the more liberal electoral law.

Between Cold War and Socio-Economic Restructuring

However, the importance of global events for political change in Syria may well have been limited, for domestic socio-economic developments offer an alternative explanation. The process of economic liberalisation which was initiated in the 1970s and relaunched in the mid-1980s contributed to a significant redistribution of wealth within the country, and to an extent even of 'economic power'.

The size of the private sector grew in absolute and in relative terms and so did the 'weight' of capital owners. It would not be surprising to see these developments reflected in the more narrowly defined sphere of politics, though in ways that are much more complex than those imagined by the champions of the liberal credo.

The relative importance of the private sector in the Syrian economy grew rapidly and substantially after a major foreign exchange crisis in 1986 which the regime ultimately identified with the shortcomings of its public sector-focused development strategy. More than from the failure as such of its public sector Syria suffered from the ways in which that sector was run and its role defined. Economic and socio-political functions had to be constantly reconciled – a combination that turned out to be unsustainable once deficits could no longer be covered through direct and especially indirect revenue from rent. This point was reached in the mid-1980s after financial aid from the major oil producers in the Arab Peninsula had continuously declined for years, largely because of their own declining oil revenues but also in part for political reasons.

From the mid-1980s onwards, the private sector was thus given a role in the economy which it had not enjoyed since the early 1960s. Although the Corrective Movement initiated after Asad's take-over in 1970 had favoured the revival of Syria's private sector, it clearly and intentionally kept it dependent on public contracts, authorisations and credits. Throughout this first period of *infitah* the private sector was active where the public sector could not be, filling gaps and to serving the material interests of vital constituencies of the regime. By contrast, the second *infitah* of the late 1980s relied on the private sector to take the lead and to pull the entire economy, public sector included, out of the crisis.[38]

By the end of the 1980s, the private sector's share in total investment, manufacturing output, export earnings and GDP equalled or even surpassed that of the public sector.[39] After a new private investment law was enacted in 1991 – law no. 10, which for the first time since the 1960s, granted important advantages to private investors not only from Syria and other Arab countries but also from the rest of the world[40] – the private completely outdistanced the public sector in terms of gross fixed capital formation. The decline of the public sector appears not only in such aggregate data but also in its dependency on essential services provided by the private sector. Major public companies such as Aftomachine had to rely on private importers to supply them with spare parts. Internal political change may therefore have been inevitable in order to accommodate these new economic and social realities.

However, while these processes of economic restructuring and their societal consequences were taking place, the Syrian regime was also exposed to mounting external pressures which often, in one way or another, resulted from the decline of the Soviet Union. At the same time, New Soviet, and subsequently Russian, foreign policies reduced support for Syria on the basis of global political considerations. Though generally supporting Syria, Moscow rejected its demand for strategic parity with Israel, not only because it would be too costly, but also because it would complicate the search for a permanent and acceptable settlement of the Arab–Israeli conflict.[41] For Syria this meant increasing vulnerability vis-à-vis Israel and its supporters, in particular in the USA.

Confronted with its own resource crisis, the USSR from the late 1980s also increasingly insisted on the repayment of Syria's – largely military – debt which over the years had reached some US $ 10–12 bn.[42] Moscow even repeatedly refused to supply Syria with spare parts for Soviet-produced military equipment, or demanded cash payment.[43] In a sense this issue highlighted once again the insufficiencies of the old economic strategy which had failed to generate the resources needed to guarantee Syria's defence capacities. More importantly, however, it showed the limits of Soviet support in general and the need to mobilise resources from elsewhere as long as they could not be generated at home.

While the strong ties between Israel and the major capitalist countries severely limited Syria's ability to obtain military aid from the latter, such restrictions applied much less or not at all to economic aid or to direct investments by international companies. The Arab countries of the Gulf also continued to be considered as important reservoirs of such resources, even though their oil revenues and financial capacities had decreased. As can be seen from the enactment of Law no 10 of 1991, and the wide publicity given to it, foreign direct investment was to play a key role in the new strategy of accumulation and development. Though certainly intended to bring about economic growth and to satisfy the growing needs of a growing population, this strategy also served to strengthen the basis on which the regime could draw internationally, not least in its conflict with Israel. In any case it had to be tuned to the interests and sensitivities of the capitalist actors who were able to provide the resources.

Close relations between Israel and the West clearly limited Syria's ability to obtain military, and to a much lesser extent, economic aid from North America, Europe or Japan. In spite of declining oil revenues the Arab world, of course, also continued to be considered as a major source of public and private economic aid. In its various forms such aid was supposed to contribute to the success of the new economic policy formulated after the mid and late 1980s; foreign direct investment was to play a key role in this strategy as can be seen from Law no. 10 of 1991. While the new economic policy itself was certainly intended to bring about economic growth and to satisfy the needs of a growing population with growing expectations, it also served to reinforce the resource basis on which the regime could draw internationally, not least vis-à-vis Israel.

At the same time, the decline of the Soviet Union increased the need for Syria to obtain diplomatic and political support from the West. In order to prevent the actual or *de facto* settlement of its conflict with Israel on unfavourable terms, the Syrian government needed to compete with Israel for support from the USA and, to a smaller extent, from Europe. As for any other state, the search for both economic and political support from the capitalist West and capitalist actors in the Arab world, implied accepting at least some of their conditions. Need, combined with the decline of its former backer, thus exposed Syria to political conditionality in its narrow as much as in a wider sense.

The USA had discontinued economic cooperation with Damascus because of its alleged involvement in international terrorism, in particular in the attempt to blow up an Israeli passenger aircraft in 1986 and the bombing of a Berlin discotheque a year later. Ever since, resumption of any sort of US aid and cooperation has remained dependent on political conditions, even though these referred to foreign rather than to domestic policy choices; policies of the latter sort were targeted only more recently by the US administration (see below).[44] European governments and institutions on the other hand very soon added human rights issues to their list of political grievances. Limited European sanctions following the two incidents mentioned above[45] were followed by a vote in the European Parliament to suspend the third and fourth bilateral financial protocols with Syria with explicit reference to the regime's poor human rights record. For Damascus this decision came at a moment when the economic crisis had reached alarming proportions and currency reserves barely covered more than a week of imports. The European Parliament finally passed the two financial protocols in October 1992[46] after Damascus had openly sided with Europe and the USA in the Kuwait crisis of 1990–91 and subsequently released several thousand of its political prisoners. Roughly another 1,000 were released in November 1995, officially on the occasion of the 25th anniversary of President Asad's assumption of power, but conspicuously close to the Barcelona conference of European–Mediterranean cooperation where the European Union, at least rhetorically, linked aid to a minimal respect for human rights and democratic procedures.[47]

Around 1992 the US administration for the first time linked the normalisation of its relations with Syria to conditions relating to the civil and political rights of Syrians citizens. In a clear-cut case of political conditionality, in June 1992 the US administration made Syrian access to preferential trade tariffs, and therefore to US markets, dependent on new labour legislation meeting 'internationally recognised worker rights' as defined by the International Labour Organisation (ILO).[48] The linkage is of considerable importance to Syria since the main direction of its foreign trade has over the years turned from the command economies of the USSR and Eastern Europe to the advanced capitalist economies of Europe and North America; in particular new private sector industries which are supposed to generate foreign exchange are actively looking for export opportunities in Europe, Japan and America.[49]

In Europe aid and cooperation with the Third World was first systematically linked to human rights issues at the time Syria traversed its economic crisis in the mid-1980s. While verbal insistence often remained at variance with actual practice, it nonetheless repeatedly coincided. The general declaration on human rights and aid of 21 July 1986 issued by the foreign ministers of the countries of the European Community (EC) did not impress the Syrian regime, but the decision of the Strasbourg assembly to freeze the two financial protocols had to be taken seriously. Human rights issues soon came to be emphasised regularly by other key Western donors and institutions, indicating that the trend turned into a new hegemonic orthodoxy. In autumn 1986 human rights issues became part and parcel of the Lomé framework and in March 1991 the European Commission requested that all foreign aid should be made conditional on the respect of fundamental human rights.[51] In 1991 and 1992 the OECD and its Development Assistance Committee emphasised the issues of democracy and governance for the granting of development aid.[52]

For Eastern Europe the policies agreed at the G–7 summit in Paris in July 1989 laid down similar conditions and inspired the subsequent PHARE programme through which the EC sought to promote the simultaneous transition to market economies and liberal democracy in the countries concerned.[53] The same year saw the publication of the famous World Bank report on the crisis of governance in sub-Saharan Africa which emphasised human and political rights as essential ingredients of good government.[54] Syria's own policies of stabilisation and adjustment formulated in the late 1980s were not negotiated with international financial institutions but were instead home-made substitutes[55] designed to avoid such an eventuality. However, there was no guarantee that the Bretton Woods institutions would not have to play a role at some stage. Already, Syria could hardly hope for much sympathy from these institutions as it had failed to repay an earlier World Bank loan, thus accumulating arrears of some $200m by 1990.[56]

In the period which was marked by declining Soviet support Damascus thus has been repeatedly confronted with political conditions on the part of external actors who controlled its access to material resources. As critical reports and comments in the official Syrian newspapers *Tishrin*, *al-Ba'th*, and *al-Thawra* confirm, the Syrian leadership was cruelly aware of the emerging new logic behind European and American development and aid policies [50] In many ways this logic recalled and yet exceeded earlier experiences in which Arab donors for political reasons withheld much needed financial aid from Syria.

Certainly nobody in Damascus intended to jump the gun, not least because there were plenty of arguments to make authoritarianism palatable to potential donors. After all, the Syrian regime had repressed Islamist opposition movements, the main bogies of European and American public opinion and the potential beneficiaries of political liberalisation. Nor did anybody in government or in the rising business community believe in any necessary relationship between economic and political markets. Nonetheless, it was clearly important to take into account new international criteria for the disbursement of crucial resources.

The Relative Importance of Causes

At this stage the question arises of the extent to which the relative liberalisation of authoritarianism in Syria was caused by economic liberalisation and its social correlates on the one hand and by global developments linked to changes in the Soviet Union on the other. The answer in a case like this will necessarily remain in part speculative, in particular when it is touches upon the importance which the decline of the USSR and the end of the Cold War may have had for economic liberalisation in Syria. Nonetheless, beyond such areas of doubt a few general tendencies appear with considerable clarity.

While global changes never exposed Syria to open external pressures for democratisation, the electoral reform of 1990 may certainly have been influenced by a general awareness among its rulers that the country needed a democratic face-lift in order to court the good opinion of potential external supporters. Political conditionality in the distribution of public international aid and improving Syria's image among key American and European players in the Middle East 'peace process' were the chief considerations in this respect. Equally, the fear of a political explosion similar to very recent instances in parts of Eastern Europe may have played its part, not least as China was the only country left which could possibly provide some material and moral support to suppress it.

Under these conditions economic liberalisation and its social correlates appear as the most important reasons for redrawing the boundaries of political participation. In the absence of sustained overt demands from influential groups within the country, political change seems to have been introduced by the regime in order to reward, please, and even functionally associate the private sector which played such an important role in and after the economic crisis of the mid-1980s.

The main beneficiaries of the new electoral law were indeed members of the business community who in 1990 won more than a fair share of the seats earmarked for independents.[57] In 1994 they again increased their share in parliamentary representation: more than 40 per cent of the independents elected were merchants, industrialists and entrepreneurs whose fortunes had risen thanks to deregulation and economic liberalisation since the 1980s.[58] In fact, the new electoral law was implicitly biased in favour of wealthy candidates who were able to fund their campaigns.without the support of parties. More generally, the decision to liberalise political participation on the occasion of parliamentary elections, which under the constitution had to be held at about that time, indicates a degree of planning rather than a spontaneous reaction to events elsewhere. The impression is reinforced by the fact that a shift in economic policies preceded political liberalisation by a few years, just the time needed to allow new forces in society to gel.

Similarly, the inclusion of private sector representatives in delegations to the Bretton Woods institutions and the open campaign for seats on the Damascus Chamber of Commerce were both a response to domestic economic change which greatly enhanced the role of the private sector. The same applies even more clearly to the informal channels of communication, representation and participation which have been established between civilian capitalists and the military establishment which itself controls large amounts of private capital.

On the other hand, the redrafting of labour legislation with a view to rendering trade unions formally independent of the Ba'th Party and of government has been initiated only in response to external pressures, in particular from the USA. The Syrian private sector will obviously benefit from access to US markets, but has never called for improving such access through a new labour law. The private sector could probably turn the existence of independent trade unions to its advantage; but considering its mainly old-fashioned patrimonial or downright non-consensual approach to industrial relations any sort of union still appears as a danger.

Equally, the partial relaxation of internal repression in the last few years is largely due to external pressures or their anticipation on the part of the regime. This applies in particular to the liberation of political prisoners, with the proviso, though, that their organisations had anyway been thoroughly destroyed in the meantime. When it occurred, the release of political prisoners or the improvement of their conditions followed a combination of external sanctions such as those voted by the European Parliament, negotiations in private, and indications that these sanctions would be rescinded. Some among the political prisoners released who had fought in Islamist movements were close to parts of the private sector; however, others such as the more 'radical' Ba'this around Salah Jadid and Nur al-Din al-Atasi (himself released only to die shortly afterwards) who were arrested when Asad launched his Corrective Movement in 1970, are still the grave-diggers of the booming private sector of the 1960s in the eyes of most business people. Nor did the business community demand the release of communists whose cause in some cases was championed by the US embassy in Damascus.[59] There is no instance in which the main beneficiaries of economic reform stressed the respect of human rights as a general principle.

The picture emerging is one in which the boundaries of political participation were redrawn largely, though certainly not exclusively, in response to social change brought about by economic liberalisation. Conversely, improvements in terms of human rights were mainly the result of external pressures or attempts by the regime to preempt such pressures. Put differently, changes at the first level of political liberalisation were primarily caused by the one of the two sets of independent variables, while changes at the second level of political liberalisation were caused by the other set of independent variables. However, while global developments prompted political change in Syria through the combination of overt pressures from outside and an awareness among the Syrian leadership that change was necessary or desirable, economic liberalisation and its distributional consequences hardly led to any similar pressures from below. Unlike changes at the level of human rights, changes in terms of political participation were thus in no way imposed on the regime. Rather they were granted by the regime in an attempt to incorporate and associate as junior partners the rising civilian part of the private sector and, to a lesser degree, a few other groups in society.[60] In line with arguments referred to earlier, the process is one of coalition-building from above, not one of pluralistic politics of pressure groups from below. Needless to say, the coalition thus built in no way resembles a 'political pact'.

The additional question as to whether reinforced economic liberalisation after the mid-1980s and its social and political consequences actually constitute a set of independent variables, is more difficult to answer. It is certainly true that the crisis of the Syrian development strategy in the mid-1980s was precipitated by a decline in material support from the major oil producing states, not from the USSR, which at the time still continued to keep up appearances. Soviet support for Damascus was thrown into question only under Gorbachev when Syria's economy was already in deep trouble. It can therefore not be argued, as it could in other cases, that the withdrawal of Soviet support contributed to the economic crisis. However, the choice of increasing economic liberalisation as the means to overcome the crisis roughly coincided with the period in which Soviet support could no longer be taken for granted and in which the public sector-based development strategy of the USSR itself had to be questioned. The remedy, rather than the malady, may have been inspired by global developments. The remedy, of course, could be adopted only because long ago the representatives of the regime, behind the smoke screen of 'Arab socialism', had themsleves opted for lucrative private enterprise.[61]

The further growth and possible emancipation of the private sector may of course reinforce claims to political participation on the part of entrepreneurs, merchants and industrialists. For this to happen, however, several obstacles would need to be overcome and various changes would have to occur. Even then only selected categories of individuals are likely to benefit from enhanced political participation and a greater respect for civil and human rights; any democratisation of sorts will hardly extend beyond groups like the business community who have or may have sufficient leverage to extract political concessions for themselves. These beneficiaries have little interest in sharing their benefits with society at large. Even if they overcome their present divisions and fears and develop into something like a bourgeoisie, they will hardly become the defenders of liberal political values as such.

The relative rise of private capital has already been accompanied by a visible decline in the influence of the institutions associated with the traditional constituencies of the regime. This applies to the Ba'th Party itself which may be viewed as a broad coalition of various social forces with a strong basis among organised labour and the salariat. Labour, of course, is hardly organised outside the public sector which is itself on the decline. While the new labour law may free trade unions from the control of the Ba'th, it will also reduce existing employment guarantees and more generally affect the rights of workers and the means available to them. Thus there will be no societal force able to redress the balance and defend the rights, including that to representation, of others than those who directly gain from economic liberalisation. Under these conditions effective demands for the generalisation of political rights and participation could only come from outside the country – a fact that would not necessarily make them popular inside, even among potential beneficiaries.

Syria in the Regional Context

In other states of the Arab East processes of political liberalisation in terms of participation or human rights seem to coincide far less than in Syria with developments in the former Soviet Union and the end of the Cold War. As indicated earlier, the chronology of events in Egypt even contradicts any positive linkage between these global developments and political liberalisation at home.

In yet other cases, chronological coincidence appears to be entirely accidental. In Lebanon, for instance, the parliamentary elections of 1992 need to be analysed in the context of the Taif agreement of 1989 and the end of the civil war.[62] In Yemen the general elections of 1993 served to sort out the internal balance of power after the northern and southern parts of the country had been reunited;[63] the end of the Cold War favoured these elections only to the extent that it favoured reunification. The return to constitutional and parliamentary life in Kuwait probably involved considerable external encouragement and pressures on the ruling Sabah family; however, these pressures were prompted less by the end of the Cold War than by the incompetence of the Sabah regime in the Kuwait crisis of 1990–91 and the popular resistance to Iraqi opposition. In Sudan, finally, the general elections of 1986 resulted from the collapse of the Nimayri regime in 1985, at a time when it was premature to proclaim the end of the Cold War; if external support was withheld from Nimayri, it was withheld in spite of the Cold War, not because of its end.[64]

In Jordan the portents of political liberalisation date back to 1984 when King Hussein, prior to any changes in Moscow, reinstated the country's parliament which had been suspended in the wake of the military defeat of 1967. On this occasion political elections were held to fill several seats which had become vacant over these years [65]. Five years later, in 1989, general elections were held in which candidates, similar to the Syrian elections in 1990, could only run as independents. According to most sources, the regime did not attempt to influence the actual election process to any significant degree. Consequently, forty-eight out of the total of eighty deputies elected were critical of key political choices of the regime or identified themselves openly with opposition forces; among the latter twenty-one deputies adhered to the views of the Jordanian Muslim Brothers. The new parliament quickly became a place of lively debate with its proceedings extensively covered and discussed by the media; it had its say in budgetary matters and in the preparation of new legislation concerning for instance taxation, the press and political parties. Accompanying the elections of 1989 was a considerable relaxation of internal repression. The press could report more freely, political prisoners were released, and opposition could be voiced more openly. Two years later in 1991, an end was declared to the state of emergency.[66]

Although the elections of 1989 coincided with the advanced decline of the Soviet Union and the end of the Cold War, they first of all reflected developments in the policies and politics of the kingdom. The way for elections had been paved by King Hussein's decision, a year earlier, to sever all administrative ties with the Israeli-occupied West Bank, thus legitimating a poll limited to the East Bank where no foreign forces could interfere in the voting. The actual decision to go to the polls in 1989 was precipitated by serious riots in Ma'an in spring and general unease about the economic policies of the regime. Like Syria, Jordan since the early 1980s had experienced an economic crisis in which decreasing financial support from the major Arab oil-producing states played an important part. Unlike Syria, however, it accepted support on conditions posed by the IMF which prompted the riots.[67] In the early 1980s the return of sorts to parliamentary life was intended to prevent the emerging economic crisis from degenerating into a political one.[68] In the late 1980s, the liberalisation of Jordanian authoritarianism was an attempt to absorb general discontent through the generalisation of limited participation; increasingly, however, it has become a strategy to incorporate as junior partners actors whose efforts are needed to keep country and regime afloat. Even though in the Jordanian context these actors may more easily be defined in 'tribal' terms, the logic is the same as in Syria.[69]

Other restrictions on political participation were removed in the parliamentary elections of 1993 when candidates could openly run on party lists. In part at least these new possibilities resulted from the party law passed by the outgoing parliament. However, the new electoral law under which the 1993 elections were conducted also changed the voting procedure in ways that favoured forces loyal to the king. The new single transferable vote procedure in practice favoured 'tribal' leaders and candidates with 'traditional legitimacy'. More importantly, it was enacted without any significant input from parliament itself, thus serving as a reminder that legislative powers continued to be vested in the executive as well. Not surprisingly, the composition of the new parliament was more to the liking of the regime.[70] Political participation remained a process managed from above as could also be seen in the drafting of the National Charter in 1991 which largely occured outside parliament. More recently, the political climate has become more repressive again, though less dramatically than in Egypt.[71]

In Egypt political liberalisation preceded the end of the Cold War by many years and has inspired an important debate which cannot even be summarised in the present context.[72] Substantial by regional standards, but nonetheless limited to strictly guided democracy, it began to take shape during the Carter presidency in the USA and was certainly not uninfluenced by its emphasis on human rights and popular participation. Without any doubt, however, the imperatives of regime consolidation and the societal correlates of new economic polices were the paramount factors in the country's transition to democratic appearances. From the moment he came into power, president Anwar al-Sadat attempted to weed out the remaining followers of his predecessor, Gamal Abd al-Nasir and to build up his own constituency or clientele. A measure of political participation contributed to the final demise of the Nasirists who continued to command support in the single party, the Arab Socialist Union; at the same time it served to reward individuals and forces loyal to Sadat. Moreover, economic liberalisation which began in earnest after the October War in 1973 and the October Paper a year later, produced new social cleavages and thus put the existing tight corporatist model to the test.

As early as 1975 'platforms' were allowed to constitute themselves within the single party; these platforms then rapidly developed into independent parties. The first multi-party elections to the Egyptian parliament after the end of the monarchy were held in 1979. At the height of the second Cold War, in 1984, new legislative elections were held, which many observers considered as a democratic watershed. Largely seen as free and on the whole unrigged, they nonetheless advantaged the regime party which was duly returned with an absolute majority. Various provisions of the electoral procedure were subsequently declared unconstitutional by the competent courts, leading to early general elections, first in 1987 and again in 1990. The fact that the regime accepted the court rulings could to an extent be seen as a confirmation of Egypt's departure from authoritarianism. However, conditions in Egypt changed soon and by mid-1992, after the assassination of the secularist writer Farag Foda, the regime was locked into a violent conflict with parts of the Islamist opposition.[73] In the face of threats and violence by parts of the opposition, political repression was reinforced on all levels including numerous arrests, disappearances, torture, scores of death sentences and campaigns against human rights organisations. At one stage even the interior minister admitted to 10,000 political detainees. New legislation drastically reduced the autonomy of professional organisations, some of which had become strongholds of Islamist forces, abolished the election of deans of faculties and of mayors, and ensured victory of pro-regime candidates in the trade union elections. In the parliamentary elections in 1995 members of the regimes National Democratic Party won a majority of 94 per cent of the seats.[74]

In the 1990s, the Egyptian government was repeatedly, though discreetly, reminded by American officials of minimal human rights standards in its fight against Islamist movements.[75] However, explicit conditionality of external support remained limited to economic reforms, and even then remained largely rhetoric.The level of aid was maintained,[76] partly to enable the government to reduce internal opposition through economic improvement. At any rate, in the eyes of many, Egypt continued to fulfil the minimum standards for democracies. Voters were regularly called to the polls and the human rights record was still better than that of Iraq. At a time when the end of the Cold War is established as some sort of unquestionable truth, the liberal values allegedly associated with it are less and less respected in Egypt. External pressures in favour of political participation and human rights are negligible if not entirely absent.

Ultimately, it may be the continued absence of any sort of political liberalisation in a number of Middle Eastern states which gives the true measure of the impact that global changes had, or failed to have, on domestic politics in the region. Despite their dependency on external support during the Kuwait war, the rulers of Saudi Arabia managed to limit representation to an appointed advisory council with no legislative powers. The House of Saud even thwarted the accreditation of a new US ambassador who previously had spoken out in favour of political reforms.

Conclusion

Beyond Syria the end of the Cold War and its causes appear to have made an even less important contribution to the liberalisation of authoritarianism than in Syria itself. Even where global and domestic developments coincide, the linkage tends to be chronological rather than logical. In these cases, and in countries where processes of political liberalisation started earlier, the end of the Cold War may have helped to consolidate such processes; however, developments in Sudan and Egypt prove that political liberalisation could be reversed even then. In Syria itself the end of the Cold War was only one of two major factors leading to political 'decompression' and in its effects remained largely limited to human rights. Furthermore, although the 'new world order' generally benefited the Arab human rights movement, it is, until this day, unable to operate in Syria.[77]

Equally important for political liberalisation in Syria, as earlier in Egypt and Jordan, were attempts by the regimes to incorporate as junior partners actors and forces which could contribute to their security and welfare. More often than not, the actors or forces concerned were owners of private capital who contributed to the relative success of economic restructuring. This is obvious in Syria and Egypt but also true for Jordan where the elections of 1993 favoured 'tribal' grandees with fortunes. Private capital was sought and enfranchised not only in countries hitherto relying on a strong public sector but also in Jordan and Kuwait where economic policies were already relatively liberal. Under both types of conditions a palliative had to be found to replace decreasing revenue from rent.

In Syria the end of the Cold War exercised a greater influence on political change than elsewhere largely because material and moral support from the pre-Gorbachev Soviet Union had enabled the regime to ignore demands for the respect of human rights in particular. In their universal definition human rights were not a priority in the old USSR and Soviet strategic interest in Syria would have in any case have relegated them to the background. Having been an ally of sorts of the losing side in the Cold War, Syria was therefore exposed to greater but certainly not great demands when it had to argue its case vis-à-vis the victors of the Cold War who defended these values at least rhetorically. Syria found itself all the more exposed to such demands as they could be used to put it under pressure with regard to other issues, in particular its relations with Israel.

Compared to other parts of the world such as Africa (see Michael Bratton's contribution to this volume) external pressures for political liberalisation have remained modest in the Middle East. The European Parliament, for instance, voted the previously frozen financial protocols for Syria not long after Damascus had released less than the majority of its political prisoners. The alleged incompatibility of Islam with democracy, deeply ingrained in European and American thought, may account for much of this attitude. However, equally important seems to be the fear that substantial political liberalisation or even democratisation might collide with the stability of regimes favourable to 'Western' interests. Not always very rationally, Islamist movements which could greatly benefit from liberalisation are seen as principally hostile to these interests. There is little doubt that once in power they would refuse to accept the present form of the Israeli–Arab peace process which is a centre-piece of American policies towards the Middle East. However, beyond that issue and an obvious disagreement about certain moral values, Western fears are largely inspired by the Huntingtonian obsession with a future 'clash of civilisations'.[78]

This obsession is certainly the major reason why the victors in the Cold War have failed to use their aid monopoly to advance political participation and defend human rights in Saudi Arabia, the Gulf and Egypt, where regimes are more or less openly fighting Islamist oppositional groups. The growing alienation in Egypt between the state and important parts of society, the initial cause of internal repression, is of course in no direct way connected to the end of the Cold War and does not point to a potential ambiguity of its effects for political liberalisation. Rather, this growing alienation is in part the product of economic liberalisation which, in the 1970s, contributed to a degree of political liberalisation. Privileging growth which probably is not sustainable, and neglecting distribution, economic liberalisation in Egypt as in most similar cases, has produced its losers, largely in the public sector, the lower levels of the administration and in addition through the partial abrogation of the land reform in the countryside. Though more than timid, the privatisation of public sector enterprises will cost hundreds of thousands their jobs while an insufficient number of new jobs is created.[79] Reactive and prophylactic repression through rigged parliamentary elections and greater government control over professional syndicates and trade unions is supposed to give the regime some respite.

Since external pressures for liberalisation were extremely limited in the Middle East, and were sometimes abandoned altogether, they also failed to reinforce internal factors to the extent to which this could happen in the case of numerous African states (see Michael Bratton's contribution to this volume). The winners of the Cold War never insisted on human rights and political participation to an extent that would have enabled internal forces to emerge, mobilise and benefit from such pressures sufficiently to bring about major changes. At best, thus, the end of the Cold War created a climate in the Middle East in which governments in certain cases pursued more readily policies of a more liberal character.

Finally, some reference should be made to the positive or negative effects the Kuwait crisis and second Gulf War in 1990–91 may have had for political liberalisation in the Arab East at large.[80] In Kuwait itself, of course, the war led to the revival of parliamentary life, though within the limits of the 1962 constitution. In Egypt, it exacerbated the conflict between the regime and many Islamist groups and their followers. In that sense, it may well have contributed to the re-authoritarisation of politics around and after 1992. However, the regime's conflict with the Islamists predated the Kuwait war and had much to do with the growing socio-economic anomies in the country. In Jordan, the 1993 amendments to the electoral law disadvantaged 'ideological' currents which had supported Iraq, but nevertheless maintained some of the achievements of political liberalisation. In Syria the regime continued to liberate political prisoners and called new elections in 1994, even though there had been substantial criticism of its participation in the coalition against Iraq. In Syria, more than anywhere else, a certain degree of political decompression decided prior to the Kuwait crisis was maintained after it.

The less uniform development of authoriatarianism in the various Arab states after the Kuwait crisis confirms the limited impact of this crisis. Concerning the erosion of authoritarian features, the end of the Cold War and economic liberalisation seem to have been factors of far greater importance. However, similar to the effects of the Kuwait crisis, those of economic liberalisation have been double-edged and sometimes reinforced authoriatarianism.

Notes

1 Definition of the 'authoritarian' system, given by R. Owen, *State, Power and Politics in the Making of the Modern Middle East* (Routledge, London, 1992) p. 38.

2 Cf. e.g. M. Farouk-Sluglett and P. Sluglett, *Iraq since 1958: From Revolution to Dictatorship* (KPI, London, 1987).

3 For a general critique of tendencies to stress 'irrationality' and 'despotism' in the politics of the Middle East or 'Orient', see, e.g., S. Bromley, *Rethinking Middle East Politics: State Formation and Development* (Polity Press, Cambridge , 1994) ch. 1; for a case study, see G. Michaud (*nom de plume* of M. Seurat) 'Terrorisme d'Etat, terrorisme contre l'Etat: le cas syrien' *Esprit* no. 94/95 (octobre–novembre 1984) pp. 188–201.

4 'Neo-patrimonialism' may be seen as the key feature of Third World politics in general, though clearly defined as 'authoritarian' in character, e.g. C. Clapham, *Third World Politics: An Introduction* (Croom Helm, London, 1985) p. 68; see also P. Pawelka, *Herrschaft und Entwicklung im Nahen Osten: Aegypten* (Deutsche Universitäts Taschenbücher, Heidelberg, 1985); for a critical discussion of this and other notions in the Egyptian context, see G. Kraemer, *Aegypten unter Mubarak: Identität und nationales Interesse* (Nomos, Baden-Baden, 1986).

5 E.g. N. Ayubi, *The State and Public Policies in Egypt since Sadat*, (Ithaca, Exeter, 1994).

6 R. A. Hinnebusch, *Authoritarian Power and State Formation in Ba'thist Syria: Army, Party, and Peasant*, (Westview, Boulder, 1990) p.322; R. A. Hinnebusch, *Egyptian Politics under Sadat: The Post-Populist Development of an Authoritarian-Modernizing State*, (Lynne Rienner, Boulder, 1988).

7 For a recent discussion of this approach, see Bromley, *Rethinking Middle East Politics,* especially p. 16ff, including his critique of E. Gellner, *Muslim Society* (Cambridge University Press, Cambridge, 1981).

8 For instance those authors who stress the specific features of Mediterranean societies, see e.g. G. Tillion, *Le harem et les cousins* (Editions du Seuil, Paris, 1966).

9 As a matter of course this need not imply neglecting cultural or other locally specific factors, see Owen, *State, Power and Politics*. A partly different universalist argument is developed by Bromley, *Rethinking Middle East Politics*. While he is as critical as Bromley of dependency theory, J. Waterbury, *The Egypt of Nasser and Sadat: The Political Economy of Two Regimes* (Princeton University Press, Princeton, 1983) is nonetheless one of the key case studies emphasising universal problems of political economy; more recently, however, Waterbury added Islam as an important cultural factor, see his 'Democracy

without Democrats? The Potential for Political Liberalization in the Middle East' in G. Salamé (ed.) *Democracy without Democrats? The Renewal of Politics in the Muslim World*, (I.B. Tauris, London, 1994) pp. 23–47. Issues of international political economy are emphasised by D. Pool, 'Staying at Home with the Wife: Democratization and its Limits in the Middle East' in G. Parry and M. Moran (eds) *Democracy and Democratization* (Routledge, London, 1994) pp. 196–216.

10 See e.g. Saad Eddin Ibrahim, *al-Mujtama'wa'l-dawla fi al-watan al-arabi*, (Markaz Dirasat al-Wahda al-'Arabiyya, Beirut, 1988). The debate is reassessed in *Middle East Journal* lix/2 (1993).

11 E.g. Hinnebusch, *Authoritarian Power and State Formation*; V. Perthes, *Staat und Gesellschaft in Syrien 1970-1989* (Deutsches Orient-Institut, Hamburg, 1990); V. Perthes *The Political Economy of Syria under Asad*, (I. B. Tauris, London, 1995); E. Picard, 'Ouverture économique et renforcement militaire en Syrie', *Oriente Moderno* lix (Gennaio–Dicembre 1979) pp. 663–76; P. Seale, *Asad of Syria: The Struggle for the Middle East*, (I.B. Tauris, London, 1988); M. Seurat, 'Les populations, l'Etat et la société', in A. Raymond (ed.) *La Syrie d'aujourd'hui*, (Centre National de la Recherche Scientifique, Paris, 1980) pp. 87–140; M. Seurat, *L'Etat de barbarie* (Editions du Seuil, Paris, 1989).

12 See e.g. H. Barkey (ed.) *The Politics of Economic Reform in the Middle East* (St. Martin's Press, New York, 1992); I. Harik and D. J. Sullivan (eds) *Privatization and Liberalization in the Middle East*, (Indiana University Press, Bloomingtion, 1992); E. Murphy and T. Niblock (eds) *Economic and Political Liberalization in the Middle East* (British Academic Press, London, 1993).

13 In this respect G. O'Donnell, P. Schmitter and L. Whitehead (eds) *Transitions from Authoritarian Rule: Prospects for Democracy* (four vols, Johns Hopkins University Press, Baltimore, 1986) may be usefully compared to Salamé (ed.) *Democracy without Democrats.*

14 E.g. Waterbury, *The Egypt of Nasser and Sadat.*

15 Term used by Raymond A. Hinnebusch, 'Liberalization in Syria: The Struggle of Economic and Political Rationality' in E. Kienle (ed.) *Contemporary Syria: Liberalization between Cold War and Cold Peace* (Tauris Academic Press, London, 1994) pp. 97–113.

16 For partly converging analyses of the relationship between economic and political change in Syria, see also S. Heydemann, 'The Political Logic of Economic Rationality: Selective Stabilization in Syria' in Barkey (ed.) *The Politics of Economic Reform*; E. Picard, 'Infitah économique et transition démocratique en Syrie' in R. Bocco and M.-R. Djalili (eds) *Moyen-Orient: Migrations, démocratisation, médiations* (Presses Universitaires de France, Paris, 1994) pp. 9–32. For Jordan see below.

17 For a critical summary of the liberal credo in the context of Eastern Europe after the Cold War, see J. Kirk Laux, 'World Economy and Democratization in Central Europe: Complementarities and Contradictions', paper presented at the 26th World Congress of the International Political

Studies association (IPSA), Berlin, 1994.

18 In 'advanced' cases, the process may be seen as a result of class formation or of taxation; for a critical summary of these views, see J. Leca, 'Democratization in the Arab World: Uncertainty, Vulnerability and Legitimacy. A tentative conceptualization and some Hypotheses' in Salamé (ed.), *Democracy without Democrats?* p. 70ff. In the present context, its own results seem to be limited to coalition-building, to regimes changing their constituencies or to the selective enfranchising of social groups and actors, see e.g. Ayubi, *The State and Public Policies*; Heydemann, 'The Political Logic of Economic Rationality' pp. 11–40; for a summary of these approaches, see E. Kienle, 'Introduction', in Kienle (ed.) *Contemporary Syria,* pp. 1–13. More generally, political effects of economic reform have been discussed by S. Haggard and R. R. Kaufman, 'Economic Adjustment and the Prospects for Democracy' in S. Haggard and R. R. Kaufman (eds) *The Politics of Structural Adjustment* (Princeton University Press, Princeton, 1992) pp. 319–50; J. M. Nelson, 'Poverty, Equity and the Politics of Adjustment', in ibid., pp. 221–69.

19 E.g. Leca, 'Democratization in the Arab World'.

20 For the impact of global changes related to the decline of the USSR, see e.g. L. Diamond and M. F. Plattner (eds) *The Global Resurgence of Democracy* (Johns Hopkins University Press, Baltimore, 1993); F. Marte, *Political Cycles in International Relations: The Cold War and Africa* (University of Amsterdam Press, Amsterdam, 1994); G. Pridham, E. Herring and G. Sanford, *Building Democracy? The International Dimension of Democratization in Eastern Europe* (University of Leicester Press, Leicester, 1994) who, however, develop an argument different from the one above. Concerning the relevance of external influences for domestic political change more generally, see e.g. M. Kahler, 'External Influences, Conditionality, and the Politics of Adjustment', in Haggard and Kaufman (eds) *The Politics of Structural Adjustment*, pp. 89–136; Pool, 'Staying at Home with the Wife'; G. Sørensen (ed.) *Political Conditionality*, (Frank Cass, London, 1993); B. Stallings, 'International Influence on Economic Policy: Debt, Stabilization and Structural Reforms', in Haggard and Kaufman (eds) *The Politics of Structural Adjustment,* pp. 41–88.

21 For earlier Syrian elections, see Perthes, *Staat und Gesellschaft in Syrien.* p. 275; E. Picard, 'Syria Returns to Democracy: The May 1973 Legislative Elections', in G. Hermet et al (eds) *Elections without Choice* (Macmillan, London, 1978).

22 Voters could delete the names of independent candidates on the list but this hardly affected the overall election result; for examples and additional details, see V. Perthes, 'Syria's Parliamentary Elections: Remodelling Asad's Political Base', *Middle East Report,* January–February 1992, pp. 15–18, 35.

23 The Hizb al-Qawmi al-Suri, known in English as Syrian Socialist Nationalist Party, is the only party not formally legalised but tolerated. One of the independent deputies is a prominent representative of this party.

24 For details, see Perthes, 'Syria's Parliamentary Elections'.

25 Parliamentary debates were widely covered in the official Syrian media, e.g. the last debates of the 5th Assembly, see *Tishrin* or *al-Ba'th*, 8–10 June 1994; for details cf. also *al-Hayat*, 3 June 1994, 12 June 1994.

26 *al-Hayat*, 27–28 August 1994, 10 October 1994; *Le Monde*, 30 August 1994.

27 *al-Hayat*, 12 June 1994, 15 August 1994, 23 August 1994, 27 August 1994, 10 September 1994.

28 *al-Hayat*, 15 August 1993.

29 See e.g. *Tishrin*, 1–5 October 1993; *al-Hayat*, 5 October 1993.

30 For these processes see the various contributions to Kienle (ed.) *Contemporary Syria.*

31 See annual and country reports published by Amnesty International in 1991, 1992, 1993, and subsequently as well *Syria: Indefinite Political Imprisonment* (Amnesty International, London, 1992); also US Government, Department of State, *Country Reports on Human Rights Practices for 1992* (Department of State. Washington, February 1993) p. 1088ff.

32 Reports by Amnesty International for the period concerned, e.g. *Syria: Indefinite Political Imprisonment*; Department of State, *Country Reports on Human Rights Practices for 1992* , p. 1088ff.

33 See *Le Monde*, 25–27 June 1993; [United Nations] Centre for Human Rights, Geneva, United Nations World Conference on Human Rights, Vienna, *Human Rights Law Journal* xiv/9–10 pp. 346–70; United Nations Information Service, press releases HR/VIE/1–39, Vienna, 1993.

34 E.g. *al-Hayat*, 10 September 1994.

35 President Asad on 26 February 1990, quoted according to Syrian Arab Republic Radio, 27 February 1990, in BBC/SWB: *The Middle East and North Africa,* 1 March 1990; see also *Tishrin,* 4 March 1990.

36 E.g. V. Perthes, 'Stages of Economic and Political Liberalization', in Kienle (ed.) *Contemporary Syria* p. 49ff.

37 For the latter notion, see S. J. al-Azm, 'Orientalism and Orientalism in Reverse', *Khamsin: Journal of Revolutionary Socialists of the Middle East* 8 (1981), pp. 5–26.

38 For a detailed account and analysis of economic developments in Syria over the 1970s and 1980s, see Perthes, *Staat und Gesellschaft*; Kienle (ed.) *Contemporary Syria.*

39 For details, see Perthes, *Staat und Gesellschaft,* p.132, and S. Poelling, 'Investment Law No.10: Which Future for the Private Sector?', in Kienle (ed.) *Contemporary Syria,* pp. 14–25.

40 One year after the promulgation of the new investment law (Law No.10/1992) private investment amounting to approx US $1.6bn roughly doubled public investment; for additional details, see Kienle (ed.) *Contemporary Syria,* p. 121ff. For recent figures, see 'Business Brief Syria', quarterly since 1995, London.

41 G. Golan, *Soviet Policies in the Middle East: From World War Two to*

Gorbachev (Cambridge University Press, Cambridge, 1990) p. 278ff; according to E. Karsh, *The Soviet Union and Syria: The Asad Years* (Royal Institute of International Affairs, London, 1988) p. 88ff, Soviet refusals of strategic parity even date back to 1985.

42 Though temporarily resolved through rescheduling, Syria military debt towards the USSR was already an issue in Asad's talks with Gorbachev in Moscow in 1987, see. e.g. Karsh, *The Soviet Union and Syria,* p. 92ff. Figures of Syrian debt owed to the USSR and its successor states vary between $10bn and $12bn due to confusions between military and civilian debt on the one hand and between amounts owed to the ex-USSR and other East European countries; see Kienle (ed.) *Contemporary Syria,* p. 124ff.

43 E.g. *al-Hayat* ,29 December 1992.

44 The annual report by the US Department of State on state-sponsored terrorism for 1995 was the first to state that Syria had not been involved in such activities for several years. However, by that time the US administration had already begun to make other types of cooperation with Syria dependent on conditions detailed below.

45 *Middle East Economic Digest*, 1 November 1986, p.4; 8 November 1986, p.30; 15 November 1986, p.31.

46 *Middle East Economic Digest*, 30 October 1992, p.39.

47 *al-Hayat*, 30 November 1995.

48 See e.g. Department of State, *Country Reports on Human Rights Practices for 1992*, p.1094.

49 For trade directions, see e.g. United Nations, *International Trade Statistics, Yearbook*, (United Nations, New York, N.Y. annual); Syrian Arab Republic (SAR), Central Bureau of Statistics, *Statistical Abstract*, (Damascus, annual); or Economist Intelligence Unit (EIU), *Country Profile: Syria*, (EIU, London, annual).

50 E.g. reactions to the G-7's 'Declaration on East–West Relations' of 1989, in these newspapers, 16–18 July 1989.

51 For details, cf. M. A. Moratinos, 'Derechos Humanos y Cooperación con el Mundo Arabe', in G. Martin Muñoz, *Democracia y Derechos Humanos en el Mundo Arabe*, (Agencia Española de Cooperacion Internacional, Madrid, 1993) pp. 257–74; K. Tomasevski, *Development Aid and Human Rights Revisited* (Pinter, London, 1993) pp. 71–82.

52 OECD, *Development Co-operation*, (OECD, Paris, 1992).

53 See e.g. Laux, 'World Economy and Democratization'.

54 The World Bank, *Sub-Saharan Africa: From Crisis to Sustainable Growth, A Long-Term Perspective*, (World Bank, Washington, 1989).

55 See Heydemann, 'The Political Logic of Economic Rationality', pp. 11–39.

56 E.g. ibid. p.17.

57 Perthes, 'Syria's Parliamentary Elections', p. 17; *al-Hayat*, 3 June 1994 and 12 June 1994. Cases in point are the Damascus deputies Badi' al-Falaha, Baha' al-Din Hasan or Ihsan Sanqar.

58 *al-Hayat*, 27 August 1994, 28 August 1994, 10 September 1994.

59 For the political complexion of those released, see Amnesty International Reports; Department of State, *Country Reports on Human Rights Practices for 1992* , p. 1089; US intervention was confirmed by interviews inside and outside Syria in 1992, 1993 and 1994.

60 For the docile attitude of the private sector, see also J. Bahout, *Les entrepreneurs syriens: économie, affaires et politique* (Les cahiers du CERMOC No. 7, Beirut, 1994).

61 For this aspect and a more detailed analysis of issues raised in the following paragraphs, see the various contributions to Kienle (ed.) *Contemporary Syria.*

62 J. Bahout, 'Liban: les élections législatives de l'été 1992', *Monde arabe: Maghreb–Machrek*, No. 139 (Janvier–Mars 1993) pp. 53–84; V. Perthes, *Der Libanon nach dem Buergerkrieg: Von Ta'if zum gesellschaftlichen Konsensus?* (Nomos, Baden-Baden, 1994).

63 Cf also: J. M. Dorsey, 'Yemen: Elections Seal the Merger', *Middle East International*, 14 April 1993, p.11; A. Lapidot, 'Yemen', in: A. Ayalon (ed.) *Middle East Contemporary Survey*, xiv, (Westview, Boulder, 1995) especially. p. 790ff.

64 See contribution by Charles Tripp to the present volume; for the 1986 elections, their background and consequences, see P. Woodward (ed.) *Sudan After Nimeri*, (Routledge, London, 1991).

65 See L. Brand, 'Economic and Political Liberalization in a Rentier Economy: The Case of the Hashemite Kingdom of Jordan' in.Harik and Sullivan (eds) *Privatization and Liberalization*, pp. 167–88.

66 For the 1989 elections and other measures of political liberalisation, see Brand, 'Economic and Political Liberalization'; L-J. Duclos, 'Les élections législatives en Jordanie', *Maghreb–Machrek* 129 (Janvier 1990) pp. 47–75; R. B. Satloff, 'Jordan's Great Gamble: Economic Crisis and Political Reform', in Barkey (ed.) *The Politics of Economic Reform,* pp. 129–52; Y. Le Troquer, 'Les islamistes, la démocratie et la question palestinienne en Jordanie après juillet 1988', *Revue du Monde Musulman et de la Méditerranée* 68/69 (1994) pp. 133–50.

67 R. Brynen, 'Economic Crisis and Rentier Democratization in the Arab World: The Case of Jordan', *Canadian Journal of Political Science* xxv/1 (1992) pp. 69–90; Duclos, 'Les élections législatives en Jordanie'.

68 Brand, 'Economic and Political Liberalization', p. 181.

69 Brand, 'Economic and Political Liberalization'; Satloff, 'Jordan's Great Gamble'; Riedel, *Demokratisierung in Jordanien.*

70 F. Charillon and A. Mouftard, 'Jordanie: les élections du 8 novembre 1993 et le processus de la paix', *Maghreb–Machrek* 144 (Avril–Juin 1994) pp. 40–54; T. Riedel, 'The 1993 Parliamentary Elections in Jordan' *Orient* xxxv/1 (1994) pp. 51–63; T. Riedel, *Demokratisierung in Jordanien: Die Parlamentswahlen 1993 am Beispiel des Wahlbezirks Al-Karak,* Diplomarbeit, Freie Universitat Berlin, Fachbereich Politische Wissenschaft, 1995.

71 Riedel, *Demokratisierung in Jordanien,* p.32.

72 Cf. e.g. R. A. Hinnebusch, *Egyptian Politics*; G. Kraemer, 'Die Wahl zum aegyptischen Abgeordnetenhaus vom Mai 1984' *Orient* xx/3 (1994) pp. 361–75; Kraemer, *Aegypten unter Mubarak:* G. Kraemer, *Die Wahl zur aegyptischen Volksversammlung vom April 1987* (Stiftung Wissenschaft und Politik, Ebenhausen, 1987); G. Martin Muñoz, *Politica y Elecciones en el Egipto Contemporaneo (1922–1990)*, (n.p., Madrid, 1992); R. Owen, 'Socio-Political Change and Political Mobilization: The Case of Egypt', in G. Salamé (ed.) *Democracy without Democrats?* pp. 183–99; A. Roussillon, 'L'Egypte républicaine: trois régimes pour une révolution', in G. Alleaume and H. Laurens, (eds), *Histoire de l'Egypte de la conquête arabe à nos jours* (Fayard, Paris, forthcoming); Waterbury, *The Egypt of Nasser and Sadat*; see also the reports by the Al-Ahram Centre for Political and Strategic Studies, on the Egyptian elections since 1984, published as *Intikhabat Majlis al-Sha'b: Dirasa wa Tahlil*, (Al-Ahram, Cairo, 1986, 1988, 1992).

73 See Roussillon, 'L'Egypte républicaine'.

74 Amnesty International and Middle East Watch, annual reports for the period concerned; for legislation concerning the press and professional organisations, see e.g. *al-Hayat,* May–August 1995.

75 See e.g. Department of State, *Country Reports on Human Rights Practices for 1992* .

76 See e.g. S. Bromley and R. Bush, 'Adjustment in Egypt? The Political Economy of Reform', *Review of African Political Economy* 60 (1994) pp. 201–13.

77 See for instance J. Paul and J. Stark, 'The Middle East and Human Rights', *MERIP-Report* 149 (Nov–Dec. 1987) pp. 2–6; N. H. Aruri, 'Disaster Area: Human Rights in the Arab World', in ibid., pp. 7–16 ; 'Ali al-Din Hillal (ed.) *al-Dimuqratiyya wa huquq al-insan fi al-watan al-'arabi* (Markaz dirasat al-wahda al-'arabiyya, Beirut, 1986); H. Megally, 'Amnesty International and Human Rights in the Arab World: A Summary of the Last Decade', in Muñoz, *Politica y Elecciones*, pp. 163–75.

78 S. P. Huntington, 'The Clash of Civilizations?' *Foreign Affairs* ixxii/3 (1993) pp. 22–49.

79 See e.g. Bromley and Bush, 'Adjustment in Egypt?'.

80 The effects of this war have been a subject of great debate in the Arab world and among scholars and intellectuals concerned with it; see e.g. Saad Eddin Ibrahim, 'Crises, Elites and Democratization in the Arab World', *Middle East Journal* xivii/2 (1993), pp. 292–306, as compared to R. Falk, 'Democracy Died at the Gulf', in T. Y. Ismael and J. S. Ismael (eds) *The Gulf War and the New World Order: International Relations of the Middle East* (University Press of Florida, Gainesville, 1994) pp. 536–48.

9 ❧ 'Good Governance' and the Ideology of Transformation

David Williams

Introduction

A perplexing and unstable world has emerged since the end of the Cold War. As countries such as Yugoslavia have disintegrated and many of the former Eastern Bloc countries have experienced precipitous economic decline, so the hard realities of potential or actual warfare have tended to replace the heady optimism of 1989. There is an increasing tendency to see the Cold War as an aberration when super-power rivalry and the nature of the Soviet regime operated to interrupt the 'normal' course of events in the international system. In this view, the ending of the Cold War has led to the re-emergence of familiar problems in the international system made more terrifying by the existence of weapons of mass destruction in potentially unstable states. This view is no doubt overplayed; the differential impact of the rapid expansion of the international economy, the dramatic development of communications, the proliferation of international organisations, and the collapse (in practice at least) of the only secular alternative to liberal capitalism, all make seemingly familiar problems more complex. Whatever the nature of these problems there is a sense that neither politicians nor academics are adequately equipped to understand them.[1]

This paper is a contribution to understanding one important area in this post-Cold War world: the relationship between developed and developing countries. It argues that recent changes in the aid policies of developing countries, especially the emergence of a concern with democracy, human rights, and 'good governance', is best understood as a return to pre-World War Two patterns in the relationship between the West and others. The imperatives of state sovereignty are being increasingly overridden by the drive to make others in the West's own image. This drive characterised colonialism and, arguably, all encounters between the West and others since the discovery of America.

While the general pattern of this relationship has altered little, at least two things have changed its appearance. In 1913 the Earl of Cromer could say with confidence that '... in the treatment of subject races, the methods of government practised by England ... are superior, morally and economically, to those of any other foreign nation.'[2] These sorts of pronouncements, utterly familiar in the age of colonialism, have been replaced by a rhetorical commitment to the self-determination of nations, so the language of the drive to transform is different, even if, as we shall see, the reality is very similar. This makes the task of uncovering the transformative drive more difficult as we will have to search below the everyday language of 'objectivity' and 'practicality' which dominates the relationship between the developed and the developing world. Second, the attempted transformation is increasingly being carried out by international organisations and Non-Governmental Organisations (NGOs), not individual states. At the forefront of this drive to transform is the World Bank. It has recently adopted, along with other donors, a set of concerns captured under the label of 'good governance'. This chapter will outline the content of this new set of concerns and suggest reasons why they have become increasingly important for the World Bank. It will argue that 'good governance' is best seen as an 'ideology of transformation', and that this has important implications for how we should attempt to understand relations between developed and developing countries after the end of the Cold War.

Good Governance: a New Consensus?

In recent years a remarkable new development consensus has emerged. At the heart of this new consensus is the view that something has gone drastically wrong with political systems in the Third World, particularly in Africa; and that this failure is a crucial reason for the lack of economic and social development (however defined). This diagnosis points to chronic economic mismanagement, corruption, bureaucratic inefficiency, personalised rule, violations of human rights and so on; and this has led to the view that aid should be used wherever possible to resolve these problems. These views are held by all of the major bi-lateral donors, most of the international organisations and almost all Western NGOs concerned with development.[3]

While there are differences of emphasis, the political reforms advocated in this new consensus include moves toward the increased accountability of Third World governments, support for none-state groups (civil society), respect for the rule of law, the need for a free press, and respect for human rights. USAID has committed itself to 'supporting sustainable African led initiatives for democratic institutions and improved governance'. This is manifested in its focus on broadening participation in development at all levels of society, supporting and strengthening democratic institutions and civil society, and supporting human rights activities.[4] François Mitterand has said that the French government would link its aid contributions to efforts designed to lead to greater liberty and democracy.[5] The German Ministry for Economic Co-operation has introduced criteria for assessing 'the kind and volume of aid for a country'. These include greater popular participation in the political process, responsible and accountable government, and respect for human rights.[6] Japan's 1992 overseas development charter says that Japan will 'implement its overseas development assistance to help ensure the efficient and fair distribution of resources and "good governance" in developing countries.' Part of Japan's 'negotiating position' with potential recipients will include consideration of moves towards democracy, respect for human rights, and political freedoms.[7] The UK position emphasises the importance of effective and honest government, political pluralism, observance of the rule of law, and specifies the need to enhance the capacity of government, curb military expenditure, promote a free press and respect human rights.[8] A recent Overseas Development Administration (ODA) Technical Note suggests that good government issues should be taken into account in all project lending. These issues include the extent of participation by those affected, the extent of institutional accountability and whether recruitment and promotion are on merit or on the basis of ethnic or individual bias. It also points to areas where ODA can work directly to support good government including support for elections, support for democratic institutions such as the judiciary and information dissemination groups, and strengthening the machinery of government through civil service reforms and technical assistance.[9]

The European Committee on Development and Cooperation has suggested that there are certain fundamental democratic and human rights which should be universally applied in Africa, and that the European Development Fund and European Union (EU) budget should be used to support the holding of elections, strengthening the rule of law, aiding the press and grassroots organisations, and promoting NGOs. In 1994, ECU 16 million was set aside for promoting human rights and democracy.[10] The Commonwealth has committed itself to the protection and promotion of 'democracy, democratic process and institutions ... the rule of law, the independence of the judiciary, just and honest government, and fundamental human rights.'[11] The Secretary General of the UN, Boutros Boutros-Ghali, has said that democratisation is the fundamental task of African leaders and that UN activities would support this process.[12]

These organisations have moved somewhat closer to the position held by many NGOs. They have always tended to promote a more 'people centred' development which focuses on issues such as participation, equality and the extension of rights. Oxfam stresses the importance of 'participatory democracy' in its work, and the securing of 'fundamental human rights' to 'priority groups' such as women, children and disabled people.[13] One World Action is 'particularly concerned' with the development of strong civil societies, free and independent media and the impartial rule of law, the legitimacy, accountability and transparency of government, and the protection of civil, political, social, and cultural rights. It 'chooses to work with parties who are committed to strengthening and deepening democratic participation in decision making'.[14] The concerns of individual NGOs are reflected in recent writing on the NGO sector in general. John Clark (who used to work for Oxfam and now works for the World Bank) argues NGOs should be concerned about 'just development', which includes concern for equity, including gender equity, democracy, which includes support for 'civil society', and social justice which includes 'full human rights'.[15]

It is significant in this regard that there has been increased cooperation between the NGO sector and official donors. Numerous formal consultative arrangements have been set up. In Sweden and Denmark NGOs sit on the board of the government development agency. The European Community set up an NGO liaison committee and the UN has a similar arrangement. Specific UN agencies such as UNDP and IFAD have senior advisers on grass-roots and NGO matters, and ECOSOC has established a committee to promote aid to cooperatives.[16] More important than this are schemes for channelling official aid through NGOs. To date, Germany, Sweden, Australia, Netherlands, Norway, Canada, Britain, France, USA and the EU all have co-financing arrangements with NGOs.[17] Many UN agencies have similar arrangements.[18] Official contributions to NGOs from all Development Assistance Committee (DAC) members rose from $12.9 million in 1970 to $200 million in 1986. Total EC contributions rose from $19.5 million in 1980 to $40 million in 1986.[19] In the UK the Joint Funding Scheme channelled £16 million through NGOs in 1989/90.[20] In 1987 the Danish government contributed $69 million to Danish NGOs, France $43.7 million in 1985, Italy $108 million in 1988/89, the Netherlands $159.2 million in 1988, and the USA $900 million in 1987.[21] These sums remain relatively small as a percentage of total overseas development assistance, about 5.3 per cent for DAC countries as a whole, though in the USA the figure is nearer 12 per cent.[22] But they have been rising rapidly and are an important indication of the 'privatisation' of the drive to transform others which is embodied in these calls for democracy and good governance.[23] It is not just that NGOs become delivery agencies in the transformation advocated by Western governments, but that, as we have seen, NGOs themselves are concerned with transforming social and political relationships in developing countries.

There are important issues here which require critical examination: first the different emphases of the various official donors, particularly the differences between the Japanese and American positions, the former being more circumspect than the latter; second, the extent to which this new rhetoric has been translated into practice; and third the numerous inconsistencies and paradoxes of these new concerns, and one might focus here on the relationship between political and economic reform, or on the differing conceptions of the state which these positions embody. While there is no space to consider these in detail here, one point is worth making.[24] Critics tend to point out that the principles of good governance have been applied inconsistently, and one only needs to look at, say, Indonesia or China to see this is right. Nonetheless, there have been some cases where actual or threatened withdrawal of aid has contributed to political changes.[25] Further these new concerns may have influenced countries in other ways by establishing 'rules' or 'norms' to which countries are increasingly expected to adhere.[26] That said, if good governance was simply about rewarding or punishing states for good or bad behaviour we would not expect this new agenda to have a great deal of impact. It is almost bound to get caught up in the practical concerns of the relations between states, particularly where there are clear economic interests at work, and in any case direct pressure on governments to reform tends to be relatively ineffective as the experience with economic sanctions shows. The drive to transform embodied in governance is, however, a transformation at much more 'micro' level – civil service restructuring, retraining of bureaucrats, legal reform, support for NGOs, election monitoring, 'civic education' programmes and the like. It is much more intrusive, much more corrosive of national sovereignty, than any attempt by western governments to influence political systems in developing countries. It is for this reason that the privatisation of this transformative drive is so important, as international organisation and NGOs generally operate at this more micro-level.

The World Bank and Governance[27]

The World Bank, unlike most of the major bi-lateral donors, has shied away from advocating multi-party democracy; though it has said that the two countries with the best economic performance in Africa, Botswana and Mauritius, both had 'effective parliamentary democracies', and that 'political legitimacy and consensus are preconditions for sustainable development'.[28] The Bank's argument is that to advocate a particular form of political system would violate its Articles of Agreement which prohibit political considerations from influencing loan proposals. There may also be a sense that multi-party democracy is not always conducive to effective economic and political reform. That said, the General Counsel of the Bank argued that internal and external political events which have 'significant direct economic effects' can properly be taken into consideration in the Bank's lending decisions.[29] We will return to this justification for the Bank's involvement in political reform later. For the sake of clarity we can divide the Bank's concerns into five areas.[30] The first four focus upon reform of the government and administration, the fifth upon the promotion of what the Bank calls 'civil society'.

Improvement of public sector management.

Here the focus is particularly upon civil service reform including restructuring and retraining, and upon 'building capacity'. Failure to reform public sector management 'progressively erodes the capacity of the state to provide economic and social services'.[31] Civil service reform should concentrate on the rationalisation of bureaucracies, where possible building in 'incentives' to performance including competition or market surrogates 'which are capable of influencing institutional performance when market competition is not possible'. These might include managerial or organisational measures to create an atmosphere of competition among units and/or individuals within organisations, or mechanisms for suppliers and beneficiaries to exert pressure.[32] African bureaucrats must be 'professionalised'. '[F]amily and ethnic ties that strengthen communal actions have no place in central government agencies, where staff must be selected on merit, and public and private monies not be confused.'[33] There is a need to provide policy analysis and economic management training to give sub-Saharan African governments 'critical expertise to analyse and articulate the region's development goals', and enable them to have a 'firmer grip on the economic destiny of their countries'.[34]

Increased accountability of government and administration.

In Africa there are few mechanisms whereby the public can 'demand and monitor' government performance. This is exacerbated by the lack of information about the state of the economy, market conditions and government policies and intentions, all of which are 'crucial for private sector calculations'.[35] Increased accountability and transparency are necessary to reduce the dangers of corruption, to improve government economic policies and to increase the efficiency and effectiveness of economic actors. There is a need to develop properly functioning government accounting and external audit systems; a need to increase the provision and dissemination of information by the World Bank, NGOs and others; and finally a need to improve the collection of information by the government itself by developing effective statistical collection techniques.[36]

Legal reforms.

The World Bank argues that an effective system of law is vital for the efficient use of resources and productive investment; in particular it reduces transaction costs and ensures property rights. The reforms advocated have an instrumental part which concentrates on the formal elements necessary for a system of laws to exist, such as a set of rules known in advance, and an independent judiciary, and a substantive part which refers to the content of laws and concepts such as 'fairness', 'justice' and 'liberty'. A 'fair' system of laws, according to the Bank, is one which is 'conducive to development'.[37]

Decentralisation of government and administration.

If undertaken properly decentralisation can lead to 'significant improvements' in efficiency and effectiveness by reducing the overloading of central government, and improving access to decision-making and participation. Efforts should be made to introduce mechanisms for increased participation ('voice') and competition ('exit') at the local level.[38] At the same time there is a need to strengthen local government capabilities by providing training programmes for regional administrators. The object should be to 'capitalise on the energies and resources of local people'.

Civil Society

The World Bank has become increasingly convinced of the importance of building a 'civil society'. This involves support for voluntary organisations and NGOs, the informal and formal economies, as well as for the more obvious groups in civil society such as universities and professional organisations. It involves the creation of a 'pluralistic institutional structure' and intermediaries between the government and the people.[39] These groups will demand better performance from the government, can hold it accountable for its actions, are important in the collection and dissemination of information about the government and the economy, and can be centres for policy analysis and formulation.

There is one further feature of the governance agenda worth noting which will be important for our analysis of governance. There is increased stress on the importance of 'building on the indigenous'.[40] 'Each country has to devise institutions which are consonant with its social values'; '... for change to be effective it must be firmly rooted in the societies concerned'; World Bank programmes must 'reflect national characteristics and be consistent with a country's cultural values'.[41] The Bank cites the examples of Japan and the South-East Asian NICs to support this view.[42] As one commentator has said, 'Japan, the Republic of Korea and Taiwan are examples of advanced economies that have achieved high levels of modern production and advanced technology while maintaining their unique national traits'.[43] The assumption I think is that other developing countries can do the same.

Why Governance?

Perceived failure of structural adjustment.

We will not be concerned here with criticising the World Bank's adjustment policies. These criticisms are numerous and include the view that such policies are 'not consistent with Africa's long-run development needs'; that there is no theoretical basis for advocating wholesale economic liberalisation; that structural adjustment fails to stimulate a supply-side response; and that the burden of adjustment falls unduly on the poor.[44] The mass of secondary literature on adjustment and the Bank's own assessments of its success or failure preclude the need for further comment here.[45] What is important is that it became clear to many within the Bank that a major reason for the limited (at best) success of structural adjustment programmes was political and institutional weakness.[46] An evaluation of structural adjustment lending undertaken in 1988 concluded that 'severe institutional and managerial weaknesses have proved unexpectedly serious constraints to better performance'.[47] The World Bank was drawn into large-scale policy reform by its structural adjustment lending and it discovered not only limited state capacities to enact these reforms, but that the failure to even try to enact them was often the result of explicitly political considerations. Most importantly, if the reforms were to be sustainable they would need to be supported by important sections of a civil society who could exert pressure on the government to continue the reform programme.

Influence of New Political Economy.

The revival of neo-classical economics in the late 1970s and early 1980s is well documented.[48] This revival was reflected in the thinking behind structural adjustment lending which encouraged much greater reliance on the market mechanism. This revival also brought with it a renewed interest in neo-classical political economy (New Political Economy, rational choice political economy). The postulates of neo-classical economics (self-interest, utility maximisation) are applied to individuals and groups within government. This leads to the view that sub-optimum economic policies are likely to be pursued because the politician or bureaucrat is more concerned with maximising some good, such as money, power, or security, rather than improving national welfare through the pursuit of 'rational' economic policies.[49] These ideas strongly influenced the World Bank. They had a direct impact with the hiring of economists convinced of the utility of these approaches, such as Anne Kreuger (to head the World Bank's research programme in 1982) and Deepak Lal.[50] The influence of New Political Economy was important for the Bank as it provided an analysis of politics and political phenomena which was immediately accessible to economists because it used concepts drawn from neo-classical economics. It also gave a simple explanation of why wrong policies had been followed in the past, and especially later in the 1980s, an explanation of why governments did not fully implement structural adjustment programmes. More importantly this profoundly cynical view of politicians and bureaucrats generates policy prescriptions, many of which we find in governance. If politicians and bureaucrats are self-seeking (attempting to maximise some good) what is required are mechanisms which recognise this, but which create incentives for good performance. Hence talk of introducing incentives into civil service, increased accountability and transparency (if you are in danger of losing your job due to bad performance, then you will perform well) and the need for a strong civil society to balance the self-seeking state.

Rethinking the state

During the same period the World Bank was reconsidering the role of the state in development more generally, and by the late 1980s the minimalist state view was giving way to a more nuanced account of the relationship between state and market. The Bank re-emphasised poverty reduction, human development and infrastructure development, in part to overcome the poor supply-side response in adjusting countries.[51] This led to the rather obvious conclusion that the state has an indispensable role in development, but it did focus attention more sharply on the kind of state that was needed and how best it could deliver these services. In a sense the Bank had simply come to realise what classical economists had always said: market led economic development requires a strong and effective state to create the conditions for capitalist development and mould a sustaining environment for private enterprise.[52] This trend was reinforced by the partial re-assessment of the Southeast Asian development experience. Pressure from the Japanese led the Bank to undertake a major study into the reasons for the economic success of the region. The subsequent report has been subject to much criticism, but it does seem to have persuaded many in the Bank of the importance of institutional factors in explaining economic success.[53] This report emerged at the same time as an assessment of adjustment in Africa and it became clear to many in the Bank that the dramatically different economic experiences of the two regions was in part explained by different institutional endowments.

Changes within the Bank.

While there are still some who maintain that the World Bank has not really changed, it seems clear that there have been real changes which help explain the rise of governance concerns.[54] The dramatic (and traumatic for many staff) re-organisation in 1987 was designed to make the Bank a 'knowledge based institution' and provide it with 'intellectual leadership in the development field'. The Bank has become more open and flexible. The number of non-economists has risen, its prestigious recruitment programme, the Young Professional Programme, is now open to non-economists, and it has hired ex-NGO personnel. The World Bank's assessment unit, the Operations Evaluation Department (OED) has become increasingly prominent because of its close relationship to the Board of Executive Directors. During the late 1980s all of OED's assessments pointed to the need to improve project and programme effectiveness through taking more account of institutional factors and increasing participation of stakeholders, and in recent years a number of mechanisms have been developed to ensure that the lessons learned by OED are taken into account in new lending. In addition the Bank has responded (grudgingly at times) to pressures from NGOs for greater accountability and participation in its development projects.[55]

The end of the Cold War.

We must be careful not to collapse congruence with causation. There were already people within the Bank concerned with the potential development problems Eastern Europe would face before communism collapsed in these countries. In addition work for the 1989 Bank report which first formulated the notion of good governance was started in 1987. So the rise of good governance concerns cannot be attributed directly to the end of the Cold War. However the end of the Cold War undoubtedly strengthened the governance agenda. There may have been a certain post-Cold War triumphalism which added to the confidence with which the Bank and other donors could promote political reforms. It certainly made it easier for the Directors of the Bank to accept the argument that political reform was a legitimate part of its activities. In addition, as many developing countries lose whatever Cold War significance they may have had, so the World Bank has assumed a leading role in determining developmental priorities, especially in Africa. The Bank has become a de facto gatekeeper for up to 75 per cent of aid to that continent, and this gives it a much enhanced ability to push for governance reforms.

Good Governance: an Ideology of Transformation

One of the dominant features of modernity is the view that the social world is malleable.[56] Institutions, structures and ways of thinking and acting are no longer seen as pre-ordained and can be altered by human effort. This view is intimately linked to a notion of progress. Not only can the existing institutions, structures and ways of thinking be changed, but they can be changed for the better. This has at least one important implication. The combination of malleability and progress entails that what does exist has no a priori value. There can be no a priori reason for maintaining it. It only has value according to the set of criteria which define progress, and if it has no value according to these criteria then it can and should be changed. The important point here is that the transformative drive embodied in governance has a conceptual foundation in the dominant ideas of modernity; it cannot be attributed to maliciousness nor simply to the desire to expand capitalism, as some critics have contended.[57] What we need to do is unpack the criteria which define progress for the World Bank, and then enable it to argue for the desirability of certain changes.

In our discussion of governance we have used a whole range of recognisably liberal concepts (both political and economic) such as civil society, the market, contracts, and accountability. It is no surprise then that the Bank's criteria of progress are derived from the liberal tradition. The term 'liberalism' is clearly problematic, and we cannot give a full scale analysis or even an exhaustive definition here. Despite the difficulties, the view taken is that liberalism denotes a field of argument, or a bounded area of dispute. It provides contested descriptions of the desirable arrangement for the 'institutional furniture' of the modern world (state, society, legal system, forms of accountability), which sit on discussions about such issues as rights and utility, as well as arguments about their limits and justifications. These in turn sit on epistemological and ontological arguments. The scope of disagreement within liberalism is different at each of these levels, and in particular there is much less disagreement at the third level than at the first and second. But at each of these levels it is possible to broadly demarcate the range of liberal positions. In addition the Bank's criteria for progress includes some form of capitalist development. Again this is a problematic term, in particular it is not at all clear in what sense we can speak of there being a 'capitalist development'.[58] But as with liberalism we might see it as a broad range of alternatives, in terms of specific policies or the international context, within which there are common features. The links between liberalism and capitalist development are extremely complex both theoretically and historically. At the level of theory it seems safe to assert that, for the Bank at least, liberal notions such as the individual, freedom, and choice, provide a justification for capitalist development. Historically the development of capitalism encourages the creation of an increasingly atomised individual, who will in turn demand freedom from government intervention, and a sphere, both economic and social, within which to choose their life patterns (perhaps the central feature of liberalism).[59] We are arguing that some form of liberal-capitalism is the basic definition of progress for the World Bank, and that it thinks within, and attempts to make others think within and act out, its basic assumptions, concepts and categories.

The state, neutrality and the good

The reforms advocated by the World Bank at the level of government and administration are presented as purely pragmatic. An effectively functioning civil service and legal system are 'basic requirements for a modern state'.[60] 'Technical considerations of economy and efficiency should guide the Bank's work at all times'.[61] There are two familiar distinctions here, between the 'technical' and the ideological, and between the economy and politics.[62] The Bank must not prescribe what is good for countries, merely what is necessary. This concern with presenting its prescriptions as objective, or merely practical, is a replication of the liberal commitment to neutrality between competing conceptions of the good; that is the idea that there is no way of deciding between the numerous incompatible conceptions of the good which individuals hold. This commitment to neutrality sits on an ontological argument which denies the existence of any one (true) conception of the good for persons, and this in turn rests on an epistemological argument about the method by which any sort of knowledge can be established (positivist and empiricist). Any attempt by the state to impose a single conception of the good will be founded on the error of supposing there is any such single conception, and will be unjust to those persons who do not share it. So the state should simply be neutral (as far as possible) between competing conceptions of the good.

There is good reason to suppose that a commitment to neutrality is unsustainable within liberal theory. In all constructions of neutrality heavily loaded assumptions about what are seen as valuable ways of life are smuggled in.[63] The commitment to neutrality itself must be sustained by an idea of why such an arrangement is good. Arguably this sleight of hand has characterised liberal thought from its beginnings. As Salkever suggests, from Hobbes onwards, 'the liberal preference for a peaceable and comfortable life is established subliminally, as it were, by repetition that appears to seek the readers complicity, rather than by an explicit argument that would risk contradicting the neutrality condition'.[64] It is difficult to avoid the conclusion that, 'the concept of right, far from being (as the liberal insists) independent of and anterior to any conception of the good, will in fact be a function of our conception of the good'.[65]

The World Bank reflects this classically liberal dilemma. It does not want to be seen to prescribe a conception of the good, for to do so would violate the neutrality principle, while at the same time in fact having such an idea of the good, which, because it is a good, can be imposed on others. Like all liberals its conception of the good triumphs. The Bank's so-called technical reforms are necessarily guided by a prior conception of the good. Governments, it argues, must provide 'rules to make markets work, and ensure property rights'.[66] The existence of a stable system of law is, 'a basic requirement for a stable business environment' and the success of investment. Without it, 'the fate of enterprises, like that of individuals, will be left to the whim of the ruling elite or clique'. Legal reform confers stability on contractual transactions and gives predictability to property rights. The bureaucracy is to be judged on, 'the degree and quality of ... [its] intervention in the running of the economy'.[67] There is here a conception of the good of social organisation and the role of the state within it, that, whatever else it is, is not neutral (nor 'objective', nor even simply 'practical'). It is of a market economy and a liberal political sphere which will ensure the proper functioning of that economy.

Civil society, tolerance and the good

In order for these reforms to be effective the Bank is supporting the development of 'civil society'. It is also arguing for the importance of building on the indigenous. This letter reflects the commitment to neutrality (there is no way of deciding between competing conceptions of the good) and is given added impetus by the imperatives of tolerance. It is not just that there is no single conception of the good, but that the choice of a good by an individual should, as far as possible, be respected. We should be wary of this. Certain features of what the Bank characterises as 'indigenous' may be conducive to the type of development the Bank wishes to see. But they may not. Family and ethnic ties are unacceptable in bureaucracies. 'African managers cannot easily escape the heavy social obligations that take up a large part of their time' (nowhere are these obligations perceived as desirable).[68] Some World Bank advisers have also pointed this out. Claude Ake has said that development projects may 'conflict with some relevant indigenous attitudes and values', Goran Hyden that there may be a need to change 'cultural traditions' to allow development to take place, and Mamadou Diouf that the lifestyle of the Senegalese elites which has had deleterious economic effects remains rooted in 'African culture'.[69]

It is clear then that tolerance of the indigenous must be bounded. Some groups, attitudes and values are to be tolerated, but those which stand in the way of development are not. The Bank is keen to build on the indigenous insofar as it is compatible with modernisation.[70]

This is not surprising as within liberal theory tolerance has always been bounded. John Stuart Mill for example sanctioned breaches of the principle of toleration in the case of children, 'uncivilised nations', in some moods at least the working classes, as well as those not 'in full possession of their faculties'. Civil society for the Bank is not to consist of ethnic or other affective groups which might stand in the way of development, but of contractual, non-affective groups such as professional associations, universities, chambers of commerce, NGOs and capitalist enterprises.[71] It is this sort of civil society which will demand and support economic and political reforms. This reflects the traditional view of civil society in liberal theory as a sphere free from state interference, and as a 'public sphere' which will monitor the activities of the state.[72] The imperatives of tolerance are overridden by a conception of the good which drives transformation.

The individual, autonomy and the good

At the heart of liberal thought is a 'free' or 'autonomous' self. This self is assumed to be capable of choosing its own life patterns, and because they have been chosen by a self capable of rational decision-making, these choices are to be respected by others (tolerated), and the state must be neutral between them. Yet we have seen already how the notions of tolerance and neutrality are problematic, and we find the same with the idea of the autonomous, rationally-choosing self. For decisions which individuals make to command respect (to be tolerated) two criteria must be fulfilled. First, in some strong sense they must be their own decisions. This effectively rules out decisions based on 'family and ethnic ties'. Second, these decisions must be 'rational'. But 'rationality' in and of itself has no content. In order to count a choice as rational, appeal must be made to some set of criteria which define what is to count as rational. To escape from this obvious circularity appeal must be made to some conception of the good, even if this is only in the form of a set of rules about what is to count as procedural rationality.[73] Either this conception of the good must be imposed on the individual, or a self must be created which already accepts this particular notion of the good. Only then can the liberal commitment to an autonomous freely choosing self be sustained.

It is not an exaggeration to suggest that it is part of the governance agenda to create the selves who will choose rationally. We have already seen how this is the case with civil service reforms which entail the breaking of affective ties and the construction of procedures for rational decision making in the areas of public administration and economic policy making.[74] The creation of these selves is also part of the justification of participation in development: 'the benefit of a participatory approach is not simply the immediate advantage of a project better tailored to the client's need, but also the impulse it gives to the long-run process of changing mentalities'.[75] Part of the reason for the rapid increase in World Bank work with NGOs is because they provide channels for this micro-level intervention to change mentalities.[76]

Knowledge, objectivity and the good

So far we have argued that the governance agenda is neither neutral, pragmatic, nor tolerant, and is concerned with transformation at the most micro-level. We must ask why it is that an organisation with intelligent, highly qualified and committed staff present this transformation as simply technical and objective. In part the reasons for this relate to the kind of knowledge accepted by the World Bank as true knowledge. Within the Bank the knowledge which is most respected is quantifiable, technical and empirical, in short, positivist. Positivist knowledge presents itself as an accurate depiction of an objective reality. It purports to generate securely known facts which can guide action. But as we have already seen the Bank's idea of facts, especially economic facts, rest on a prior account of the good. If the market mechanism is deemed a good way of organising economic affairs, then it is possible to generate facts about it. But these facts do not stand independently from the conception of the good.

We can see that neutrality, tolerance, the free-choosing self and a positivist view of knowledge are tied together. A positivist epistemology generates scepticism about the existence of a single conception of the good. This then justifies neutrality between, and tolerance of, the conceptions of the good which individuals rationally choose. But we can also see that they are all problematic notions; we can see that underlying them is a conception of the good of political, economic, social and individual life. Governance is a 'transformative ideology': it has a clear conception of the desirable future; it provides a way of identifying obstacle to this future; it generates strategies to overcome these obstacles; and finally it presents this transformation as simply objective.

Conclusion

If this analysis has cogency several conclusions seem to follow. First, we should attempt to overcome the crippling divide in the discipline of politics between 'political theory' and 'political science'; the former concerning itself (often in minute detail) with the works of political thinkers, the latter with the 'real world'. As Alasdair MacIntyre has put it, 'there ought not to be two histories, one of political and moral action and one of political and moral theorising, because there were not two pasts, one populated only by actions, the other only by theories. Every action is the bearer of more or less theory-laden beliefs; every piece of theorising and every expression of belief is a political and moral action.'[77] We must attempt to integrate our accounts of action and our accounts of theory. We need to accord some kind of causal and interpretative place to theory or 'ideas' more broadly, and this means escaping from analytical schemas which insist that 'interests' are the key to explaining all interactions in the international system.[78]

Second, the characterisation of governance as an ideology of transformation has implications for our understanding of the political reform agendas of other donors including NGOs. All are informed by a conception of the good, which drives their desire to do good to others by transforming them. In this respect they, and the World Bank, are following in a long line of encounters between the West and others, from the discovery of America to African colonisation. As Tzvetan Todorov has so clearly demonstrated, the Spanish, in their encounter with the Aztecs were informed by a moral imperative that 'one has the right to impose on others what one considers as the good, without concern as to whether or not this is also the good from the other's point of view.'[79] This moral imperative was at work in the attitude of the Earl of Cromer and his fellow colonialists, and it is still at work today in the operations of the World Bank; only now it is disguised behind notions of objectivity, neutrality and tolerance which soothe our worries about the difficult normative questions which arise. It is this transformative drive which is the key to understanding the relations between the developed and developing world in the post-Cold War era.

There is a final conclusion which is perhaps of more immediate relevance. As we can see from our analysis of governance, respect for the sovereignty of other countries is overridden by the imperative of transformation. During the Cold War two things happened which pushed this transformative drive into the background. First, relations between the West and the Third World were often determined by the day to day demands of pursuing national interest. Second, the promise of independence was that countries would transform themselves, albeit with some help from the developed world. The end of the Cold War has reduced the importance of the Third World, and especially Africa, in the calculations of national interest. The failure to achieve self-transformation justifies outside intervention. As John Stuart Mill put it, some nations had 'not got beyond the period during which it is likely to be for their benefit that they should be conquered and held in subjection by [civilised] foreigners'.[80] While conquering may not yet be a viable option (Haiti? Somalia?) the agenda is still the same.

Notes

1 I would like to thank the participants at the conference where the first draft of this paper was presented. I owe particular thanks to Eberhard Kienle for his constructive and encouraging comments.

2 Earl of Cromer, 'The government of subject races', in *Political and Literary Essays: 1908–1913* (Macmillan, London, 1913) p. 4.

3 Many NGOs are critical of the World Bank, especially its structural adjustment programs. See John Clark, *Democratizing Development* (Earthscan, London, 1991) ch. 12. This criticism has intensified with the '50 Years is Enough Campaign'. See some of the contributions to John Cavanagh, Daphne Wysham and Marcos Arruda (eds) *Beyond Bretton Woods* (Pluto, London, 1994). But to the extent that NGOs agree with much of the political agenda of the bank (even if they disagree about its scope) there seems to be a remarkable consensus.

4 US AID African Bureau, African Voices i/1 (1992) p. 2. See also Carol Lancaster, 'Governance and development: the views from Washington', *IDS Bulletin* xxiv/1 (1993) pp. 9–15.

5 Interview with François Mitterand, *Le Monde*, 20 June 1990.

6 Klemens Van de Sands and Ralf Mohs, 'Making German aid more credible', *Development and Co-operation* i (1992) p. 4.

7 Ryokichi Hirono, 'Recent trends and debates on Japan's ODA', paper presented at the ODC/ODI/NSI conference, Bellagio, July 1993.

8 See Douglas Hurd, speech given at Overseas Development Institute, June 1990; Linda Chalker, speech given to the Wilton Park Conference on Good Government in Africa, January 1992; and Linda Chalker, 'Aid and poverty', *Journal of International Development* iv/1 (1992) pp. 87–93. The Labour Party position is very similar; Anne Clwyd, 'The Labour Party policy

on overseas development', *Journal of International Development* iv/1 (1992) pp. 94–102.

9 Overseas Development Administration, 'Taking account of good government', *Technical Note* 10 October 1993.

10 *The Courier*, 140 (1993) p. 46.

11 Emeka Anyaoku, 'The Commonwealth and the challenge of democracy', *Development Policy Review* x/1 (1992) pp. 99–106.

12 United Nations, *Africa Recovery* vii/2 (1993) p. 6.

13 Oxfam, *Field Directors' Handbook* (Oxford University Press, Oxford, for Oxfam, 1990), pp. 16, 65.

14 One World Action, 'Good Governance: report of One World Action seminar', London, March 1994.

15 Clark, *Democratizing Development*, pp. 26–33. See also, David Korten, *Getting to the 21st Century: Voluntary Action and the Global Agenda* (Kumanan Press, Connecticut, 1990) and John Friedman, *Empowerment: the Politics of Alternative Development* (Blackwell, Cambridge, Mass., 1992).

16 OECD, *Voluntary Aid for Development: the Role of Non-governmental Organisations* (OECD, Paris, 1988), pp. 79–97.

17 Paul Burnell, *Charity, Politics and the Third World* (Harvester Wheatsheaf, London, 1991), p. 211.

18 OECD, *Voluntary Aid for Development*, pp. 94–7.

19 OECD, *Voluntary Aid for Development*, pp. 148–9.

20 Mark Robinson, 'An uncertain partnership: the ODA and the voluntary sector in the 1980's', in Anuradha Bose and Paul Burnell (eds) *Britain's Overseas Aid Since 1979* (Manchester University Press, Manchester, 1991), p. 162.

21 Charities Aid Foundation, *Charity Trends*, 14th ed (Charities Aid Foundation, Tonbridge, 1991), pp. 154–65.

22 Burnell, Charity, *Politics and the Third World*, p. 210.

23 See Report by the General Audit Office to the Ranking Minority Member, Committee on International Relations, House of Representatives, 'Foreign Assistance – PVOs contributions and limits', December 1995.

24 See Richard Jeffries, 'The State, Structural Adjustment and Good Government in Africa', *Journal of Comparative and Commonwealth Studies* xxxi/1 (1993) pp. 20–35, and Geoffrey Hawthorn, 'How to ask for Good Government', *IDS Bulletin* xxiv/1 (1993) pp. 24–30.

25 See Michael Bratton, 'International versus Domestic Pressures for Democratisation in Africa', this volume.

26 With reference to elections see Tom Young, 'Elections: for what and for whom?', *Africa* lxiii/3 (1993) pp. 300–12.

27 Here I do not consider the actual lending which is generated by this ideology of transformation. I am engaged in a larger study which will explore these issues.

28 World Bank, *Sub-Saharan Africa: From crisis to sustainable growth* (World Bank, Washington, 1989), p. 60.

29 Ibrahim Shihata, *The World Bank in a Changing World: selected essays* (Martinus Nijhoff, Dordrecht, 1991), p. 75.

30 I am aware that the World Bank is not a monolithic organisation. Much more work needs to be done on how these governance concerns are formulated and disputed within the Bank. The real problem here is of having an adequate conceptualisation of the bank as an actor. Like all organisations it is clearly more than the sum of its parts, and it does seem plausible to say the Bank 'acts'. Yet it is probably wrong to treat is as the same type of agent as a person. The difficulties here are methodological. For the moment it might be best to characterise the bank as having a kind of 'quasi-intentionality' in terms of directedness. I am indebted to Sudipta Kaviraj for suggesting this sort of conceptualisation.

31 World Bank, *Governance and Development*, p. 12.

32 Arturo Israel, *Institutional Development: Incentives to Performance* (Johns Hopkins University Press for the World Bank, London, 1990).

33 Edward Jaycox, 'Capacity Building: the missing link in African development', address to the African–American Institute conference on African Capacity Building: effective and enduring partnerships, Reston, Virginia, May 1993.

34 World Bank, Africa Region Technical Department, *A Framework for Capacity Building in Policy Analysis and Economic Management in sub-Saharan Africa* (World Bank, Washington, 1989).

35 World Bank, *Governance and Development*, pp. 14, 39.

36 World Bank, *Governance and Development*, pp. 46–7, World Bank, *Sub-Saharan Africa*, p. 58. See also, *World Bank Policy Research Bulletin* iii/2 (1992).

37 Shihata, *The World Bank in a Changing World*, pp. 81–8, World Bank, *Governance and Development*, pp. 29–39.

38 World Bank, *Governance and Development*, p. 49; World Bank, *Sub-Saharan Africa*, p. 58.

39 World Bank, *Governance and Development*, p. 49, World Bank, *Sub-Saharan Africa*, p. 61, and World Bank, *A Framework for Capacity Building*, p. 6.

40 The idea of there being an 'indigenous' in modern Africa is clearly problematic, but thus far the Bank does not seem to have addressed this.

41 World Bank, *Governance and Development*, p. 12, World Bank, *Sub-Saharan Africa*, pp. 60, 193. See also *World Bank News* xiv/2 (1995).

42 World Bank, *Governance and Development*, p. 8.

43 Mamadou Dia, 'Development and cultural values', *Finance and Development* xxvii/4 (1991) p. 12.

44 Francis Stewart, 'Are adjustment policies consistent with Africa's long-run development needs?', *Development Policy Review* ix/4 (1991) pp. 413–39; Paul Mosley, Jane Harrigan and John Toye, *Aid and Power* vol 1 (Routledge, London, 1991); John Toye, *Dilemmas of Development* (Blackwell, Oxford, 1987) and Michael Lipton 'Requiem for Adjustment Lending',

Development Policy Review viii/4 (1990) pp. 437–43.

45 See Mosley et al., *Aid and Power*, vol 1, pt 3. For the latest (and extremely controversial) bank assessment see World Bank, *Adjustment in Africa: Reforms, Results and the Road Ahead* (Oxford University Press for the World Bank, Oxford 1994).

46 World Bank, *World Development Report* 1990, p. 115, Shihata, *The World Bank in a Changing World*, p. 53.

47 World Bank, *Adjustment Lending: an Evaluation of Ten Years of Experience* (World Bank, Washington, 1988), p. 3.

48 See Toye, *Dilemmas of Development.*

49 See Michael Staniland, *What is Political Economy?* (Yale University Press, New Haven, 1985); John Conybeare, 'The rent-seeking state and revenue diversification', *World Politics* xxxv/1 (1983) pp. 25–42; and Merillee Grindle, 'Positive economics and negative politics', in Gerard Meier (ed.) *Politics and Policy Making in Developing Countries* (ICS Press, San Francisco,1991).

50 See Deepak Lal, 'The political economy of the predatory state', DRP paper 105 (World Bank, Washington, 1984). See also Anne Kreuger, 'The political economy of the rent seeking society', *The American Economic Review* lxiv/3 pp. 291–303.

51 See the bank's *World Development Reports* for 1990 and 1994.

52 Arthur Goldsmith, 'The state, the market, and economic development: a second look at Adam Smith in theory and practise', *Development and Change* xxvi/4 (1995) pp. 633–50.

53 World Bank, *The East Asian Miracle: economic growth and public policy* (Oxford, OUP for the World Bank, 1993) For a critical commentary see the contributions to *World Development* xxii/4 (1994).

54 The cynical view of changes within the bank is most often put forward by NGOs.

55 This pressure has often been channelled through the US congress. See Catherine Gwin, *US Relations with the World Bank: 1945–1992* (Brookings Institute, Washington,1994).

56 Again I am indebted to Sudipta Kaviraj here.

57 Cheryl Payer, *The World Bank: a critical analysis* (Monthly Review Press, New York, 1982).

58 At least one would have to identify the features common to all forms of 'capitalist' development, while recognising the important differences between, say, the USA and Japan.

59 There are difficult issues here. For a presentation of a kind of minimal case in terms of their historical relationship at the level of theory see Quentin Skinner, 'Some problems in the analysis of political thought and action', in James Tully (ed.) *Meaning and Context: Quentin Skinner and his critics* (Polity Press, Cambridge,1988).

60 Shihata, *The World Bank in a Changing World*, p. 85.

61 Shihata, *The World Bank in a Changing World*, p. 95.

62 This replicates the fact/value distinction within liberal thought. The 'facts' of the economy are incontrovertible. It is impossible to decide between 'values' in the political world.

63 See Richard Bellamy, *Liberalism and Modern Society* (Polity Press, Cambridge, 1992), ch. 5 for useful demonstrations of this.

64 Stephen Salkever, '"Lopp'd and Bound": how liberal theory obscures the good of liberal practices', in R. Bruce Douglas, Gerald Mara and Henry Richardson (eds) *Liberalism and the Good* (Routledge, London, 1990), p. 171.

65 Susan Mendus, *Toleration and the Limits of Liberalism* (London, Macmillan, 1989) pp. 119–20. See also Charles Taylor, 'Atomism', *Philosophical Papers ii* (Cambridge University Press, Cambridge, 1985).

66 World Bank, *Governance and Development*, p. 6.

67 Shihata, *The World Bank in a Changing World*, pp. 87–90.

68 Pierre Landell-Mills, 'Creating transparency, predictability and an enabling environment for private enterprise', paper given at Wilton Park Conference on Good Government in Africa, January 1992.

69 See their contributions to World Bank, *Long-term Perspective Study* Vol 3 (World Bank, Washington, 1989).

70 Pierre Landell-Mills, 'Governance, civil society and empowerment in sub-Saharan Africa', paper prepared for the Annual Conference of the Society for the Advancement of Socio-economics' May 1992.

71 World Bank, *Sub-Saharan Africa*, p. 191, and Landell-Mills, 'Governance, civil society and empowerment'.

72 Charles Taylor, 'Modes of civil society', Public Culture 3 (1990). See also Jurgen Habermas, *The Structural Transformation of the Public Sphere* (Polity Press, Cambridge, 1989).

73 Though there are difficulties, I think, in arguing that a conception of procedural rationality can stand without the support of more substantive conceptions of the good.

74 For a more substantial argument along these lines see David Williams, 'Governance and the discipline of development', paper presented to the panel discussion 'The Politics of Governance', at the Development Studies Association Annual Conference, Dublin, September 1995.

75 Landell-Mills, 'Governance, civil society and empowerment'.

76 David Williams, 'Liberalism and development discourse' *Africa* lxiii/3 (1993).

77 Alasdair MacIntyre, *After Virtues* (Duckworth, London, 1981).

78 See Manfred Bienfeld, 'The new world order: echoes of a new imperialism', *Third World Quarterly* xv/1 (1994) pp. 31–48.

79 Tzvetan Todorov, *The Conquest of America: the question of the other* (Harper Collins, New York, 1992) p. 154.

80 John Stuart Mill, 'A few words on non-intervention', *Essays on Politics and Culture*, ed. Gertrude Himmelfarb (Peter Smith, Gloucester, Mass., 1973).

10 ↝ Indian Communism: Re-defining Identity and the Struggle for Democracy

Harihar Bhattacharyya

In his post-mortem of communism, Zygmunt Bauman writes:

> The fall of communism was a resounding defeat for the project of a total order, an artificially designed, all-embracing arrangement of human actions, and their setting. In short, the fall of communism signalled the final retreat from the dreams and ambitions of modernity.[1]

The collapse of communism, according to Bauman, was a symptom of post-modernity and an issue of how to live without totalising alternatives.[2] Communism, as he rightly says, is a thoroughly modern phenomenon which is based on the assumption that a good society can only be found in a carefully designed, rationally managed and thoroughly industrialised society: 'communism was modernity in its most determined mood and most decisive posture'.[3] Bauman's post-modernist frame seems useful for examining the current dilemmas of Indian communism which remains, like communism, generally, a modern phenomenon.

In studying Indian communism after the end of the Cold War, two interlinked issues must be considered. First there is Indian communism's 'own' problematic in which it desperately searches for an appropriate identity, as its old identity has been threatened and eroded due to the global crisis in communism. Second, the subject is relevant for a consideration of the regeneration of Indian democracy, particularly in the wake of the growing disintegration of the Congress Party (so far the ruling party of Indian democracy), the reactionary communal challenges posed by such forces as the BJP, and the growing liberalisation of the Indian economy since 1992. The first two factors have been responsible for the uncertainties in Indian democracy, which is much needed for the successful implementation of the liberalisation programme. At this conjuncture, Indian communists reappear as the consistent and honest defenders of India's parliamentary democracy. The material bases of the communists' claim to be the promoters of democracy are provided by their experience in running the state level administrations in West Bengal, Kerala and Tripura where the masses have slowly worked their way into the party and the self-government institutions such as the *panchayats*. Paradoxically, the communists' 'democratic practice' offers more effective scope for the successful operation of liberalisation programmes in India. India's 'reformed' communists hold the key to the regeneration of Indian democracy.

Indian communism today is at a crossrods. The collapse of communism in the former Soviet Union and Eastern Europe – which marked the end of the Cold War – has plunged Indian communism into a crisis. The symptoms of this crisis are already surfacing. Indian communism, which is still in its over-long pre-revolutionary period, is much threatened today. It is searching desperately for an identity, as its old identity is eroded by the global crisis of communism of which it remained a part. Its judgement of the events leading to the disintegration of the erstwhile Soviet Union and the collapse of communism in Eastern Europe is one instance of assertion of identity. On the other hand, it has begun to revise itself in terms of newer ideas, beliefs and assumptions. It is searching for new meanings of communist modernity within the overall totalising framework and goal. Its neo-modernity is supposed to co-exist with its old modernity, at least in some very vital respects. In short, Indian communism, in its drive for neo-modernity, has introduced anachronisms into its theoretical assumptions, but that is the proof of a threatened movement's need for survival and identity.

The Indian communists' participation in the Cold War was disastrous for the movement itself. The hot waters of the Cold War rather than Soviet revolutionary help were to become, in the post-war period, the life blood of communism in many post-colonial societies including India. While the social reality at home might have been marked by class conflicts, the latter seemed to have been 'understood' in the language of either Soviet or Chinese communism. Indian communism's over-dependence on 'global' communism meant, as Sen Gupta rightly stressed, that 'neither Moscow nor Peking has hesitated to sacrifice the communists of other countries for the sake of Soviet or Chinese national interests'.[4] As a result, the 'achievements' of socialism (or its 'wonders') were to become the proofs of the validity of Marxism. A crude, empirical reasoning then replaced any truly scientific (that is, critical) analysis of Marxism and socialist systems. In short, the Cold War corrupted the Indian communist movement and emptied it of all real content. The movement became dependent on the dynamics of the Cold War. It maintained a weak and regionalised existence, mostly as a loyal opposition. Not surprisingly, with the break-up of the USSR and the collapse of communism in Eastern Europe, Indian communism finds itself in a near-total ideological and theoretical void affecting the organisation and the movement deeply.

The present state of Indian communism, which was born in the 1920s, is quite complex.[5] Apart from the two major communist parties, the Communist Party of India (CPI) and the Communist Party of India (Marxist) or CPI(M), there are many small and regionalised leftist groups such as Forward Bloc (FB), Forward Bloc (Marxist) (FBM), Revolutionary Socialist Party (RSP), Revolutionary Communist Party of India (RCPI), Socialist Unity Centre of India (SUCI), Communist Party of India (Marxist–Leninist – popularly known as 'Naxalites')[6] and so on. While many of these are post-1947 developments, the most powerful of the communist parties today, the CPI(M), came into being in 1964 after splitting from the CPI.

Alhough they have one of the oldest communist movements in the world, Indian communists have yet to capture power at the all-India level. However, beginning with the south Indian state of Kerala in 1957, they have been exercising 'governmental power' by capturing state level administrations through electoral victories. In 1995, they were running the state level administrations in two Indian states – West Bengal (since 1977 continuously) and Tripura, in India's northeast, since 1978 (discontinuously). This communist experiment with governmental power at the state level is a unique experience in the history of the world communist movement. It signifies a marriage, however inconvenient, between communist class struggle and bourgeois administration. Of all the groups and parties, the Communist Party of India and the Communist Party of India (Marxist) are the only major groups which really matter for present purposes.

The CPI

The Communist Party of India (CPI), which was born in the early 1920s in the former Soviet Union, has a membership today of 467,205, or 205 less than its 1989 figure of 467,539 [7].The party's latest party congress reports lament the fact that the 'party is today suffering from serious weakness'.[8] The class composition of CPI membership (Table 1) shows that the industrial working classes form only a small proportion of its membership, although the other proletarian elements predominate among its members (industrial workers, poor peasants and agricultural labourers taken together account for 71.6 per cent of the total).

The same, however, cannot be said of the class composition of the CPI leadership, which is dominated by non-proletarian elements (Table 2). Of the delegates, as many as 51.3 per cent possessed university degrees, suggesting further the profoundly middle and upper class origins of the party leadership. Organisationally, the party has stagnated recently, and the party congress blamed the leadership for this: 'Thinking inside the party from top to bottom was that organisational problems are not as important as the political problem. Organisational issues can wait. This is the political psychology of leadership.'[9]

The CPI, then, is a communist movement in which proletarian elements predominate in the membership but over which they have little control because the leadership is dominated by non-proletarian elements, particularly the middle classes, both urban and rural. This is damaging for the health of a true communist party, but significant for the current shifts in the movement in the wake of the demise of socialism in the former USSR and Eastern Europe. For the CPI, which has remained for long a more or less consistently pro-Soviet party, the demise of socialism in the former Soviet Union has been traumatic. It has yet to recover from the shock. Its current political discourse is as much dominated by an assessment of why socialism failed as by a search for an alternative identity. Like the CPI(M), it is a much-threatened communist party. As far as its assessment of the demise of socialism is concerned, the party, first of all, admits to its failure to understand the process of socialist reconstruction in the former USSR, a failure, it must be stated, which was related to the very loyal nature of the party itself. The party believes that behind the break-up of the USSR lay the factors of 'ethnic and nationalist' rivalries: 'You can blame anybody, you can blame wrong policies followed by Gorbachev which accelerated the movement towards disintegration. The state has been torn apart on the basis of ethnic and nationalistic rivalries' [10]

Table 1: Class Composition of CPI Membership (1991)

Class position	Per cent share
Industrial workers	12.3
Poor peasants	26.8
Middle peasants	6.9
Rich peasants	0.3
Rural labour	32.5
Middle classes	2.9
Students	1.8

Source: *CPI 15th Party Congress Documents* (New Age, New Delhi, 1993),

Table 2: Class Composition of Delegates to the 15th Party Congress

Class Position	Per cent share
Working class	15.5
Middle classes	35.8
Agricultural labourers	4.5
Middle peasants	20.0
Rich peasants	2.4
Landlords	1.2
Poor peasants	16.7

Source: Ibid.

By way of self-criticism, the party has said that although it had been 'firmly convinced that the nationality question had been solved in the Soviet Union' this was 'not the whole truth'.[11] The party's assessment stressed both the internal factors ('we have overlooked and glossed over the negative features of the Soviet Union')[12] as well as the international factors, that is, the potential of capitalism to utilise the achievements of science and technology in further developing the forces of production. As the party self-critically wrote: 'There was the wrong belief that the general crisis of capitalism and its special crisis would lead to capitalism's imminent collapse.'[13]

For the party then, the 'inevitable breakdown' thesis of capitalism has to be abandoned. On the contrary, it links the present crisis of communism to prospering capitalism. The 'negative features' mentioned above refer to the following: (1) The restriction of democracy, misapplication of the concept of dictatorship of the proletariat, and the wrong belief that class struggle intensified as socialism grew. (2) Bureaucratic centralisation in the economy. The system of centralised planning became a fetter and the elimination of all forms of property by one form of state or collective ownership acted as a brake on development. (3) The identification of the state and the party. (4) The gulf between ideology and actual practice.[14] In the party's assessment, the 'gross mistakes of the Gorbachev's Leadership' as much as the 'deepening crisis of the model of socialism' plus the rapid growth of nationalism and secessionism were the essential elements of the 'negative features' mentioned above.[15] Despite the collapse and crisis of socialism, the CPI does not consider that this is the end of socialism and socialist strategy,[16] since, for the party, 'Marxism is immortal because it is true and valid'.[17]

The following aspects of the new CPI thinking may be considered an aid to understanding the party's reconstruction of socialism. First, the party believes it ought to have a 'proper line' on the question of ethnic rights, ethnic determination and ethnic efforts to assert an identity.[18] This suggests that it is now unhappy with Stalin's theory of the national question, for so long the most sacred Marxist tract on the problem for the party. As the Fifteenth Party Congress (1992) reports, the party adopted the following resolution on the nationality question: 'our party would unhesitatingly uphold the aspiration of every nationality and ethnic group for developing its own linguistic-cultural identity'.[19]

Second, so far as the mobilisation of the working class is concerned, the party emphasises broader trade union unity and suggests that all left trade unions be merged into one. Chaturanan Mishra, a CPI veteran parliamentarian, wrote that Indian communists 'surely should begin to merge their mass organisations into one body'.[20] Nonetheless, the party's idea of the role of the working class still remains classically Marxist, as the party says that despite the changes in the working class, 'its essence as the *class capable of social initiative*' (my emphasis) has not changed.[21] For the CPI, the working class is still the agent of social transformation of a socialist nature.

Third, the CPI defines its model of socialism with a pronounced 'Indian' stress. 'The CPI stands by the goal of socialism. We do not regard Marxism–Leninism as a doctrine or dogma where the final truth has been spelt out. We value all that is positive and progressive in the thought and culture in India.'[22] Furthermore, 'there can be no models – socialist or democratic. We have to integrate Marxist theory with the specific conditions in India.'[23] The struggle to extend and defend India's bourgeois parliamentary democracy is the main task of Indian communists, and the precondition for the struggle of socialism.[24]

Fourth, Chaturanan Mishra has pinpointed three features of new CPI thinking. First, the party has attempted a new approach to some extent, in its programmatical statement: the party's welcome of the abolition of the license-permit raj in India, and of the import of foreign capital are evidence. Second, on the ideological question, the party has sought to seek sustenance in India's noble traditions, historical experience, rich cultural heritage and valuable teachings of great social reformers and thinkers of the country which the party believes will help to cultivate scientific temper and social ideals. Third, on the organisational question, the party has changed its views and incorporated this in the preamble to the party constitution. This reads: 'minority opinions on substantial political issues shall be made known to all party units and party members'.[25]

Finally, and most importantly, the party shows in its reconstruction of socialism a clear preference for the model of socialism currently practised in China under Deng's leadership.

'We note with keen interest the spectacular development that is taking place in China – its high rate of economic growth, its fast expanding trade and favourable balance of payments, its policy of opening up to the world without impairing self-reliance, its method of integrating planning with socialist market etc.'[26]

The party does not want to accept the charge of reformism in advocating the Chinese path, as it believes that nobody can charge Vietnam with reformism for inviting foreign capital for, 'The Chinese like the Vietnamese are not opposed to large-scale import of foreign capital.'[27] In the arena of global politics, the party believes that 'it is communist China that will challenge the hegemony of the USA in the next century'.[28] The CPI's support for the Chinese model is based on the replacement of a unitary public ownership structure with a multiple ownership system consisting of state, collectives, and individual and foreign funded enterprises.[29] The Chinese claim that there is no contradiction between a socialist economy and a market economy – as does the CPI. Mishra quotes approvingly from the following statement from the *Beijing Review* of 22 November 1993 (p.33): 'Experience proves that solely adopting a planned economy fetters productivity.'[30]

The CPI(M)

Since its emergence from the split in the CPI in 1964, the CPI(M) has grown both in terms of its membership and its influence over larger sections of society. From 1964–92 the number of party members gew from 118,683 to 579,666. In its three decades of existence. the party has grown almost six-fold. The growth patterns of the CPI(M) show two discernible phases. First, during 1964–78 (that is, until the arrival of the CPI(M)-led Left Front governments in West Bengal, Tripura and Kerala) the growth was fairly respectable with one negative period during 1964–68. Second, in the post-1978 period, the party has grown by leaps and bounds. – in fact, most growth has occurred in the later phase. The party in its Salkia Plenum at Howrah (West Bengal) in 1978 issued a call for building a mass revolutionary party, and this is cited by the party as the cause of such expansion. On closer analysis, however, a combination of factors, such as lowering the standard and criteria of membership, and the state level communist administration which evidently attracted opportunists, affected the quantitative growth in membership of the party. Since 1978, internal party sources have lamented the decreasing standards of party members, and the lack of discipline, ideological training and collective leadership, as well as egotism, individualism, and so on. It can indeed be argued that most of the growth in the party has been at the expense of the quality of membership. The 14th Party Congress of 1992 noted with alarm that: 'By the practice of communists, the distinction between a proletarian party and the bourgeois parties must be distinct in the eyes of the people. This is one way of assessing the quality of party membership.'[31]

Thus, the growth of the movement in terms of membership must be judged very cautiously. Nor should it be forgotten that, overall, the party's 579,666 members in 1992 were still dwarfed by India's total population of 860 million.

Another notable feature of the communist movement represented by the CPI(M) is that, to some extent, the party has penetrated areas beyond its traditional home of West Bengal, Kerala and Tripura. Today, most of India's states and regions have some CPI(M) units and members. Many of these units have also registered some growth in membership since 1978: Gujarat from only 150 to 1,052 in 1991, Assam from 3,424 to 10,696 in 1991, and Rajasthan from 1,339 to 3,626 in 1991. Organisationally, the CPI(M) has grown into a truly national party – in fact more national than Congress, which has lost organisational touch with many regions of India.

Two distinctive limitations of the growth process of the CPI(M) can hardly be overlooked. First, the party still suffers from unevenness in the regional distribution of its membership. For instance, in 1991, the party had 189,732 members in West Bengal and only 15,500 in neighbouring Bihar, which is larger than West Bengal in size and population. Similarly, it had 227,424 members in Kerala and just 70 in Goa in 1991. Second, the party membership is still largely concentrated regionally in West Bengal, Kerala and Tripura (a small state), which account for most of the party members. These three states have also witnessed a close association between the rise of communist-led state governments and the growth in party membership.

In the post-1978 period, the party has penetrated into so far unpenetrated Hindi speaking areas, but the maintenance of party discipline there has equally been a harder task. As was openly admitted in its 14th Party Congress reports of 1992, 'defiance of party decisions' has become a feature of party life. For instance, in Uttar Pradesh, six party members were expelled for contesting elections defying party decisions in the 1989 Assembly elections. The party reports also noted that in many cases elections are paramount for members; and the organisational task is ignored.[32] In the three states in which CPI(M) has been or is in power now (that is West Bengal, Kerala and Tripura), the situation is no better. The 14th Party Congress complained that 'parliamentarism' and 'crass opportunism' had spread in the party, and had eroded the communist consciousness. Hankering for posts in elected bodies such as municipalities, *zilla parishads* (District Councils) or the Assembly leads to 'groupism'. Individual egos and vested interests vitiate collective functions. These become issues of internal party struggle.[33]

The above very brief account of the development of the CPI(M) up to 1992 suggests that the party organisationally is in a bad shape. This has occurred despite its quantitative growth. So far as ideology is concerned, the situation is no better: for years what passed as Marxism for the party rank and file was nothing but the achievements or 'wonders' of socialism. A true recourse to Marxist literature, or critical analysis, was never undertaken. The absence of 'theoretical knowledge' among the rank and file is now acknowledged in inner party sources and in interviews with party leaders. In short, the party has hardly been ready to absorb the shocks and to face up to the challenges following the demise of socialism in the USSR and Eastern Europe. World events have threatened its identity.

As in the case of the CPI, the CPI(M)'s political discourse is dominated by an attempt to assess the causes of the break-up of the USSR and the collapse of communism in Eastern Europe. To put it differently, these events have led to important changes in the understanding and policies of the CPI(M). The party's admission of its failure to understand properly the processes of disintegration of socialist systems, and hence to predict the downfall of socialism, is one aspect of the party's self-critical analysis. Linked to this is the party's de-emphasis of information supplied by governments and parties of the former socialist systems, which were seen to be faulty and the source of misunderstanding. The party had always highlighted the achievements of those socialist systems. Another source of the party's misunderstanding was the famous 'Statement of 1957 and 1960 of 80 Parties' which emphasised 'socialism as the decisive factor shaping world developments' and overlooked the potential of world capitalism. As the CPI(M) General Secretary H. S. Surjeet self-critically wrote: 'Such a conclusion … grossly underestimated the potential of world capitalism, both of its capacity to further develop productive forces as well as its capacity to adapt itself to changed circumstances.'[34] The party thus clearly links the decline of communism to prospering capitalism.

In the party's assessment, socialism declined because 'distortions took place in the process of socialist construction.'[35] The dictatorship of the proletariat, which is not constant or immutable, was carried over subsequently, and this obstructed the widening and deepening of socialist democracy. As a result, what emerged was not people's participation but growing bureaucratism, violation of socialist legality, and the suppression of individual liberty and freedom.[36] Thus, it is argued, it is not Marxism–Leninism which is to be blamed, but the results of accumulated distortions and revisionist deviations in applying Marxist–Leninist principles to building socialism, and the deformation of socialist democracy.[37] E. M. S. Namboodiripad, a former general secretary and now a Politburo member, blamed 'leadership' for the demise of socialism. For him, 'ivory tower leadership' was responsible for 'deviations in building socialism and in the activities of the state, deviations in the method of organising socialist economy and deviations in the ideological education of the people,[38] it is the confirmed belief of the party that Marxism has not been challenged. To the party the philosophy of Marx is not irrelevant because Marxism is a science, and a developing one. Although the reverses of socialism, in party belief, 'have altered the world balance of forces in favour of imperialism for the moment,' capitalism's inevitable collapse is assumed. Surjeet even believes that there has been a further intensification of the central contradiction between imperialism and socialism.[39]

What, then, have been the effects of the demise of socialism on the CPI(M)? How has the party felt them? How does the party try to emerge from the crisis? How does it reconstruct its version of socialism? As an answer to the above we will present two types of evidence: interview materials and data from a select group of Burdwan District Committee CPI(M) members, including the secretary, who is also a West Bengal State Committee member of the CPI(M) and archival data from party documents including some internal party sources. The same set of questions were presented to each of the interviewees: they were asked to reflect on the effects of the decline of socialism on the party, and on the present state of the movement. Two interview responses are given in summary form as representative samples.

> Tendencies that led to the downfall of the CPSU remain here: absence of criticism and self-criticism from top to bottom. Rectification that is undertaken is 'nominal' and ritualistic for fear of promotion. There is the need for real self-criticism. Democratic centralism implies a balance, but this is upset always in favour of centralism. Now, inside the movement

the democratic aspect is encouraged; democratic opinion is assessed. As a corrective, purgation of undesirable elements is going on. After the demises of socialism, the ideological basis of the party has been weakened. Many inside the movement now question the socialist ideal, especially its applicability. It is now difficult to present socialism as a virulently cohesive force against deviation. As a rectification, the basics of Marxism are being read and discussed keeping in mind the particular situation of India. In studying them, the format or schema is abandoned.

As a result of the slogan of forming a mass party, the party grew enormously in the last ten years. A new generation has entered the party. There is a problem of ideological orientation for them. Today, the problem is all the more acute. On party organisation, we in the past emphasised the abstract principle, an *a priori* model of party organisation. Now the emphasis is laid on the link between this abstract principle and concrete reality (praxis). Earlier, we had a command system. Now the very leadership is encouraging the balance between democracy and centralism. The process has begun. On the nationality question, the basic (Leninist–Stalinist) model remains valid. Its application is wrong. Ethnicity is a new realisation, but its solution is possible only in socialism. On the individual, the problem is very real inside the movement. Theoretically, collectivity is emphasised, but practically the individual is overemphasised. This created dejection among cadres who saw themselves as cogs in the wheel. A centralised party in a democratic framework is not possible in all cases. Democracy is now emphasised; the urge is coming from within the party. The prospect of a socialist revolution in India is bleak. The harmful effects of electoral politics with their corrupting influences are eating into the vitality of the party organisation.[Interview with Mr J.Bhattacharyya, DCM and editor of *Natun Chithi*, the district party organ, on 14 April 1994, at Burdwan].

Indian communism is in crisis today. We have two levels of Marxism corresponding to two levels inside the party: rank and file, and leadership. In the post-War period, the general people were attracted to the cause of Marxism because of the achievements of socialism which also remained the Marxism for the rank and file. For them now, there is a void. The leadership feels the void ideologically and theoretically. The CPI(M) was never 100 per cent pro-Soviet or Chinese: it pointed out the revisionist policy of the CPSU or CPC. The wrong implementation of socialist policy backed by a revisionist policy was the cause of the demise of socialism although we could not predict its downfall. The CPI(M) still holds on to the masses because it has been warning of the danger of revisionism.Inside the movement, new theoretical questions are being asked. There will be changes in the Party Programme in the next congress (1995). Being aware of the consequences of one-party rule, the issue of a multi-party system in People's Democracy will not be ignored. India has had a long tradition of democracy so we communists see this as very important. The command structure of the party is questioned inside the movement. How to restore democracy in democratic centralism is the question. We are re-reading the classics of Marxism with emphasis on the role of the superstructure. Lenin did not tell us to follow his model of a single party which seemed justified in the conditions of Russia. We can not avoid foreign capital in People's Democracy, and cannot confiscate the entire monopoly capital. The crisis of communism in India should be seen in the expansion of communism into new areas (which is more difficult now): communism is less attractive to intellectuals; for the newer sections, there is today restricted spontaneity about the ideal: the masses are now not automatically coming into our fold as before'. (Interview with Mr. N.Sen, Secretary of Burdwan District Committee of the CPI(M) and West Bengal State Committee member, 6 April 1994).

The CPI(M)'s Reconstruction of Socialism

The 14th CPI(M) Party Congress resolution of 1992 defined 'socialism in the Indian conditions as a system wherein people's power would be supreme and socialist economic structure will be based on socialist means of production and central planning. Various forms of property can and will exist, but the decisive form will be that of socialist ownership of the means of production. Under socialism, the right to dissent, freedom of expression and plurality of opinion will flourish.'[40] The party explains that the right to dissent within socialism should not be interpreted to mean that it abandons the class character of the state or the leading role of the party. For the party, the communist party is the vanguard of the working classes in revolution and post-revolutionary reconstruction: it continues to lead the state. The real value of dissent is thus minimised by maintaining the centrality of the communist party in socialism.

Like a classical Marxist party, the CPI(M) does not abandon the principle of central planning. On the contrary, it still believes that central planning lays the basis for the socialist state to discharge its social and economic responsibilities to the people. All that the party objects to is 'over-centralisation' which is bad and stifles initiative and innovation.

The party retains the idea of a centralised state in its conception of the nationality question in India. On the nationality and ethnicity question, the party shows signs of new thinking when the 'deep roots', 'durability, and 'powerful social and ideological appeal' of such identities are recognised.[41] However, as regards a solution, the party seems to assert the old cliché: regional autonomy is to exist within a strong, centralised nation-state.[42]

For the CPI(M), class struggle is the basis on which the struggle for democracy and socialism will be organised. The party rejects the priority of human value over class struggle. Nonetheless, for the CPI(M), India's 'bourgeois' parliamentary democracy is today the ideal political arena for conducting its struggle for socialism:

> Conditions in this country are favourable for the effective use of the bourgeois parliamentary democratic system in the interest of developing the struggle for proletarian statehood. We stand for the strengthening in the interest of the common people, of bourgeois democratic parliamentary system. In India, the proletarian class and general democratic movement has been developing under the conditions of the flowering of bourgeois parliamentary democracy which creates the conditions for the steady development of the Indian working class. There is therefore no stereotype model to be indiscriminately applied in all countries.[43]

The CPI(M)'s parliamentary illusions in the above passages are beyond doubt.

The CPI(M) has not yet formally abandoned the principle of the dictatorship of the proletariat, but the indication of change is obvious: 'Neither the dictatorship of the proletariat nor the dictatorship of people's Democracy is to be applied in other countries including India'.[44] Namboodiripad believes that it is now time that Marxist–Leninists throughout the world inevitably take a 'second look at the fundamental concepts of Marxism–Leninism'. For him and the CPI(M), the basic premises of Marxism are: class struggle, the leadership of working class in progressive movements, proletarian internationalism and *the variegated ways of building socialism in various countries*.[45] On closer analysis, however, Namboodiripad's views are little more advanced than the more formal views of the party. In its formal restatement of Marxism, the party says that 'on the application of Marxism in socialist society' it will consider 'four guarantees: dictatorship of the proletariat, primacy of Marxism–Leninism, socialist means of production, and the communist party leadership.'[46] In the light of the latter, the CPI(M) is a hardcore Bolshevik party, and its model of socialism is Stalinist.

However, the party's views on other aspects, such as the market, are not so consistently classical Marxist or Bolshevik. The party is right (in the capitalist sense) to assert that 'it is unscientific and ahistorical to conceive of a market independent of state interference or even control.' However, the party does not sound Marxist when it states: 'It would be erroneous to conclude that under socialism, the market will cease to exist.' Any student of Marx would know that Marx was opposed to the market even under socialism, and could not conceive of the possibility of a 'socialist market'. But, for the CPI(M), commodities are produced in socialism, and hence the market exists under socialism. The party even is ready to give the market a distributive role: 'Under socialism, the market is one of the means for the distribution of the social product.'[47]

This shift towards the market is actually the result of the party's recent tilt towards the Chinese model of socialism, which should be understood as part of its identity search. Echoing the modernisation model of Deng's leadership, Namboodiripad writes:

> Borrow from capitalism but use it in the interest of socialism. Permit the penetration of capitalism in certain sections of the economy but only under the overall control of the socialist state led by the communist party.[48]

Variants of the Chinese model of 'market socialism' are being practised in Korea, Cuba, and Vietnam. The party upholds the banner of socialism of these countries because 'they are trying to evolve their own path of advance to socialism ... in consonance with the concrete situation in their countries'. The CPI(M) finds the future of world socialism in these countries, since 'they would be making a positive contribution to the evolution of new forms of socialism in the developed and developing capitalist countries of the world.'[49]

Significantly enough, an entire issue of *The Marxist*, the party's theoretical journal (xi/4 [1993]) was devoted to the publication of three documents, one each from the South African, Vietnamese and Chinese Communist parties, with the note 'we hope this material would be of interest and use to our readers'. These three documents have much in common in respect of new ideas and beliefs relating to multiple ownership systems in socialism, the pitfalls of state ownership, the plurality of socialism, and more importantly, the need for the market. The most important aspects of the Chinese documents merit some attention:

1. 'The structure of planned economy is gradually being replaced by the socialist market economic structure';

2. 'The establishment of this structures aims at enabling the market to play a fundamental role in resource allocations'.
3. 'Development is an essential criterion. We should take care to be steady and discreet and stay clear of massive losses and *social upheavals.*' (My emphasis).[50]

Both the South African and Vietnamese communist parties have extended their support to the market model of socialism. The Vietnamese Communist Party has proposed that 'the state-run economy has failed to play well its leading role in production and circulation'.

Like the CPI-affiliated AITUC, the CPI(M) led CITU in its eighth National Conference (3 March 1994) called for 'broader trade union unity'. This did not mean the merger of all trade unions (as proposed by the CPI) which would amount to a 'confederation of all central trade unions as the task of the time'.[51] Whatever CITU's reasons may be, its own trade union movement cannot be said to be in a happy state. In its review of the 'Trade Union fronts', the 14th Party Congress of the CPI(M) complained of 'Bureaucratism as infecting the trade union fronts',[52] and the painful fact that 'party members are not doing communist style of work on the trade union front'.[53]

> Functioning of the trade unions is still dominated, by and large, by economism. Party building in many unions and industrial centres is not given priority by party committees. The party must directly intervene to generate socialist consciousness in the working class.[54]

Conclusion

Indian communism is today in deep crisis. The symptoms of this crisis are indicated by the public pronouncements of communist parties, in their identity searches which are profoundly contradictory, and more clearly, by the 'private beliefs' of communist leaders, as the interviews with them suggest. Confronted with the challenges to their identity, Indian communists are considering a number of areas of change in their patterns of movement, in organisation and assumptions. The movement is deeply threatened by world events which have created an ideological as well as a theoretical void inside the movement. The negative impact on the movement has already born fruit: deviation from party disciplines, dismissal from the party, lack of growth in membership (in the case of the CPI), bureaucratism and absence of quality of membership of parties.

On closer analysis, the changes involved in the reconstruction of socialism in the cases of both the major communist parties are contradictory. The contradictory nature of changes in the reconstruction of Indian communism are, however, suggestive of its current preference for a particular model of socialism, globally speaking. Interestingly enough, the global model that Indian communism strives to embrace is as contradictory as the local one. For instance, in the case of the nationality question, Indian communists are now ready to recognise the special 'ideological and social appeals' of such 'enduring' identities, but the solution of the problem is still found in a framework which is as Stalinist as before: the strong, centralised nation-state, and an essentially non-political definition of the nation. The CPI will now allow, in its organisational matters, 'minority opinions on substantial political issues' to be known to other members, but this change is only microscopic because this is to operate within the framework of a Bolshevik model of party organisation which is marked by ultra-centralisation. While the CPI abandoned the concept of dictatorship of the proletariat as early as 1958, the CPI(M) still retains it as the defining feature of a Marxist party.

The Indian communists' reconstruction of socialism is far removed from that of analytical Marxists. G. A. Cohen, the father of analytical Marxism, believes that in the light of historical experience the Marxist 'ideal' needs to be rethought.[55] Not only that, 'the lines of the movement for socialism, traditionally conceived as a movement centrally of the industrial working class, also need to be redrawn. Transformations in the class structure of western capitalist society necessitate a new conception of the agency for socialist change'[56] For Indian communists, Marxism is valid, immortal, true and all-powerful. Despite the fundamentally different socio-economic universe existing in India, and more particularly the fact that Indian communism is led by the non-working class elements (that is, the middle classes, urban and rural), for Indian communists the working class is still the central agency capable of social initiative and of leading an Indian revolution. Indian communists are blind to the limitations of classical Marxism.[57]

Indian communism's current shift towards the Chinese model of market socialism is the most important area of changes in its ideal of socialism, and strongly suggests the identity that the movement now tends to acquire. Indian communism's present shift towards 'market socialism', which Cohen would call an 'unthinking and fashion-driven rush',[58] takes it to the argument of the 'structuralists' which Petras and Vieux identify as one of the two dominant arguments explaining the global decline of communism today.[59]

The argument of the structuralists may be summed up as follows: capitalism is still a dynamic and creative force, the failures of socialism are pre-determined by the very 'structures' of the world economy, the crisis of socialism was built around the contradiction between stagnant socialist economies and opportunities for growth of productive forces through opening to the market. The 'structural' realities responsible for the decline of the revolutionary left are capitalist dynamism, the growth of productive forces, the centrality of the world market, and so on.[60] The current Chinese model, it is said, is informed by this argument. 'What matters is production' is the watchword for the ideology of the Chinese regime, which has prioritised the development of productive forces independent of social content. Petras and Vieux believe that this model paves the way for conversion to capitalism.[61] The implications for Indian communism's tilt towards 'market socialism' of the Chinese variety should thus be clear.

For our purpose, the process is inherently contradictory. Some years ago, G. S. Jones, in his analysis of the Tiananmen Square massacre of June 1989, drew our attention to the contradictory nature of the Chinese modernisation process, of which market socialism is an offshoot:

> Modernisation was declared a priority, foreign investment was welcomed, and tens of thousands of students were sent abroad. The emergence of a new rich class was openly encouraged, and even the army was urged to contribute its support through its involvement in business activities. Yet at the same time, the Marxist–Leninist organisation of state and party was kept largely unchanged.[62]

According to Jones, the Chinese modernisation process gave birth to socio-economic forces which the 'Marxist' political system failed to accommodate. The result was the very violent resolution of conflicts at Tiananmen Square. In their reconstruction of socialism Indian communists have only reproduced this Chinese model with all its contradictions.

Prospects

Sudipta Kaviraj has rightly remarked that the 'collapse of the Soviet

Union should force radicals to rethink some of the basic issues of Marxist theory.'[63] This is something which is glaringly missing in the current agenda of Indian communism. The CPI(M) thinks its job amply done by directing its committees, before the ensuing party congress in April 1995, to pay attention to the induction of elements from working class and agricultural labourers' families, and women, in forming party committees.[64] The party also wants to highlight the failures and successes of democratic centralism and utilisation, by party members of the party and the administration for personal gains, favouritism on the basis of personal loyalty etc. in the coming Congress.[65] Such measures, however, are all conceived within the old framework and do not touch upon the more fundamental issues of Marxism.

Charges of corruption are publicly brought in to sharper light by party veterans, 'pampered bureaucracy' is publicly attacked, lack of ideology among party members is openly lamented by party leaders and concentration of powers in a few hands also resented,[66] but we are yet to witness a real debate on an alternative model of socialism which is also philosophically regenerative and politically based on a radicalised democracy, or one which seeks to delegitimise the state institutions and centres of power.[67] Jürgen Habermas, the foremost Marxist in the west today, advocates the restoration of the 'public sphere' and the construction of a 'democratic dam' against the encroaching state in the context of the West.[68] The idea is more relevant to the realities of India, which see the presence not only of an omnipotent state but also the rise of a whole series of social movements centring around such issues as women, ecology, ethnicity and so on. These construct identities not only against the state (or nation), but they are also based on a suspicion of totalistic revolutionary programmes.[69] If the experience of the CPI(M)'s West Bengal unit is any indication, then the sorry state of the movement is unable yet to offer a radical breakthrough. The late Rabin Sen, a CPI(M) veteran from West Bengal, lamented the miserable working class representation in the party's West Bengal unit (only 9.9 per cent) and was critical of the upsurge of membership since 1977, describing the new members as 'self seekers, opportunists and [an] undesirable element'. He was a little disillusioned about the 'creeping parliamentary cretinism inside the organisation.'[70] Nirupam Sen, secretary of the Burdwan District Committee of the CPI(M), was at pains to observe the near absence of ideological conviction among party members in his succinct yet satirical summary of the state of the party:

> In our party, everybody, from leaders to cadres, are very busy. Some are ministers, some are MLAs (Members of Legislative Assembly) and MPs, some are members of the management of cooperatives, governing bodies of schools, and colleges. Smaller leaders beyond the pale are also equally as busy. The common people throng them for hundreds of reasons. As a result, they are busy all through the day. Now, if some one asks them: have you read yet the party's organs such as the dailies *Ganashakti* or *Deshitaisi*, the answer will be 'had a look at the headlines of newspapers', and they immerse themselves in daily business. Almost everybody follows this practice.[71]

A radical breakthrough, though much desired, is unlikely to flow from this movement, but the renewed relevence of Indian communism for the defence of democracy in India can hardly be underestimated.[72]

Notes

1 See Z. Bauman, *Intimations of Post-Modernity* (RKP, London, 1992), p. 178.

2 Ibid., p. 156.

3 Ibid., pp. 166–7.

4 See B. Sengupta, *Communism in Indian Politics* (Cambridge University Press, New York and London, 1972) pp. 440–2.

5 See T. J. Nossiter, *Marxist State Governments in India* (Pinter, London and New York 1988) for a concise summary of this complex communist movement.

6 The available literature on the smaller communist parties suggests that they share a lot of common gound in their assessment of why socialism failed in the former USSR and Eastern Europe although in matters of lessons they differ somewhat. For instance, the Socialist Unity Centre of India (SUCI), a small leftist party based mostly in some pockets of West Bengal districts, suggests that 'the crisis [in socialism] cropped up owing to some erroneous and revisionist formulations of the 20th Congress of the CPSU'. A hard-core Stalinist organisation, and the only leftist party outside the Left Front in West Bengal, the SUCI defines its 'Marxist' task as, among other things, building 'a strongly centralised monolithic Leninist party to combat modern revisionism': for more details see 'Theses on International and National Situation', first Congress of SUCI (25–29 March 1988) and *Proletarian Era* (SUCI organ) xxxv/6, 1 November 1991, especially 'Marxism–Leninism Lives For Ever', by Nihar Mukherjee. For the Forward Bloc (FB) socialism will now have to be 'more humane, democratic and participative'. The FB, a Left Front ally, also shows a pro-China tilt: 'achievements recorded

in [the] People's Republic of China through application of the theory of socialist market economy, and economic progress in Vietnam ... have falsified the prophets of doom for socialism': (Resolution of the Central Committee Meeting, 6–7 February 1994, unpublished).

7 *Fifteenth Party Congress Documents* of the CPI (New Delhi, 1993), p. 103.

8 Ibid., p. 103

9 Ibid., p. 105.

10 Indrajit Gupta, CPI General Secretary, in his paper 'Communist Party of India' in *Contemporary World Situation and Validity of Marxism* (CPI-M Publications, New Delhi, 1993) p. 346

11 Ibid., p. 345–6.

12 Ibid., p. 205.

13 Ibid.

14 Ibid., pp. 39–40.

15 Ibid., pp. 50–1.

16 35th Session of AITUC, Patna, 11–15 March 1994 (Unpublished Reports).

17 Gupta, 'Communist Party', p. 199.

18 Ibid., p. 346.

19 *15th Party Congress Report* of CPI, p. 27.

20 See his, 'Indian CPs and New Communists', *Mainstream*, 12 March 1994, p. 26.

21 Gupta, 'Communist Party', p. 204.

22 Ibid., p. 213.

23 Ibid.

24 Ibid., pp. 213–14.

25 *Mainstream*, 12 March 1994, p. 27.

26 Gupta, 'Communist Party', p. 204.

27 *Mainstream*, 12 March 1994, p. 26.

28 Ibid.

29 Ibid.

30 Ibid.

31 *Documents of the Fourteenth Congress of CPI-M* (CPI-M, New Delhi, 1993), p. 169.

32 Ibid.

33 Ibid.

34 H. S. Surjeet in his paper 'Communist Party of India' in *Contemporary World Situation and Validity of Marxism* (CPI-M Publications, New Delhi, 1993) p. 24.

35 See E. M. S. Namboodiripad, 'An Experiment that failed', *Social Scientist*, xxix/12 (1991) p. 3.

36 Gupta, 'Communist Party', p. 110.

37 *Documents of the 14th Congress of CPI-M*, p.4. See also H. K. S. Surjeet, *An Outline of the History of the Communist Movement in India* (CPI-M, New

Delhi, 1993), p. 193.

38 See *Sharmik Andolan* ('Working Class struggle') (monthly organ of CITU, Unif, West Bengal, February 1990, p. 40.

39 *Documents of the 14th Congress of CPI-M*, p. 1.

40 Ibid., p. 11.

41 P. Karat, 'The Concept of Regional Autonomy and its Concrete Application in India', *The Marxist* (CPI-M theoretical journal) xi/2 (1993) p. 30.

42 Ibid., p. 31.

43 Namboodiripad, 'Experiment', p. 17.

44 Ibid.

45 Ibid., p.19.

46 See *Marxbadi Path* (Marxist Path) no. 3 (February 1989) (CPI-M, Calcutta), p. 6. Although the party has not abandoned the concept of dictatorship of the proletariat in the light of later developments, changes in this respect can be observed. The 14th Party Congress opined that 'the dictatorship of the proletariat is not constant or immutable' (p. 110).

47 *Documents of the 14th Congress of CPI-M*, p.121.

48 Namboodiripad, 'Experiment', p. 13.

49 Ibid., p.15.

50 See *The Marxist*, xi/4 (1993).

51 T. D. Gupta, 'Meeting Challenge of Economic Reforms', *Economic and Political Weekly*, 30 April 1994, pp.1057–8. Gupta has highlighted some of the problems of left trade union movements which stand in the way of any real unity between CITU and AITUC.

52 *Documents of the 14th Congress of CPI-M*, p. 161.

53 Ibid., p.149.

54 Ibid. The situation on the peasant front is equally bad from the standpoint of the proletarian elements. The 14th Congress lamented: 'We have not been able to build up a strong movement for seizure of surplus land and benami land in most of the state' (p. 151).

55 See G. A. Cohen, 'Is There Still a Case for Socialism?' *Social Scientist*, xx/12 (1992) p. 3.

56 Ibid.

57 See, for instance, the critique as developed by Perry Anderson in his *Considerations on Western Marxism* (Verso, London, 1979).

58 Cohen, 'Is There Still a Case?', p. 6.

59 See, J. Petras and S. Vieux, 'The Decline of Revolutionary Politics: Capitalist Detour and Return of Socialism', *Journal Of Contemporary Asia*, xxiv/1 (1994). The term 'Structuralist' is used in general terms, and not in an Althusserian sense.

60 Ibid., pp. 2–3.

61 Ibid., p. 8.

62 G. S. Jones, 'Crisis of communism', *Marxism Today*, July 1989, p.9.

63 S. Kaviraj, 'Marxism and the Darkness of History', *Development and*

Change, xxiii/3 (1992).

64 See 'Party Letter', No.5, 1994 (West Bengal State Committee of the CPI-M, September 1994: internal document).

65 Ibid.

66 For the public complaints of Nripen Chakrabarty (CPI-M Politburo member and ex-Chief Minister of Tripura, 1978–88) see *The Statesman*, 4 and 29 December 1994. See also, *Ganasakti* and *Deshitaishi* festival issues (CPI-M, Calcutta, 1994) for criticisms of the party by Nirupam Sen (Secretary. Burdwan District Committee of the CPI-M).

67 See J. Habermas, 'Concluding Remarks' in C. Cahlon, (ed.) *Habermas and the Public Sphere* (MIT Press, Cambridge, Mass., 1992), and H. Wainwright, *Arguments for the New Left: Answering the Free Market* (Blackwell, Oxford, 1994).

68 Habermas, 'Concluding Remarks', p. 450

69 S. K. White, *Political Theory and Post-Modernism* (Cambridge University Press, Cambridge, 1991), pp.11–12.

70 See his 'We and Our Organisations' (in Bengali), *Deshitaishi* Festival Number 1994.

71 See his 'Ideological Crisis and our Party', *Deshitaishi* Festival Number 1994, p. 200. However, this 'ideology critique' of the leadership should not be taken at face value. There is a profoundly political dimension to it which should not be missed. Rosa Luxemburg's following statement, made in the wake of her fight against Bernstein's revisionism, is a pointer to this: 'It is, therefore, in the interest of the proletarian mass of the party to become acquainted, actively and in detail, with the present theoretical controversy with opportunism. As long as, theoretical knowledge remains the privilege of a handful of academicians in the party, the latter will face the danger of going astray. Only when the great mass of workers take the key and dependable weapons of scientific socialism in their own hands will all the petty bourgeois inclinations, all the opportunist currents come to naught. The movement then will find itself on sure and firm ground': Rosa Luxemburg, *Reform or Revolution* (Pathfinder, New York, 1970) pp. 9–10. For her, the whole question was related to the predominance of petty bourgeois elements in the party, especially its leadership: 'The question of reform or revolution, of the final goal and movement, is basically is another form, but the question of the petty bourgeois or proletarian character of the labour movement' (p. 9).

72 The 15th Party Congress of SPI-M (Chandigarh, 1995) does not show much improvement in radical organisational breakthrough, but 'democracy' has received even greater emphasis, so far as the inner party structures are concerned. While this may be symptomatic of the relative lack of democracy in the internal operation of the movement, this renewed emphasis - shown openly in the party documents - indicates strongly the shift currently taking place in the movement. The following passages from the 'Political Organisation Report' (1995) serve as a few representative

examples. 'The conferences held at all levels were conducted with greater stress on inner party democracy' (p. 70). 'Strengthen inner party democracy within the framework of democratic centralism' (p. 78). 'Resorting to bureaucratism or imposition of the decision of the majority faction in the name of centralism etc., will only worsen the situation and do harm to the party' (p. 71). However it must also be pointed out that the movement still has to go a long way to some up with a really fresh, regenerative theory of democracy because the current stress on democracy of the party is conceived within the old framework of a centralised Leninist–Stalinist political theory. If one keeps the West Bengal experience in mind, this political theory has informed the political practice of the communists in representative institutions which they run, and in all cases democracy as a deliberate practice has been the causualty. I have discussed this in my book, *Micro-Foundations of Bengal Communism* (Ajanta, Delhi, forthcoming).

11 ~ The African Left After the Cold War

Christopher Clapham

Defining the African 'Left'

In politics as in ordinary life, the categories 'left' and 'right' do not denote fixed and immutable positions, but can, rather, be defined only in terms of the particular situation arising at a given time; you have only to turn round for everything that was on your right to be on your left, and vice versa. In order to assess what has happened to the left in Africa since the end of the Cold War, and to speculate about the prospects for its revival, it is therefore necessary to situate 'leftness' within the context of African political life, and then to examine how this has been affected by developments both within Africa and outside.

In a broad sense, the left has characteristically been defined by its opposition to established structures of power, and by the attempt to articulate alternative forms of political and economic life, dedicated to the welfare of the mass of the population, by which these structures could be replaced. A systematic ambivalence has then been built into the idea of leftness, as a result of the ineluctable tendency of these alternative systems to create new power structures in their turn, and thus new targets against which the struggle for popular welfare had to be directed. The 'project' of the left is in this sense inherently dialectical, and its placement in any specific context depends on the way in which its current adversaries are identified.

In the context of the 'Third World', which had very evidently been incorporated into, and subordinated to, the global system created by European imperialism and capitalism, the left could initially most readily be defined in terms of opposition to this system, and of an attempt to create alternatives which were viewed as meeting the needs of the exploited populations of the subordinated regions. These alternatives, however, normally entailed the creation of powerful state authorities, capable of withstanding pressures from a capitalist-dominated international system, which rapidly came to constitute a new potential source of exploitation and target for leftist dissent. Sometimes, Third World state authorities could be treated as no more than the local representatives or 'compradors' of the global capitalist system, and in these cases the struggle against global power structures could be equated with opposition to the domestic political order. But even regimes which were incontestably 'leftist' in the context of one stage of the dialectic were open to challenge as the situation changed.

Within this broad framework, the peculiarity of the left in Africa lay in the low level of development which inhibited the creation of the kind of indigenous power structure against which the left had defined itself in much of Asia and Latin America, as well as in Europe. In particular, most of Africa lacked a class structure that was clearly anchored in control over productive economic resources. Only in South Africa, where a relatively high level of articulation of productive forces was combined with a peculiar relationship between race and class, and in Ethiopia, where a very low level of articulation was associated with an indigenous class structure based on the control of land, was it possible to define a revolutionary left in the sense in which this would be understood in other parts of the world. These two states were consequently the only ones in sub-Saharan Africa to have generated a domestic communist party of any importance, though the Stalinist projects to which the Workers' Party of Ethiopia and the South African Communist Party were committed proved drastically unsuccessful in the Ethiopian case and have been abandoned in the South African one. Instead, power structures in Africa were based on control of the state, and this created peculiar problems for 'leftist' ideologies which had characteristically looked to state power as a counterweight to the economic power of dominant classes.

In the absence of any substantive basis for a politics of class, the left in Africa was characterised by three main projects, each of which could be regarded from one perspective as a form of opposition to established power structures and an attempt to devise more acceptable alternatives, but each of which could likewise eventually be regarded as an instrument of domination. These may broadly be defined as a project of liberation, a project of state construction, and a project of international alliance.

The *project of liberation* most obviously encompassed independence from colonial or settler rule, and the establishment of states governed by their indigenous inhabitants. In a sense, *any* independent African state was a worthy object of leftist support, regardless of its internal power structure – a proposition delightfully illustrated by the enthusiastic support provided for Emperor Haile-Selassie, at the time of Mussolini's invasion of Ethiopia in 1935, by one of the 'left' communists, Sylvia Pankhurst, against whom Lenin had directed his attack on this 'infantile disorder'.[1] Once the principle of decolonisation had come to be almost universally accepted, a more specifically leftist territory was marked out by support for those African 'nationalist' leaders whose domestic political base was most populist in nature, and whose opposition to colonialism was most strident. These were in turn most likely to opt for projects of state construction which enjoyed leftist support. As the unwillingness of white settlers and some colonial regimes (notably Portugal) to concede African majority rule became clear, the project of liberation was extended to support for those African movements which sought independence through insurgent warfare against these regimes, and could in turn be linked with Maoist doctrines of liberation war.[2]

Once 'liberation' from colonial or white minority rule had been achieved – and in most of sub-Saharan Africa this happened both quickly and relatively painlessly – the project of the left was converted into an agenda for government, and raised all of the classic problems associated with leftism as an ideology of power, rather than of protest.[3] The second and central element of the African leftist was then as a *project of state construction*, which in turn was closely associated with particular conceptions of political and economic development. Though the project of state creation was common to all new African states, it took its most strident form in the more leftist regimes, which could continue to deploy a unifying anti-colonial rhetoric which was rapidly dropped after independence by most of those regimes which swiftly established close post-colonial connections with their former metropoles. The greater the extent to which independent governments distanced themselves from the colonial past, moreover, the greater their anxiety to ensure their control over potential sources of 'neocolonial' opposition. Politically, all leftist regimes were committed to single-party states, which combined a high level of centralism with a strong emphasis on personal leadership, and an authoritarian attitude to dissent. Percipient left-wing observers recognised from a very early stage that many of these regimes would scarcely have qualified for leftist status in an ideological setting less dominated by the struggle against European rule and global capitalism.[4]

Only a small minority of African leftist regimes, however, opted for a Leninist vanguard party, and a formal attachment to Marxism–Leninism. The emergence of a group of such regimes in the mid-1970s was commonly taken to mark a 'second phase' of African socialism, following the first phase immediately after independence. In several cases, however – as in Benin, where it was locally dubbed Laxism–Beninism – the commitment to 'scientific socialism' was more rhetorical than real.[5] Only in Ethiopia under the Mengistu Haile-Mariam regime of 1977 to 1991 can one find an African government with an articulate Marxist–Leninist structure and programme, and the capacity – for a while, at least – to implement it.[6] The Leninist model nonetheless presented an attractive scenario to quite a number of African leaders, most appealingly in the form presented by North Korea, which appeared to have achieved by this means the level of total social control, allied to adulation of the leader, to which African leaders unavailingly aspired. Only in the exceptional case of Ethiopia, likewise, did any leftist African government adopt a Stalinist doctrine of nationalities as a means of combining tight central control with a recognition of ethnic differences within the national population. First introduced in a heavily controlled form in the later years of the Mengistu government, this was far more systematically implemented under the EPRDF regime which displaced it. Bizarrely, though for understandable reasons, the most thoroughgoing attempt to combine centralised state-building with a doctrine of national self-determination was to be found in apartheid South Africa.

A further and very considerable ingredient of the state creating project was as a strategy of economic control.[7] This readily combined an opposition to international capitalism which linked it to global leftist ideologies, with a determination to bring previously externally managed resources into the hands of the regime, and in the process both to foster a state-directed programme of rapid economic development, and also – more crudely and practicably – to provide a patronage basis for the regime and a means of gratifying the economic aspirations of those who managed it. Central economic planning provides the perfect example of ideology as a form of legitimation which at the same time meets the interests of those in power. Again, it should be pointed out that there were right-wing as well as left-wing variants on the theme of national developmentalism; however, only South Africa had the domestic capitalist class and the elite attitudes required to reproduce anything approximating to the kind of 'capitalism in one country' sought by military regimes in Latin America. For most capitalist African states, a rightist development ideology necessarily involved a close association with external businesses and the international market.

The third element in African leftism as it existed before the end of the Cold War, and the most governmental of all, was as a *project of international alliance*.[8] This certainly had its origins in the need to find a counterweight to the continuing power of the formerly colonial European states and the United States in Africa, and in the relative freedom of action that could be created by balancing each of the major global blocs against the other; and though the USSR and its allies were quite unable to displace the West as a source of economic linkages for Africa, they provided valuable support in the struggle for liberation. By the Angolan war of the mid-1970s, however, many of the advantages of the USSR as a counterweight to Western dominance had been exhausted, and the attractions of a Soviet alliance came to consist very heavily in its effectiveness as a source of armaments. Soviet (and Cuban) military support for the MPLA government of Angola against Unita and its allies could plausibly be presented as the continuation of a liberation war, especially given the level of direct South African intervention on the other side. Similar support for the Mengistu regime in Ethiopia, against opponents led by the Eritrean and Tigrayan Peoples' Liberation Fronts which themselves had Marxist–Leninist origins, could have no such rationale, and represented a peculiar expression of Marxism as an ideology of militarist repression.[9]

Significant elements of left-wing projects in other parts of the world were effectively excluded. There was virtually no emphasis on class, except perhaps in the peculiar case of the Ethiopian revolution and in the immediate post-independence period in a number of states where rural elites had been associated with the colonial regime. Nor was there any discernible emphasis on either justice or equality, except in an international context. Ideologies of human rights, which had enjoyed a respectably leftist ancestry in the European political tradition, were deployed almost exclusively as part of a 'right-wing' (and US-supported) attack on African statehood. Socialism, as it developed in Africa, became a means of justifying the monopoly state, and the power of the urban elites who derived their status from it.

The Collapse of the Statist Left

All three of the projects associated with the left in Africa were terminally undermined by the end of the Cold War. The project of liberation was in one sense achieved, with the transfer of power in South Africa, but in another sense proved to be unattainable. The acceptance by the African National Congress, at an early stage of the South African transition, of a market economy operating in close contact with global capitalism was no more than a recognition of the inevitable. Regardless of the ANC's previous commitment to a socialist South Africa, which reflected the ideological pre-eminence of the South African Communist Party within the movement, this would all too evidently by the late 1980s have been a recipe for economic collapse. Other would-be socialist African states had recognised the same reality from the start, in some cases such as Nkrumah's Ghana after early attempts to build up trade relations with the CMEA. No African state was remotely in a position to implement the strategies of autonomous development attempted in Burma or Khmer Rouge Kampuchea. Even the Soviet Union's closest Africa allies, Angola and Ethiopia, remained firmly within international trading networks dominated by the Western states – in Angola's case through oil exports to the United States, in Ethiopia's through coffee exports largely to Western Europe, and an increasing dependence from 1984 onwards on Western relief grain.

Socialism as a strategy of economic development through centralised state control had collapsed several years before the end of the Cold War, in the debt crisis of the early 1980s and the subjection of almost all sub-Saharan states to external economic management through IMF and World Bank structural adjustment programmes. Up until the dismemberment of the Soviet Union and Yugoslavia, however, it had been possible to conceive a socialist road to nation-building, through the recognition of the cultural identity of the different 'nationalities' of which African states, like their socialist models, were composed, coupled with the maintenance of a powerful central government. The collapse of what had once appeared to be one of the world's few effective systems of multiethnic government, revealing ethnic hatreds not merely unhealed but even intensified after a long period of communist rule, may well prove in the long run to have been an even more dispiriting lesson from the fall of communism than its failure as a model of economic development. And finally of course, the third pillar of the African leftist project, the role of the USSR as a source of arms and counterweight to the West, simply disappeared.

The failure of the African left, moreover, was not simply a failure of power – the defeat of a potentially viable and morally sustainable ideal, by the forces of global capitalism which it was simply not strong enough to resist. It was also, and more basically, an *ideological* failure: the policies which 'socialism' had been used to promote, whether in its stricter Marxist–Leninist form or in the less rigid and coherent versions supposedly designed to correspond to local circumstances, provided no plausible means of attaining the objectives to which they were ostensibly directed. The cruellest gap between ideological rhetoric and reality was presented by the failure of Nyerere's policies of socialism and self-reliance in Tanzania, not only to improve the welfare of the Tanzanian people, who remained amongst the poorest in Africa, but even to achieve self-reliance: Tanzania remained, next only after Mozambique and Guine-Bissau, among the most aid-dependent states in the world.[10] Finally, and most damaging of all, it was a *moral* failure: policies which resulted not only in impoverishment, but in often appalling levels of state-inflicted suffering, had lost any claim to the legitimacy conferred by concern for the public welfare on which any ideology of the left must ultimately rely.

The African Left in a Post-Cold War Era

The period of political reopening in Africa after 1989, which resulted in a massive (though temporary) explosion of popular political participation, and the holding of multiparty elections in the great majority of African states, provided the opportunity for previously suppressed or ignored political forces to bring themselves to public attention. During this process, in sharp contrast to the previous surge of participation during the 1950s, no distinctive left-wing voice made itself heard at all. The new political parties that competed for popular support included none that had any discernibly socialist message, or which looked to economic development through any other mechanism than the international market. The new parties professed overwhelmingly liberal ideologies, often expressed (as in the Zambian Movement for Multiparty Democracy) in terms of a simple reactive opposition to the old single-party states. Even though the MMD was led to victory in the 1991 elections by a trade unionist, most of its leadership, like that of virtually every other party, came from such elite professions as the law and academic life.[11] Even in the South African elections of April 1994, where themes drawn from the traditional left might have been expected to enjoy a resonance which they had lost in other parts of the continent, the support achieved by the sole explicitly left-wing party, the Pan-African Congress, was negligible. The only discernibly new social forces revealed by democratisation were religious ones, in the form not only of Islamic fundamentalism but also – and more importantly in much of Africa – of Christian revivalism.[12]

When, however, one looks beyond the dearth of discernibly left-wing movements on the current African political scene to the social and economic conditions which have characteristically given rise to a politics of the left, there is no difficulty in identifying such conditions in modern Africa. They are found, firstly, in a continuing level of immiseration and inequality which might well be expected to produce a reaction of a classically leftist kind directed against the educated class which has managed to retain an extraordinary level of dominance in independent Africa. Since African state elites have, as already noted, used 'socialism' as a means of legitimating their own access to the benefits of state power, this would require the discrediting of such 'old leftist' ideologies and their displacement by 'new leftist' alternatives geared to a different (and possibly drastically reduced) conception of the state. Such ideologies would also be able to draw on the resentments aroused by the subordination of Africa to Western capitalist states, a subordination which has been greatly intensified (and made much more explicit) in the aftermath of the Cold War, and which has as yet failed to produce the benefits promised by economic liberalisation and political reform – and seems unlikely to do so. Potentially at least a new African left could also draw on environmental issues – the failure of statist political and economic systems to manage the environment has been as evident in much of Africa as in the former Soviet bloc – as well as on demands for devolution to local-level management and for a recognition of local identities.

But while the potential for the revival of an African left is in a sense evident, it is much less clear how such a movement would organise itself in social and political terms, or, still more important, what kind of project for a new and preferable social order it could articulate. Political action in Africa has overwhelmingly been the preserve of those groups who wanted to gain something from the state. People who did not stand to gain anything from the state have tended simply to withdraw from it, rather than attempt to reform it; given the relative ease of the 'exit' option, and the virtual impossibility of reform, this has been a perfectly rational response.[13] Political activity has accordingly been dominated by clientele networks, which have been organised in order to establish channels for the distribution of state benefits, under the control of elite politicians; 'socialism' in its statist form was an ideology perfectly attuned to this function. The resurgence of multi-party democracy was likewise seized on with relish by excluded elites, who saw in it their opportunity to make another bid for power. It gave rise to no movements evidently concerned to create a different kind of state, to which clientelist organisation would be irrelevant, nor was it clear how any such movement could gather the constituency needed for it to take power. The very lack of effective economic development in Africa has impeded the emergence of new social strata – like the bourgeoisie in industrialising European states, or the new democratic forces in east Asia – with an interest in creating new mechanisms through which to manage and at the same time limit political power.

Such attempts as there have been to create a new basis for governance in current African politics have emerged not from among the leaders of electoral parties, but from two other sources of political initiative. One of them, exemplified by the Rawlings phenomenon in Ghana, is a radical military regime with a populist mission geared to an attack on urban and bureaucratic privilege through the restructuring of the economy with assistance from the IMF and World Bank. These two international institutions form so much part of the demonology of the 'old left' in Africa that it is hard to conceive of any regime which maintains close links with them as having any leftist credentials at all; but if the old state to which the old left is inextricably linked is seen as part of the problem which any 'new left' must address, then an external alliance with powerful money-bearing institutions may not be such a bad place to start.

The second potential starting point is from some at least of the guerrilla insurgent movements which have flourished in parts of Africa as the state has decayed, and which have succeeded in capturing state power in some half-a-dozen African states. Several of these movements, including notably the NRA in Uganda, the EPRDF in Ethiopia, and the EPLF in Eritrea, had authentic leftist origins, with an educated leadership which attempted to apply to Africa some of the lessons of revolutionary guerrilla warfare promoted by Mao and Giap. They may be sharply distinguished, not only from 'nationalist' movements designed to liberate African territories from colonial or white minority rule, but also from the personalist or 'warlord' insurgencies found in such states as Liberia and Somalia. Whereas warlord movements (including also Renamo and Unita) had an appalling record in destroying states without being able to put any alternative structure in their place, the leftist ones for the most part proved remarkably effective in taking over and exercising power, and have been responsible for most of the attempts to rethink the role of the state in Africa.

The major problem facing such regimes lies in the difficulty of devising any new 'project' or programme of action which would have a distinctively leftist character. Not only have the old projects dropped out of sight, but the exigencies of the international situation make some alliance with global capitalist powers almost unavoidable. The NRA and EPLF do not appear to have gone far beyond attempting to reconstruct a state on the ruins left by warfare in Uganda and Eritrea respectively, while attempting to retain Western support by announcing a commitment to private sector economic management, as they seek to deflect pressures to establish multi-party political systems. The EPRDF has attempted an innovative form of reconstruction, through a scheme of ethnic decentralisation which harks back to its old commitment to a Stalinist nationalities policy; but the whole exercise has been caught between the dangers of Yugoslav-style fragmentation on the one hand, and the EPRDF's refusal to give up any of its own control on the other.

In short, if the essence of 'the left' lies in a concern for the welfare of the poorest members of a society, in an attack on privilege, and in an attempt to devise principles for the reconstruction of political and economic life in terms of some fairer model, then the scope for leftist movements in Africa is obvious. Much of the agenda for such movements may well consist in destroying the institutions of the monopoly state which a previous generation of leftists sought to establish. But in Africa as elsewhere, a viable alternative project for a new leftist alliance remains extremely elusive.

Notes

1 See V. I. Lenin, *Left-Wing Communism, an Infantile Disorder* (Moscow, Progress, 1968) Ch. 9; a generation earlier, still more remarkably from a late twentieth century perspective, the anti-imperialist left wing of the British Liberal Party had supported the white Afrikaner settlers in the Anglo–Boer War of 1899–1902.

2 Though there is a massive leftist literature in support of decolonisation, the work first of Fenner Brockway and subsequently of Basil Davidson deserves special mention. See Fenner Brockway, *African Socialism* (Bodley Head, London, 1963): Basil Davidson, *Which Way Africa? The Search for a New Society* (Penguin, Harmondsworth, 1964).

3 For general studies of 'socialism' or 'communism' in Africa, each inevitably corresponding to the era in which it was written, see William H. Friedland and Carl G. Rosberg, *African Socialism* (Stanford University Press, Stanford, 1964): C. G. Rosberg and T. M. Callaghy, (eds), *Socialism in Sub-Saharan Africa: A New Assessment* (University of California, Berkeley, 1979): Barry Munslow, (ed.), *Africa: Problems in the Transition to Socialism* (Zed, London, 1986): Marina and David Ottaway, *Afrocommunism* (Africana, New York, 1986): Arnold Hughes, (ed.), *Marxism's Retreat from Africa* (Cass, London, 1992). For a work which attempts to identify African political movements which may be regarded as leftist, see Donald I. Ray, *Dictionary of the African Left: Parties, Movements and Groups* (Dartmouth, Aldershot, 1989).

4 Amongst the first of these was Frantz Fanon in *The Wretched of the Earth*, first published in 1961, whose appraisal of 'the pitfalls of national consciousness' was influenced by his position as ambassador of the Provisional Government of the Algerian Republic in one of the classic leftist states, Kwame Nkrumah's Ghana; other leftist commentators often retained an embarrassingly indulgent attitude towards personal rule in African 'socialist' states.

5 See Chris Allen, '"Goodbye to all That": The Short and Sad Story of Socialism in Benin', in Arnold Hughes, (ed.), *Marxism's Retreat from Africa* (Cass, London, 1992).

6 I have examined this project in Christopher Clapham, *Transformation and Continuity in Revolutionary Ethiopia* (Cambridge University Press, Cambridge, 1988).

7 This gave rise to a substantial leftist literature, which was marked by often intense polemics between 'classical Marxist' and 'dependentist' schools.

See, for example, Colin Leys, *The Rise and Fall of Development Theory* (James Currey, London, 1996) for a post-mortem on this literature.

[8] This is more systematically examined in chapter 4 of this volume.

[9] This is a phenomenon which has been described by John Markakis as 'garrison socialism'; see Markakis, *National and Class Conflict in the Horn of Africa* (Cambridge University Press, Cambridge, 1987) chs 8 and 9.

[10] World Bank, *World Development Report 1994*, Table 19.

[11] See Carolyn Baylies and Morris Szeftel, 'The Fall and Rise of Multi-Party Politics in Zambia', *Review of African Political Economy* 54 (1992).

[12] See Paul Gifford, 'Some recent developments in African Christianity', *African Affairs* lxxxxiii/373 (1994) for a useful general discussion of this phenomenon.

[13] See Jeffrey Herbst, 'Migration, the Politics of Protest, and State Consolidation in Africa', *African Affairs* lxxx/355 (1990) and Jean-François Bayart, 'Civil Society in Africa', in Patrick Chabal, *Political Domination in Africa*, (Cambridge University Press, Cambridge, 1986) for two discussions of 'exit' in African politics.

Index